Trading Financial Futures:
Markets, Methods, Strategies, and Tactics

John W. Labuszewski

John E. Nyhoff

WILEY

JOHN WILEY & SONS

New York • Chichester • Brisbane • Toronto • Singapore

Library of Congress Cataloging in Publication Data:

Labuszewski, John.

    Trading financial futures : markets, methods, strategies, and
tactics / John W. Labuszewski, John E. Nyhoff.
      p. cm.
    Bibliography: p.
    Includes index.
    ISBN 0-471-60675-8
    1. Financial futures. 2. Hedging (Finance) 3. Put and call
transactions. I. Nyhoff, John E. II. Title.

HG6024.3.L325   1988
332.64'4—dc19   87-28570
                                                      CIP

Printed in the United States of America

10 9 8 7 6 5 4 3 2

Foreword

The commodity futures industry has witnessed dramatic changes over the past decade.

In the 1970s, industry growth was primarily attributable to the agricultural futures trade, but industry impetus shifted in the early 1980s. Today the term "commodity" has been extended to include markets such as fixed income, foreign exchange, and stock index instruments. By the mid-1980s, these *financial* commodity markets accounted for the bulk of industry volume.

Recent years have witnessed record numbers of security dealers, commercial and investment bankers, fund managers, and corporations employing financial futures in order to hedge transactional risk exposures and seek yield enhancement opportunities.

They do so for a simple reason: These markets represent powerful, efficient, and flexible tools for a variety of trading and risk-management purposes. But like any other tool, if they are improperly used, they will not serve the intended purpose.

This book is intended to serve as a springboard for successful entry into the financial futures markets, providing the reader with a firm theoretical and practical grounding in these exciting and important new markets.

THOMAS H. DITTMER
Chairman
Refco Group Ltd.

February 1988

Acknowledgments

The authors would like to express their sincere appreciation to our colleagues who made immeasurably valuable contributions to this effort. In particular: Takashi Aragane, Mutsuo Asaba, Suzanne Bishopric, Kyo Cho, Dennis Collins, Robert J. Dantone, Maryrose Dombrowski, H. Patrick Faust, Yusuke Ikeda, Dennis L. Heskel, Michael P. Kamradt, Yasuyuki Kato, Heidi Labuszewski, James F. Meisner, Ikunori Morita, Marion Nyhoff, Horoiku Sago, Motoaki Sakaguchi, Yasuhiko Sawa, Diane E.G. Spikes, Yoshiki Suzuki, Keisuke Taguchi, Takeshi Sugihasi, Toshiki Tsunoda, Yasuto Tsuruta, and to the many others who supported this effort but whose contributions may have been inadvertently overlooked.

Special recognition must be extended to our employer, Refco Group Ltd.; its chairman, Thomas H. Dittmer; and its president, Tone Grant. Thank you for your generous support, infinite patience, and constant encouragement during the preparation of this publication.

JOHN W. LABUSZEWSKI

JOHN E. NYHOFF

February 1988

Contents

1 Introduction to Financial Futures   1

Mechanics of a Futures Contract, 1
Order Flow, 11
Questions, 14

2 Fundamental Market Factors   16

Significance of Fundamental Analysis, 16
Questions, 22

3 Technical Analysis with Futures   24

Why Technical Analysis?, 24
Interpreting the Bar Chart, 30
Elliot Wave Theory, 52
Intraday Trading Techniques, 66
Trend-Following Systems, 70
Questions, 81

4 Cost of Carry   83

A Simple Carry Model, 83
Quantifying the Model, 88
Yield Curve Analysis, 92
Questions, 99

5 Discount and Interest Bearing Securities   101

Treasury Auction Procedures, 101
Time Value of Money, 104
Present and Future Values, 109

Annuities, 113
Treasury Bill Prices and Yields, 117
Yield Measures and Volatility Properties, 120
Duration and Price Sensitivity, 126
Questions, 130

6   Playing the Treasury Futures Basis   132

The Delivery Experience, 132
Tracking the Basis, 134
The Implied Repo Rate, 150
Questions, 154

7   Financial Futures Spread Relationships   156

Intramarket Spreads, 157
Intermarket Spreads, 170
Questions, 182

8   Hedging with Financial Futures   184

Cash Instrument Hedgeability, 185
Identifying the Hedge Ratio, 185
Hedging Short-Term Interest Rate Risk, 201
Regression-Weighted Hedge Techniques, 208
Questions, 221

9   Asset/Liability Management with Futures   225

Macroasset/Liability Management, 225
Microasset/Liability Management, 227
Asset or Liability Hedge?, 229
Duration Analysis, 230
Questions, 231

Answers to Questions   233

Index   239

1

Introduction to Financial Futures

Since the early 1970s, a variety of futures contracts based on "financial commodities" has been introduced with a great deal of success. Futures on instruments as diverse as fixed income, equity, and foreign exchange markets have proven their value as effective risk-management and trading vehicles.

These contracts represent tools which may be used to accomplish a variety of investment purposes, but like any other tool, if improperly used, these contracts will not perform the desired function. The intent of this chapter is to introduce and discuss the fundamental terminology and concepts associated with the most popular of the financial futures markets.

MECHANICS OF A FUTURES CONTRACT

This section reviews the contract terms and conditions associated with the most heavily traded fixed income, stock index, and foreign exchange futures contracts offered on domestic commodity exchanges.

Before we review these terms, however, a more fundamental question arises: What is a *futures contract?* A futures contract may be thought as a commitment to transact an exchange of a specified quantity and quality commodity, security, or other fungible instrument sometime in the future.

A *futures contract* represents a contract between two parties, convey- ing to one party the commitment to sell and to the other party the commitment to buy, a specific quantity and quality of a fungible instrument during some future delivery month or on some future date.

For example, a Japanese yen futures contract calls for the delivery of 12,500,000 yen during the months of March, June, September, or December.

Let us see how this generalized definition applies to the trade of a variety of financial instruments. In the interest rate field, we shall consider the T-bond, T-note, T-bill, and Eurodollar futures contracts.

Foreign exchange contracts include the Japanese yen, deutsche mark, Swiss franc, Canadian dollar, and British pound. Equity-based stock index futures include the Standard & Poor's 500 (S&P 500), New York Stock Exchange Composite (NYSE Comp), and Value Line Composite Average (VLCA). While this is not an exhaustive list, it does in fact cover the most popular of these financial instruments.

Futures and Forwards

A futures contract is often considered quite similar to a "forward contract." But futures and forwards are different in many respects.

A forward contract may be thought of as a negotiated commitment between two parties who come together for the purpose of transacting what may be an isolated exchange. The integrity of these contracts is generally *not* guaranteed other than by the credit worthiness of the two principal parties. Moreover, they are generally not "fungible;" that is, once the transaction is entered, it may only be offset by mutual agreement of both parties.

A futures contract is traded pursuant to very specific terms and conditions. In the United States, these terms and conditions are established by commodity exchanges and subject to regulatory requirements imposed by the Commodity Futures Trading Commission (CFTC).

These transactions are administered and backed by a centralized clearinghouse or clearing corporation established by the exchange. The clearinghouse formally stands as buyer to every seller and seller to every buyer. Trades are executed on the exchange by brokerage firms designated as "clearing members" and booked to the account of the customer.

Because futures contracts are standardized, they may easily be offset; that is, an individual may buy or "go long" futures and subsequently sell at the prevailing market price prior to entering the delivery process. As a result, the original commitment to buy is cancelled. An individual may also sell or "go short" futures and subsequently buy at the prevailing market price prior to entering the delivery process. Again, this series of transactions means that the original commitment to sell is cancelled.

Long-Term Interest Rate Futures

The first exposure many have to interest rate futures is through the financial pages of a newspaper. T-bond and T-note futures share many similarities in the way they are reported.

Bond Futures
(September 26, 1986)

Months	Open	High	Low	Settle	Change
Dec.	94–15	95–28	94–04	95–21	+ 14
Mar.	93–13	94–29	93–06	94–22	+ 13
Jun.	92–21	93–27	92–08	93–22	+ 12
Sep.	91–17	92–30	91–12	92–24	+ 11
Dec.	90–19	92–03	90–19	91–29	+ 11

Bond and note futures call for delivery of debt securities during the months of March, June, September, or December, extending outwards more than two years into the future.

Traders who go short (sell futures) are committed to make delivery of $100,000 face value securities; traders who go long (buy futures) are committed to take delivery of the $100,000 face value securities.

All contracts are quoted in percentage of par in minimum increments of one thirty-second ($1/32$d) of one percent. Since these contracts cover $100,000 face value, each full percentage point equals $1,000. December futures settled in our example at 95–21. This is equivalent to $95,656.25 (95 and $21/32$ds percent of $100,000). A minimum price fluctuation or *tick* equals $31.25 ($1/32$ of 1 percent of $100,000).

On this day, December futures rallied by $14/32$ds. At $31.25 a tick, this means that futures advanced $437.50 from the previous day's settling price.

Many futures contracts impose a limit on the maximum amount by which the price may fluctuate in a single day. In the case of bond and note futures, movement is limited to 3 points or $3,000 above or below the previous day's settlement price. Thus if the market settles at 95–21, the next day's possible daily range in December is between 92–21 and 98–21.

Bond and Note Delivery Grade

Delivery months, price quotations, contract size, price limits, and margins are uniform for bond and note futures contracts. The securities which may be delivered against the contracts are what differs.

Bond futures call for the delivery of *nominally* 8 percent bonds which mature or are noncallable for at least 15 years from the date of delivery. Note futures call for the delivery of nominally 8 percent Treasury securities which mature within 6½ to 10 years from the date of delivery. (See Table 1.)

Long-Term Interest Rate Futures Contract Specifications*

	Bonds	Notes
Unit/	\$100,000 face value T-bonds	
Grade/	Bonds w/ "nominal" 8% coupon w/ at least 15 years from earliest of call or maturity date.	Notes w/ "nominal" 8% coupon w/ 6-1/2 to 10 years to maturity date.
Delivery/	Federal Reserve book entry wire transfer. Invoice price based on futures × conversion factor.	
Quote/	In percentage of par in minimum increments of one thirty-second (1/32) of a point, or \$31.25 per "tick," *e.g.,* 94–01 or 94–01/32nds.	
Daily limit/	Ninety-six thirty-seconds (96/32nds) or \$3,000 per contract above or below the previous day's settlement price.	
Hours/	8:00 A.M. to 2:00 P.M. & 6:00 P.M. to 9:00 P.M. (Chicago time).	
Months/	March, June, September or December	
Last trading day/	Seven (7) business days prior to the last business day of the month.	
Last delivery day/	Last business day of the month	

*Contract terms and conditions subject to change.

These contracts are based on nominally 8 percent instruments, but this does not imply that shorts are required to deliver 8 percent coupon securities. Bond futures, for example, permit the delivery of *any* bond which does not mature and is not callable within 15 years from the date of delivery regardless of the coupon. At any given time, there may be upwards to 30 different securities varying widely in coupon and maturity which meet that qualification.

Clearly, high-coupon securities are worth more than comparable low-coupon securities. Thus the "invoice price" paid by buyer to seller upon delivery is to reflect the varying values of different coupon and term securities.

Bond and note futures employ a "conversion factor" invoicing system to reconcile these differences to the standard 8 percent coupon. Upon delivery of a note or bond, the "principal invoice price" is calculated as the futures settlement price times $1,000 times the conversion factor.

$$\frac{\text{Principal}}{\text{Invoice Price}} = \frac{\text{Futures}}{\text{Settlement}} \times \$1,000 \times \frac{\text{Conversion}}{\text{Factor}}$$

Conversion factors equal the price of the bond or note to be delivered to yield 8 percent, so securities with coupons in excess of 8 percent will have conversion factors greater than 1.0. Securities with coupons under 8 percent will have conversion factors less than 1.0.

Example: The conversion factor for the delivery of the 14 percent bond of 2006–11 against the December 1986 bond contract equals 1.5903. This implies that the 14 percent bond is worth roughly 160 percent of an 8 percent bond. If December futures settle at 95–21, the principal invoice price may be calculated as follows:

$$\text{Principal Invoice Price} = \frac{95.65625}{(95^{21}/_{32ds})} \times \$1,000 \times 1.5903$$
$$= \$152,122.13$$

Example: The conversion factor for the delivery of the 7 1/4 percent bond of 2016 against the December 1986 bond contract equals 0.9155. This implies that the 7 1/4 percent bond should be worth roughly 92 percent of an 8 percent bond. The principal invoice price may be calculated as follows.

$$\text{Principal Invoice Price} = \frac{95.65625}{(95^{21}/_{32ds})} \times \$1,000 \times 0.9155$$
$$= \$87,573.30$$

Interest accrued since the last semiannual interest payment date is added to the principal invoice price, arriving at a final price which the short invoices the long upon delivery.

The conversion factor invoicing system is intended to provide for the economic delivery of any of the deliverable securities. In practice, however, a single security generally stands out as "cheapest (most economic) to deliver" in light of the relationship between cash and futures prices.

Example: The 14 percent bond may be purchased in the cash market for 153–14 or $153,437.50 for $100,000 face value; the 7 1/4 percent bond may be purchased for 95–17 or $95,531.25 for $100,000 face value (not including accrued interest). Compare these values to the principal invoice prices found previously.

		Cash Price	Invoice Price	Difference
14%	–11	($153,437.50)	$152,122.13	($1,315.37)
7 1/4%	–16	($95,531.25)	$87,573.30	($7,957.95)

This implies that if you deliver the 7 1/4s, a loss of $7,957.95 will result. Delivery of the 14s results in a loss of only $1,315.37, so the 14s are more economic or cheaper to deliver than the 7 1/4s.

Futures prices tend to correlate most closely with the price of the cheapest-to-deliver cash security. What makes one security cheaper to deliver than another? While the conversion factor system goes a long way towards reconciling the price of a particular security with the 8 percent standard, there are certain biases which may render a single security as cheapest.

When yields are in excess of 8 percent, the conversion factor system tends to slightly favor the delivery of relatively low-coupon, long-maturity securities. When yields are less than 8 percent, high-coupon, short-maturity securities may become cheaper.

Cash market biases play a strong role as well. For example, some investors prefer discount as opposed to premium securities for tax reasons. The shape of the yield curve is also influential.

Futures Margin Requirements

December bond futures were trading in our previous example at 95–21 or $95,656.25, but this is not the amount needed to establish a futures position. When you establish a futures position, long or short, you are required to make an "initial" margin deposit. Initial margins may be deposited in cash, Treasury bills, or other qualifying securities.

Once an initial margin is deposited, futures traders "mark-to-market;" that is, they are required to pay any losses and entitled to collect any gains daily in cash. "Variation" margins must be met in cash. However, these variation margin payments are only required if the account balance falls below the "maintenance" margin level.

Example: A long futures position is established at 95–21. Assume that an initial margin of $2,500 may be required. (Margin requirements change from time to time—consult your broker for current requirements.)

On the next day, futures decline $500 to 95–05. Now there is only $2,000 in the account. Still, no additional funds are required because the maintenance margin is $2,000.

On the next day, futures decline another $500 to 94–21. The trader must now replenish the depleted account to the initial level with a $1,000 cash deposit.

On the next day, futures rally $500 to 95–05. This releases $500 to the trader's account in cash.

Futures margins are unlike stock margins. When you purchase stock, you may margin up to 50 percent of that purchase; that is, you make a down payment equal to at least one-half the value of the stock and borrow the balance at interest from your broker. When you buy or sell futures, however, you do not assume an equity interest in any particular instrument. You have simply entered into a commitment to make or take delivery of a particular commodity or security.

As such, futures margins may reflect a much lower proportion of the value of the underlying instrument. Futures margins may be thought of as good faith deposits or performance bonds, not as a down payment on the purchase of equity. Because futures are marked-to-market daily, they are intended to cover one day's maximum price movement.

Stock Index Futures

The three most significant stock index-based futures contracts are the Standard & Poor's 500, the New York Stock Exchange Composite, and the Value Line Composite Average. These contracts are offered at the Chicago Mercantile Exchange, the New York Futures Exchange, and the Kansas City Board of Trade, respectively.

The S&P 500 is a capitalization-weighted index of 500 stocks listed on the NYSE. These 500 stocks are selected "with the aim of achieving a distribution by broad industry groupings that approximates the distribution of these groupings in the NYSE common stock population." (Standard & Poor's Corporation.)

The NYSE Comp is also a capitalization-weighted index. This index includes all 1,500 plus common issues traded on the NYSE.

The VLCA is an equally-weighted geometric average of 1,700 plus stocks traded on the NYSE, AMEX, and OTC markets. The VLCA is the broadest index of the three discussed here referencing many "secondary" stocks.

The threat, if not the actual realization, of deliveries is said to drive futures "in-line" with the underlying cash market. Yet stock index futures do *not* call for the physical or actual delivery of stock; maturing contracts are settled in cash (a "cash settlement") at the spot value of the index.

Long and short positions are marked-to-market (entitled to collect any gains and required to pay any losses) on every day a position remains open. On the last trading day, mark-to-market procedures are observed except that, subsequent to the last trading day, positions are stricken from books and disappear.

Composition of Stock Indexes

Index	Underlying Stocks	Computation
S&P 500	500 companies representing 80% of NYSE capitalization	Capitalization or market-weighted
NYSE Comp	All NYSE issues	Capitalization or market-weighted
VLCA	About 1,700 stocks representing 96% of dollar value of U.S. equities	Equally-weighted, geometric average

The cash settlement system is a necessary development in the context of stock index futures. Consider the alternative—the delivery of a basket of all the stocks represented in the index. This, of course, is quite impossible where you may have upwards to 1,700 stocks represented in the index.

The following table illustrates how stock index futures may be quoted.

S&P 500 Futures
(September 26, 1986)

Months	Open	High	Low	Settle	Change
Dec.	230.40	234.50	229.75	231.95	+ .60
Mar.	231.00	235.35	230.70	233.15	+ .85

Stock index contracts are quoted in terms of index points, generally in minimum increments of one-twentieth index point (0.05). Since the S&P 500, NYSE Composite, and VLCA contracts are valued at $500 times the index, each full point equals $500. Thus a minimum price fluctuation or tick equals $25.00 (0.05 × $500).

Stock Index Futures Contract Specifications*

	S&P 500	NYSE Comp	VLCA
Unit/	$500 × Standard & Poor's 500	$500 × New York Stock Exchange Composite	$500 × Value Line Composite Average
Delivery/	Cash settlement based on spot value of the index		
Quote/	0.05 points or $25/contract	0.05 points or $25/contract	0.05 points or $25/contract
Daily limit/	None		
Hours/	8:30 A.M.–3:15 P.M. (Chicago time)		
Months/	March, June, September or December		
Last trading day/	Thursday before 3rd Friday of month	3rd Friday of month	Last business day of the month

*Contract terms and conditions subject to change.

Short-Term Interest Rate Futures

T-bill and Eurodollar futures traded on the Chicago Mercantile Exchange are based on $1 million face value short-term debt instruments. The T-bill contract calls for the delivery of 13-week (91-day) bills; the Eurodollar contract is settled in cash based upon a survey of 90-day London InterBank Offered Rates (LIBOR).

These contracts mature during the months of March, June, September, or December, extending outwards more than two years into the future. They are quoted in terms of the "IMM index." The IMM index is equal to 100 less the yield on the security; that is, if the yield equals 7.55 percent, the index equals 92.45. The minimum price fluctuation equals 1 basis point or 0.01 percent. Based on a $1 million face value 90-day instrument, this equates to $25.00.

Eurodollar Futures
(September 26, 1986)

Months	Open	High	Low	Settle	Change
Dec.	93.96	94.03	93.88	94.01	−.02
Mar.	93.85	93.93	93.78	93.90	−.01
Jun.	93.62	93.70	93.55	93.67	−.02
Sep.	93.26	93.35	93.20	93.32	−.03
Dec.	92.80	92.94	92.78	92.92	−.03
Mar.	92.44	92.54	92.40	92.52	−.03

On this day, December futures fell by 2 basis points. At $25.00 a tick, this means that futures declined $50.00 from the previous day's settling price.

Short-Term Interest Rate Futures Contract Specifications*

	Eurodollars	T-Bills
Unit/	$1 million face value 90 day Eurodollar time deposits	$1 million face value 13 week T-bills
Delivery/	Cash settlement based on a survey of LIBOR rates	Actual delivery of 13 week week bills
Quote/	In terms of the "IMM index" or 100 less the yield. E.g., a yield of 7.55 is quoted as 92.45. One basis point (.01) equals $25.	
Daily limit/	None	None
Hours/	7:20 A.M. to 2:00 P.M. (Chicago time)	
Months/	March, June, September or December	
Delivery day/	Cash settlement on 3rd Monday of month	Delivery occurs during a 3 day period beginning with the Thursday of the contract month on which a previously auctioned 1-year and 6-month T-bill has 3 months to maturity.

Foreign Exchange Futures

Futures are also available on a variety of foreign currencies. The most popular are futures based on the British pound, Canadian dollar, deutsche mark, Japanese yen, and Swiss franc. These contracts are traded at the Chicago Mercantile Exchange. They uniformly call for the actual delivery of currencies on deposit at designated foreign financial institutions during the months of March, June, September, and December.

The following table illustrates how yen futures may be quoted.

Japanese Yen Futures
(September 26, 1986)

Months	Open	High	Low	Settle	Change
Dec.	0.6493	0.6507	0.6486	0.6490	+ 0.0005
Mar.	0.6517	0.6522	0.6506	0.6508	+ 0.0005
Jun.	0.6546	0.6546	0.6546	0.6527	+ 0.0004

These contracts are quoted in "American" terms, that is, in terms of dollars per foreign unit. For example, the foregoing table quotes the yen in terms of U.S. dollars per 100 yen. This differs from the typical interbank practice of quoting foreign exchange transactions in terms of foreign unit per U.S. dollar.

Of course, you can convert these quotes from dollars per foreign unit to foreign units per dollar by simply taking the reciprocal. December yen closed at $0.6490 per 100 yen. The reciprocal equals 154.08 yen per dollar.

Given that the yen contract is based on 12.5 million units, the December contract is valued at $81,125. A minimum price fluctuation equals $0.0001 per 100 yen. This equates to $12.50 per tick.

Foreign Currency Contract Specifications*

	British Pounds	Canadian Dollar	Deutsche Mark	Japanese Yen	Swiss Franc
Unit/	25,000 BPs	100,000 CDs	125,000 DMs	12,500,000 JYs	125,000 SFs
Delivery/	Delivered in the country of origin at a bank designated by the clearinghouse				
Quote/	$.0005/BP or $12.50	$.0001/CD or $10	$.0001/DM or $12.50	$.000001/JY or $12.50	$.0001/SF or $12.50
Daily limit/	None				
Hours/	7:20 A.M.– 1:24 P.M.	7:20 A.M.– 1:26 P.M.	7:20 A.M.– 1:20 P.M.	7:20 A.M.– 1:22 P.M.	7:20 A.M.– 1:16 P.M.
Months/	March, June, September or December				
Last trading day/	The Monday before the 3rd Wednesday of the month				
Delivery day/	3rd Wednesday of the month				

*Contract terms and conditions subject to change.

ORDER FLOW

The first time visitors to a futures exchange witness the daily trading session, they are often much confused by the apparent chaos, noise, and commotion on the floor. But upon closer study, they begin to realize that there is a method to the madness, that what they see is really a very organized form of chaos.

Role of the Local

Futures trade in a manner known as "open outcry," an open auction environment where a number of traders may simultaneously be voicing a bid and an offer. Only members of the exchange are permitted to participate directly in the auction-like proceedings which take place on the floor. Exchange members are independent businessmen who make a living by trading commodities.

There are two basic types of participants or "locals" on the trading floor: the floor trader (scalper) and the floor broker. Brokers are by far the less numerous of the two categories of participants. They stand in the pit and execute trades on behalf of outside customers. In return for this service, they accept a fee for each contract traded.

Traders or scalpers essentially act as market makers. Sometimes these traders take a position in the market either long or short in anticipation of a bullish or bearish price movement. Most of the time, however, they are content to attempt to take the bid/ask spread out of the market; that is, they stand ready to buy or sell in order to capture the bid/ask spread.

Scalpers, for example, will buy at the bid against market orders to sell. Then they will look for market orders to buy against which to sell. If they succeed in trading against a market buy order by selling at the offer, they will have captured the bid/ask spread. Because there are a large number of scalpers operating competitively, this bid/ask spread is typically very tight.

They are at risk, however, during the time between the point at which they bought at the bid and are able to sell at the offer. If, for example, the market falls between those two transactions, the scalper is subject to grave risk. If market conditions become extremely unstable, the bid/ask spread may be slightly increased.

These floor traders, therefore, perform a valuable service; by taking the opposite side of customers orders, they assure that these outside orders will be filled quickly and at a narrow spread. While the activity of these locals is often the center of attention on the part of people visiting an exchange floor for the first time, it is important to realize that this activity is intended primarily to serve the needs of outside customers.

Order Routing

How do these customer orders reach the trading floor? A customer with an account open with a futures broker typically calls the broker and verbally conveys an order. That order is recorded and stamped with the time at which it was received by the broker.

That order is then conveyed directly to the order desk of the brokerage firm for execution on the floor. Many large brokerage firms wire the instructions associated with smaller orders or retail orders to the floor. Large orders are typically conveyed verbally through a telephone line to a clerk at the firm's order desk.

The clerk records and time stamps the order. It is handed to a floor messenger or "runner" or is signalled by hand to the floor broker in the pit who will execute the order. Once executed, the information surrounding the order is conveyed backwards through the original chain to the customer.

At the end of the day, locals on the floor who have executed business on the floor take their transaction cards to the brokerage firm which is clearing their trades. These cards are submitted to the exchange clearinghouse at which point the clearinghouse attempts to match buyers and sellers. For every buyer there must be a seller; every seller must have a buyer.

If these cards fail to match—if the details recorded in connection with each transaction do not coincide—the trade does not clear. If, subsequent to a number of opportunities to reconcile the trade, it does not clear, it becomes an "out-trade" and is not valid. Once a trade clears, the clearinghouse formally stands as buyer to every seller, seller to every buyer.

Acceptable Orders

A variety of different types of orders may be accepted on the floor of the exchange. These orders may vary in terms of the price and the time at which they are executed. Typical orders are described next.

A *market order* is simply an open order to buy or sell. Once placed, the broker has discretion to buy or sell at the best available price prevailing in the pit. A customer might expect a market buy order to be filled at the prevailing offer, a market sell order to be filled at the bid.

A *limit order* is specific with respect to the price at which it may be executed. For example, one may place a limit buy in the bond futures market at 98–10. This means that the transaction may only be executed if the broker is able to buy at 98–10 or less. A limit sell at 98–12 may only be executed if the broker is able to sell at 98–12 or more.

A *stop* or a *stop loss order* is generally placed in conjunction with an order to establish a new position. Assume, for example, that you establish a long position at 98–10. You may place a stop sell order at 98–04 *below* the market, or if you sold at 98–12, you may place a stop buy order at 98–16 *above* the market.

A *market if touched order* is an instruction to the broker to execute the buy or sell order at the best available price if the market trades at a particular price at least once.

Orders may also be placed instructing the broker to buy or sell at a particular time of day. For example, a *market on open order* (MOO) instructs the broker to buy or sell on the opening. A *market on close order* (MOC) instructs the broker to buy or sell at the close.

A *one cancels the other order* (OCO) may be thought of as two limit orders or a limit and a stop order. If one of the two orders is executed, the other becomes invalid. Assume, for example, that the bond market is at 98–10. You may put in a limit order to buy at 98–05 and a stop buy at 98–15. If the limit order is executed, the stop is cancelled or vice versa.

A *discretion order* is much like a limit order in that it instructs the broker to buy or sell at a particular price. However, it provides the broker with some discretion or range in which to execute the order.

QUESTIONS

1. Which statement is true?
   (a) A futures contract requires the long to make and the short to accept delivery of a specific commodity.
   (b) A futures contract represents a commitment to make and a commitment to take delivery of a specified instrument at a specific strike price.
   (c) A futures contract is the same as a forward contract.
   (d) All futures contracts are quoted in percent of par.
   (e) A futures contract is a formalized commitment to make and take delivery of a specified instrument between the short and long, respectively.

2. The face amount specified in a Chicago Board of Trade bond contract . . .
   (a) Is the same as in a CME Eurodollar futures contract.
   (b) Varies depending upon the maturity and coupon of the bond actually delivered.
   (c) May be found by referencing the conversion factor.
   (d) Is fixed no matter what the coupon and maturity of the bond actually delivered.
   (e) Equals $1,000,000.

3. Match the futures contract with the face amount of the delivery unit:

Japanese yen	$1 million face value
British pounds	125,000 units
S&P 500 futures	12.5 million units
6½- to 10-year T-note	25,000 units
90-day T-bill futures	$100,000 face value
West German mark	$500 × index

back to the seller within a short period of time. Often these transactions are concluded on an overnight basis. A matched sale or reverse repo transaction is just the opposite of a repo agreement. The Fed sells securities, taking cash out of circulation with the understanding that it will repurchase the securities in the near future.

Effectively, then, a repo or a matched sale means that the Fed is either lending money to or borrowing money from capital market participants. The interest rate is effectively implied in the difference between the purchase and sale prices. These transactions are executed by the New York branch of the Federal Reserve banking system. Typically, these open market actions commence at 10:30 A.M. CST. This kicks off what is known as "Fed intervention hour."

The Fed may also implement its policies by adjusting the "discount rate." This is the rate at which members of the Federal Reserve System may borrow from the Fed at the "discount window." The impact associated with an upwards or downwards adjustment in the discount rate is obvious.

Further, the Fed may adjust bank reserve requirements. Requiring banks to retain more of their funds in reserve causes money to become tighter, and rates may increase. Reducing the reserve requirements causes money to become looser, and rates may decrease.

Inflationary Pressures

Inflation and interest rates tend to fluctuate in loose tandem. In other words, investors will demand higher returns in periods of high inflation to compensate for the eroding value of the dollar. Returns may be expected to moderate when inflation is low or negative.

Historically, it has been observed often that long-term Treasury yields have maintained a 2 percent premium over inflation rates, that is, "real" rates of return have averaged about 2 percent. In the early to mid-1980s, however, real rates of return far exceeded this historical level, and it is a matter of conjecture whether this relationship will reestablish itself on a long-term basis.

This means that interest rate traders should be careful to monitor inflationary indictors such as the consumer and producer price indexes (CPI and PPI) closely. These statistics are made available on a monthly basis, but they represent lagging indicators insofar as they measure inflationary trends prevailing in the month prior to their release. Changes in money supply may have a significant impact upon inflation, but as just indicated, shifts in money supplies tend to lead inflation by perhaps six to twelve months.

Industrial Activity

Industrial activity is monitored quite closely by various federal agencies and private organizations throughout the month. In broad terms, as industrial activity heats up, commercial loan demand increases, driving rates upwards. If industrial activity falls off, commercial loan demand falls and rates decline.

These commercial market activity statistics may be classified on the basis of whether they represent leading, lagging, or concurrent indicators, that is, whether they purport to forecast market activity, are reported subsequent to the market activity they represent, or are reported simultaneously.

Perhaps the most significant of all leading indicators is the Commerce Department's Index of Leading Economic Indicators. This index represents a composite of twelve different leading indicators including net business formations, orders for plants and equipment, and the Standard & Poor's 500 stock index. It is released monthly and closely followed.

Some of the more common of the lagging indictors are gross national product (GNP), retail sales, and housing starts. GNP is released on a quarterly basis. It represents the value of all goods and services produced in the prior calendar quarter. Retail sales reflect consumer cash and credit transactions. However, retail activity may be anticipated by watching statistics regarding orders for consumer goods and materials. Housing starts may be used as a proxy for mortgage loan demand. But data regarding the issuance of new housing permits provides an advance look at the same information.

Summary

As a general rule, there is a strong connection between money supplies, inflation, and productivity. Money supplies should strike a rough balance between the price of goods and services available and their production. If one element in the equation changes, something else must change to maintain the balance.

For example, if productivity increases while money supplies remain constant, general price levels must decline. If money supplies increase while production remains constant, general price levels should increase, as measured by CPI or PPI.

However, it is not sufficient to know that a particular economic statistic is moving upwards or downwards. Presumably, the marketplace as a whole anticipates these movements. These expectations are reflected in futures prices. Thus in order to realize a profit as a result of changing fundamental conditions, you must attempt to identify how the actual statistical release will vary from marketplace expectations!

This suggests that unless a financial futures trader has a very keen appreciation for current economic events, it may be quite dangerous to hold a market position when a fundamental news item is scheduled to be released. If nothing else, the calendar of forthcoming economic statistical releases should be referenced to identify when one should stay out of the market.

Economic Statistics

Indicator	Released	Effect	Reason
Money supply up. (M1 = cash in circulation, checking, NOW, ATS, mutual savings. M2 = M1 plus money market accts, time deposits, overnite repos, Euros.)	Thursday 3:15 CST	Yields up	Excess growth in money causes inflation and fear that Fed will tighten
Fed buying bills		Yields down	More money in system
Fed tightens		Yields up	Availability of funds for lending restricted
Fed does repos		Yields down	Fed puts money in system by purchasing securities
Fed does reverse repos or match sales		Yields up	Fed takes money out of system by selling securities
Fed raises discount rate		Yields up	Increase in rates between Fed and member banks means increase in rates
Increase in supply of bonds	Reported in press daily	Yields up	Greater demand for credit
CPI up	Late in mo. for prior mo.	Yields up	Inflationary
PPI up	First week of mo. for prior mo.	Yields up	Inflationary, indicates increased demand
GNP down	Quarterly revision at mid-month	Yields down	Economy slowing, Fed may loosen

Economic Statistics *(Continued)*

Indicator	Released	Effect	Reason
Housing starts up	Mid-month for prior month	Yields up	Growth in economy, demand for mortgage funding, other goods
Industrial production down	Mid-month for prior month	Yields down	Slow economy, Fed may ease
Inventories up	Mid-month for prior month	Yields down	Inventory levels indicates relative pace of demand and production
Leading indicators up	Late in month for prior month	Yields up	Leading indicators are advance signal about economic health
Personal income up	Mid-month for prior month	Yields up	Higher income, more consumption, more demand, inflationary
Retail sales up	Mid-month for prior month	Yields up	Indication of economic growth
Trade balance up	Late month for prior month	Yields up	Dollar strengthens, anticipates foreign demand
Unemployment up	First Friday for prior month	Yields down	High unemployment indicates lack of economic expansion

QUESTIONS

1. What three *general* factors impact upon U.S. interest rates?
   (a) Federal Reserve policy, concurrent economic indicators, and money supply.
   (b) Leading economic indicators, CPI, and M1.
   (c) Inflation, industrial activity, and Federal Reserve policies.
   (d) Industrial activity, Fed market intervention, and GNP.
   (e) None of the above.
2. Which of the following factors is *not* referenced to construct the Leading Indicators Index?
   (a) Dow Jones Industrial Average.
   (b) Net business formations.
   (c) Net change in inventories on hand and on order.

    (d) Cash in circulation plus checking accounts, NOW, ATS, mutual savings plus money market accounts, time deposits, overnight repos, and overnight Euros.

    (e) New building permits for private housing units.

3. Indicate whether the following factors can be expected to result in a rise (+), fall (−), or have no effect (NE) on interest rates.

    (a) Fed does match sales: _____

    (b) PPI is down: _____

    (c) Housing starts are up: _____

    (d) Personal income is down: _____

    (e) Unemployment is down: _____

    (f) GNP is up: _____

    (g) CPI is down: _____

    (h) Leading economic indicators are down: _____

    (i) Corporate tax rates are going up: _____

    (j) Fed is buying bills: _____

    (k) Fed is tightening: _____

4. Follow fundamental market activity for the next month by referencing a calendar which indicates when key economic statistics will be released. Prior to each new release, identify figures for that statistic over the past two to three months. What does the street anticipate with respect to the probable level of each figure? Compare the actual number to the street's anticipated number and see how the market reacts.

3
Technical Analysis with Futures

Technical analysis covers an extremely broad spectrum of concepts and techniques. Many technical methods are quite complex, relying on reams of statistical information. Other technical methods may be simple and may even appear to be without firm grounding.

One thing which is clear is that technical analysts have achieved prominent recognition in the futures markets over the years. In fact, technical forecasting methods are probably more widely followed and prompt more trades in the futures markets than any fundamental indicators.

This is evident when you consider there are hundreds of commodity trading advisors (CTAs) offering their funds management services largely on the strength of their technical market forecasting expertise. As such, the market is driven in accordance with technical factors. The bottom line is you cannot afford *not* to pay attention to these interesting and potentially quite rewarding technical forecasting methods.

WHY TECHNICAL ANALYSIS?

Technical forecasting techniques have been in use in one form or another at least as long as organized markets have existed. But technical methods are not the only means by which one may attempt to gain an insight into potential future market movements. This section attempts to answer the question: Why should I be interested in technical analysis? We will discuss the distinction between a technical and fundamental approach to market forecasting as well as some of the origins of technical trading methods.

Fundamental and Technical Analysis

Technical and fundamental analysts have often been at odds regarding the validity and relevance of the two approaches to market forecasting. Let us discuss the role that each method may play in a trading situation and why technical analysis plays so prominent a role in many futures trading applications.

Fundamental analysts are most concerned with the question "why?" Why does the market move the way it does? What fundamental economic conditions may cause the market to fluctuate upwards or downwards? In other words, fundamental analysts busy themselves studying cause and effect relationships.

Technical analysts believe that the market price already incorporates all *known* fundamental information. As new economic data is released, it is incorporated into the market price level efficiently and almost instantaneously; therefore, it becomes difficult to trade profitably on the strength or weakness of known fundamental information. You should focus instead on a study of the price level and patterns in price movements directly!

The market trades from day to day on the strength or weakness of *unknown* fundamental factors, more specifically, on the strength or weakness of what traders believe these factors will portend as they become known. More than anything else, therefore, the market trades on the basis of market psychology—the bullish or bearish attitudes of market participants in the aggregate.

Many academics question the validity of technical trading methods although these same academics often warmly embrace the "random walk" theory. The random walk theory suggests that market prices respond as fundamental market information is made known quickly, efficiently, and without serial autocorrelation.

The absence of serial autocorrelation in a price series, specifically, in a series of price movements, is said to occur because today's fundamental economic release may bear little correlation to tomorrow's fundamental economic release. Random walk theorists believe, therefore, that market prices fluctuate unpredictably and randomly over time.

This, however, is not inconsistent with the technical viewpoint that the market may fluctuate considerably between the points in time at which fundamental information is made known. During those intervals, market perceptions become more important than the most recently issued bit of fundamental market news.

Random walk theorists may assert that market movements are random and unpredictable, but a simple inspection of any chart book will probably satisfy most observers that the market tends to move in trends. Not only does the market tend to move in trends, but pricing patterns tend to repeat themselves and are witnessed over and over again. There are very few if any traders, for example, who have never seen a "head and shoulders" formation, and very few who are unfamiliar with the traditional interpretation and pricing implications of the pattern.

If the market trends and behaves in accordance with repeating patterns, traders take action accordingly. If many traders rely on similar technical systems (and there is evidence to suggest that most trend-following systems will trigger buy or sell recommendations in rough unison), technical analysis becomes a kind of "self-fulfilling prophecy."

If you believe the market will advance or decline and you buy or sell accordingly, the market *will* tend to rise or fall (particularly if there is a large number of like-minded traders). Many of the "principles" of technical analysis are quite unusual and seem to lack a common sensical basis, but if enough traders believe that a given technique will work, it will in fact work! If technical analysis is useful at all, therefore, it is because traders believe it will provide useful information. Their subsequent actions enforce those predictions!

This implies that one should be concerned only about methods which fall in the mainstream of technical thought. Other, more arcane methods cannot work because too few traders will utilize those methods and therefore enforce their predictions.

Technical Analysis and the Futures Markets

Most of the technical work which has been done throughout the years has centered on the stock markets. In particular, famous analysts such as Charles Dow and Ralph Nelson Elliot concentrated exclusively on equity markets. Nonetheless, a case may be made that technical analysis is more relevant in the context of the futures markets than in any other segment of the marketplace.

This fact is due largely to the fact that futures trade on extremely low margin requirements relative to the value of the underlying instrument. It is not uncommon for the margin on a futures contract to be anywhere between one to five percent of the total value of the delivery instrument. Compare that to the minimum 50 percent margin requirement associated with stocks.

Futures traders enjoy extreme leverage compared to equity traders, but these comparisons do not tell the entire story. When you buy stock, that 50 percent minimum margin requirement represents a down payment on the purchase price of the stock. The balance is typically borrowed at interest from the broker. This is appropriate because when you purchase stock, you acquire an equity interest in the issuing firm.

When you buy (or sell) futures, however, the difference between the value of the commodity and the margin or the "unpaid balance" is not lent at interest. This is because the margin associated with futures transactions serves an entirely different purpose than a stock margin.

A futures margin simply represents a "good faith deposit" or "performance bond." It is intended to secure the integrity of the contract by covering the risk associated with a single day's price movement. The margin need only cover a single day's maximum possible risk because margins are administered daily; that is, there are no paper profits or losses because traders mark-to-market daily. Profits or losses are distributed or paid daily and in cash.

But the *initial* margin is deposited in the form of collateral; this collateral is in the form of securities, generally T-bills, on which the futures trader continues to earn the interest. Thus there is no explicit opportunity cost associated with the initial purchase or sale of futures; futures traders enjoy 100 percent leverage!

Because of this extreme leverage, futures traders cannot afford the luxury of a "buy and hold" strategy. Equity traders may buy a stock and hold it in the face of adverse market movements because they know they have already paid the full purchase price. Futures traders, however, may not be able to fund variation cash payments associated with a losing futures position.

Futures trading, therefore, is much more of a short-term proposition. Because futures positions are not likely to be held for an extended period of time, *timing is paramount!* A futures trader who is right in the long term but wrong in the short term loses money. Futures traders who are wrong in the long term but right in the short term usually make money. The "trick" is to be right in the short term!

This means that technical analysis may be much more important than fundamental analysis in the futures markets. Fundamental analysis may provide useful insights in the long term. But often short-term market trends run contrary to long-term trends. Technical analysis is a tool which is much more useful in the short term.

Dow Theory

If any single individual may be credited with the introduction of modern technical thought, it is probably Charles Dow. Dow was an owner and editor of the *Wall Street Journal* in its early, formative years. Dow's "theory" appeared in a series of editorials carried by the paper in the late 1800s until Dow's death in 1904.

Some people may question the relevance of Dow's ideas in an age of advanced telecommunications, computerized trading methods, and extremely fast-paced markets. Yet much of his work endures today and has heavily influenced vastly disparate schools of financial thought.

Among Dow's achievements was the introduction of a series of stock market indexes, one of which became known as the Dow Jones Industrial Average (DJIA). The first of Dow's stock averages, published initially on July 3, 1884, was an eleven-stock rail average.

In 1885, that average was expanded to include twelve rail stocks and two industrials. By 1896, the composition of the average was altered such that it contained exclusively industrial stocks. Finally, by October 7, 1896, Dow created two averages: a twelve-stock industrial and a twenty-stock rail index.

Dow relied heavily upon these indexes for technical forecasting purposes. In particular, Dow believed that it was more worthwhile to study the movement of the indexes than movement in any individual stock. He believed that the price of any individual stock may be affected heavily by unique factors which may not impact upon other firms. In order to identify broad market trends, therefore, it was important to focus on the averages. Furthermore, Dow believed that bullish movement in either the rail or industrial average should be confirmed by similar action in the other index.

Although Dow is not generally credited with the idea, it is clear he recognized that the risks associated with any individual stock were a function of general economic conditions as well as conditions which might uniquely impact upon a given stock. He recognized early what has become an axiom in modern financial thought: The total risk associated with any given stock is comprised of "systematic" and "unsystematic" market risks. Systematic risks refer to those general economic factors which impact upon all stocks to one degree or another. Unsystematic risks may uniquely affect a given firm with little or no impact upon other firms.

These ideas represent a cornerstone of the "capital asset pricing model" (CAPM). The CAPM was hammered out largely in the 1950s and early 1960s by a variety of academics who might have little sympathy for many of Dow's theories. Nonetheless, they owe a large debt of gratitude to Dow. In particular, it is interesting to note that systematic market risks are measured today by stock market averages or indexes such as the Dow Jones Industrial Average or the Standard & Poor's 500!

Not only did Dow's thought feed into the CAPM, but his work also deeply affected other financial theorists of quite a different ilk. Ralph Nelson Elliot, a leading technician of the 1930s whose theories are known cumulatively as "Elliot wave theory" and have enjoyed a resurgence of interest in recent years, was a student of Dow theory.

Dow believed that market movements may be categorized as primary, secondary, or minor trends. A minor or "near-term" trend may be considered broadly as movement which lasts anywhere from two to three days to two to three weeks. A secondary or "intermediate-term" trend may last from two to three weeks or two to three months. A primary, major, or "long-term" trend may last upwards from two to three months.

Elliot believed that he refined these ideas considerably. In particular, Elliot was far more specific in identifying various trends. In addition to the primary, secondary, and minor trend, Elliot refers to trends of smaller duration—the minute, minuette, and subminuette. Furthermore, Elliot has identified trends of larger degree in the cycle, supercycle, and grand supercycle, which may last upwards to 200 years!

Dow also suggested that a primary trend breaks down into three stages: (1) the accumulation stage, (2) the technical trend-following stage, and (3) the distribution stage. Let us consider a primary bull trend. The accumulation stage represents the initial stage of a primary market movement. This is where the "smart money" begins to take a position by buying the bull trend. The technical trend-following stage occurs later when a variety of technical trading systems confirm the existence of a trending market and trigger buys. The distribution stage is the final upward surge where the "smart money" begins to take its profits.

Elliot wave theory is based primarily upon the idea that the market moves in distinguishable patterns. In particular, the market may rally in a bull market in a five-step pattern and subsequently correct itself in a three-step pattern. These "5s" and "3s" represent the core of the Elliot wave theory (see Figure 3–1).

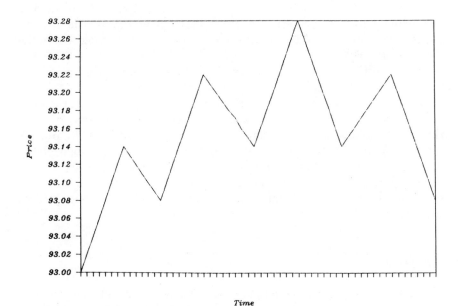

Figure 3–1   Elliot's fives and threes.

The five-step upward movement is denoted with the numbers 1, 2, 3, 4, and 5. The subsequent corrective phase is denoted with the letters a, b, and c. These 5s and 3s may be referred to as the "numbered" and the subsequent corrective "lettered" phases.

The numbered phase breaks down into three "impulse waves"—waves 1, 3, and 5 in the general direction of the market trend. The intervening waves 2 and 4 represent "corrective waves." The point is that these three impulse waves 1, 3, and 5 are highly reminiscent of Dow's accumulation, technical trend-following, and distribution phases.

It is difficult to imagine two schools of financial thought more divergent than the capital asset pricing model and Elliot's wave principle. Both of these concepts, however, owe much to the original work of Charles Dow, the "great-great-grandfather of technical analysis."

INTERPRETING THE BAR CHART

Technical analysts have often been distinguished into two camps, *chartists* and *statisticians*. A statistician relies upon a numerical approach to technical market forecasting. A chartist relies upon trends and patterns observed in a graphic representation of market behavior.

One of the most commonly referenced types of charts is the *bar chart*. A bar chart provides a vast wealth of information about market price movements, volume, and open interest. It is characterized by a series of vertical bars which depict the lowest price traded on a given day and the highest price traded on a given day against a horizontal axis depicting sequential dates. To the right of the bar, a short tick or slash is used to indicate the closing or settlement price of the day. Sometimes a similar slash is used to the left of the bar to indicate the opening price of the day.

Bar charts often incorporate information regarding volume (in the form of bars at the bottom of the chart) and open interest (a line running through the bars at the bottom of the chart). In addition to providing information about price, volume, and open interest, bar charts provide information about market volatility and timing. Volatility may be observed in the height of the vertical bars. Timing may be observed in terms of the horizontal length over which a trend or pricing pattern persists.

The Trend

The first and foremost issue in the minds of many technical traders centers about the existence or nonexistence of a *trend*. A trend may be bullish, bearish, or sideways (neutral).

A bullish trend is indicated by a series of successively higher and higher peaks coupled with a series of successively higher and higher troughs, that is, higher highs and higher lows (see Figure 3–2). A bearish trend is indicated by a series of successively lower and lower troughs coupled with a series of successively lower and lower peaks, that is, lower lows and lower highs (see Figure 3–3).

> The *trend* is found by studying peaks and troughs in market movements. A bullish trend is characterized by a series of higher peaks and higher troughs; a bearish trend is confirmed by a series of lower troughs and lower peaks.

Trends may be enforced by the existence of "support" or "resistance" in a bullish or bearish market, respectively. Support may be thought of as buying pressure as the market falls into a trough or a "reaction low." Resistance may be thought of as selling pressure as the market rallies into a peak or a "reaction high."

Areas where support or resistance may be encountered may be estimated by drawing a "trendline" on the chart. A bullish trendline (support) may be found by connecting a straight line under a series of higher and higher troughs. A bearish trendline (resistance) may be found by connecting a straight line over a series of lower and lower peaks. When connecting

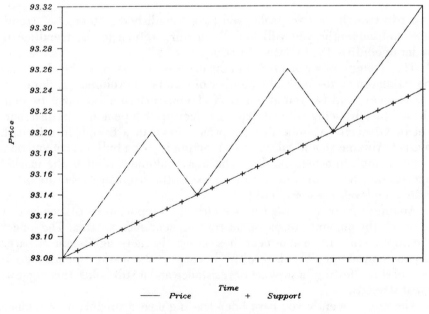

Figure 3–2   Bullish trend.

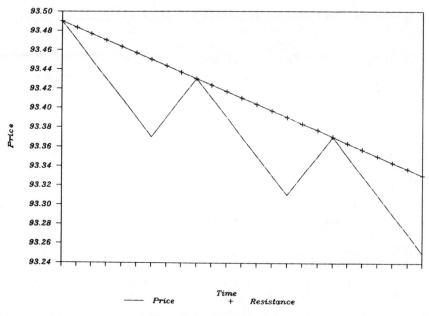

Figure 3–3   Bearish trend.

just two troughs or two peaks, you have established a "tentative" trend-line. Subsequently, you will look for a third return to the trendline in order to confirm the tentative trendline.

The strength of a potential support or resistance area on the chart may be estimated on the basis of a number of factors: (1) volume, (2) duration, (3) recency, and (4) round numbers. Trends may, for example, be confirmed by advancing volume driving prices up to a peak in a bullish market or advancing volume driving prices down to a trough in a bearish market. Volume should fall off on a reaction low in a bull market and on a reaction high in a bear market. The more volume traded as the market approaches the support or resistance levels, the stronger those support or resistance levels are considered.

Another way of assessing the strength of a support or resistance level is to watch the amount of time spent trading near such an area. The longer the time spent trading at or near these areas, the more significant that area may be considered. This is intuitive because if the market spends a great deal of time "testing" a support or resistance and it still holds, this suggests great strength.

The more recently you have been trading near a support or resistance area, the stronger that area is likely to be. This is intuitive in the sense that if support or resistance at any particular area has held firm in the recent past, it is likely to remain firm in the near future.

Finally, traders often associate a great deal of significance with round numbers. For example, a bond futures quote of 100 percent of par (100–00) is more likely to have some psychological significance than a quote like 99–23. In fact, the famous commodity and stock analyst W.D. Gann spent a great deal of time looking at the value of round numbers. He would break a range into halves, thirds, quarters, and eighths, assessing less and less significance to each successively finer and finer division.

Consider, for example, a situation where Eurodollar futures are trading between 93.00 and 94.00. Gann might break that range into halves, identifying 93.50 as a potentially significant support or resistance level. Other potentially significant areas might be 93.33 and 93.67 (thirds); 93.25 and 93.75 (quarters); and 93.12, 93.37, 93.63, and 93.88 (eighths).

How can you tell whether these levels will represent support or resistance? If the market is above the level, it may provide support; if the market is below the level, it may provide resistance! This is a variation of the idea that once broken, support becomes resistance; once broken, resistance becomes support.

As a rule, it is probably best to avoid placing limit orders precisely at a support or resistance level which is deemed significant. If a significant support or resistance level is hit, the market may react strongly with a sharp advance or decline. This may mean that your broker will be unable to fill a limit order at the specified price. It is usually best to place a limit buy order just above a support level and a limit sell order just below a resistance level in order to assure a fill.

But why should these perceived support or resistance areas be expected actually to hold? Some observers say that there are three kinds of market participants: longs, shorts, and the uncommitted. All three groups are psychologically committed to enforcing support in a bull market.

Longs are looking for the next dip to a support level in order to add to an existing profitable long position. Shorts are looking for the next dip as a good opportunity to cut their losses. Finally, the uncommitted are looking for the next dip in order to establish a new position and participate in the bullish trend.

Support and resistance are said to be characteristic of a bull and a bear market, respectively. Many traders, however, identify lines which run parallel to bull and bear trendlines. By connecting a series of higher and higher peaks in a bull market, you have identified a bullish channel (see Figure 3–4). A series of lower and lower troughs may be connected in a bear market and identified as a bearish channel (see Figure 3–5).

A *channel* is found by studying peaks and troughs in market movements. A *bullish channel* is identified by connecting a series of higher and

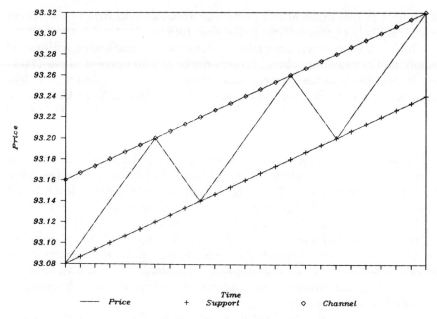

Figure 3–4   Bullish trend.

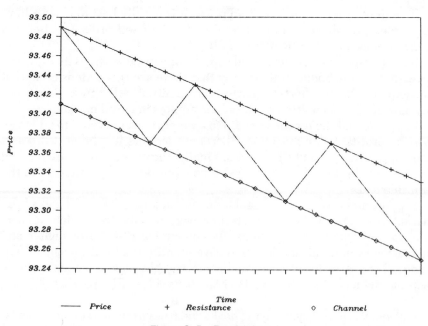

Figure 3–5   Bearish trend.

higher peaks in a bull market; a *bearish channel* is identified by connecting a series of lower and lower troughs in a bear market.

While channels are frequently identified in bull and bear markets, they are generally weaker and more "ragged" than the support or resistance levels that they parallel. These channels should run parallel to the support or resistance levels and may provide a useful indication of where to take profits. For example, a long in a bull market may buy on the troughs and take profits on the peaks; a short in a bear market may sell on the peaks and take profits on the troughs. But the market may not always reach the channel level. Often, the first sign of a reversal is the failure of the market to achieve a channel level.

What happens if a trendline should be broken? A broken support or resistance level is a necessary condition to signal a reversal of the market trend, but it is not a sufficient condition. Trendlines are often penetrated, and yet the market continues to trend in a bullish or bearish direction. As a result, many analysts apply "filters" to help them determine whether any given penetration constitutes a legitimate break of the trendline.

For example, a penetration of a trendline on an intraday basis is generally not regarded as significant. Many analysts look for a penetration of a trendline on the market close or settlement. Some analysts are not convinced unless the market trades through a support or resistance level for two or three consecutive days. Others are not convinced unless that break accounts for perhaps 2 to 3 percent of the previous market trend, measured from the lowest trough to the highest peak achieved during the duration of the trend.

Assume, however, that a trendline is broken, satisfying the added rigor of a filter application. This still does not necessarily suggest that the trend itself is broken. It may simply mean that the trendline as drawn is "unsustainable." A trendline can be unsustainably steep or even unsustainably shallow.

A "sustainable" rate of advance or decline is thought to be measured as a 45-degree angle. Forty-five degrees is meaningless in and of itself. Obviously, the size of one's graph paper makes a great deal of difference with respect to the angle. The point is, however, that the "common wisdom" attributes significance to a 45-degree angle. For better or worse, if a sufficiently large group of traders ascribe significance, the weight of their market opinion may constitute a force with which to be reckoned.

This suggests that it is better in many cases not to design your own charts. Rather, it may be better to subscribe to a popular chart service which develops charts (generally on a weekly basis) which are used by a large number of traders. By relying on those commonly referenced charts, you will be assured that you are working with a common reference.

As a result, it is common to "fan up" trendlines drawn initially at too shallow an angle or to "fan down" trendlines drawn at too steep an angle. One rule of thumb, however, is that once you have penetrated three "fanned" trendlines, trend reversal is imminent. ("One, two, three strikes, you're out!")

How far can the market be expected to travel on a valid trend penetration? Many analysts rely upon "percentage retracement" guides. The first issue is: How far can a market trend be retraced? Obviously a movement can only be *retraced* up to 100 percent of the original movement. But once a retracement or reversal begins, analysts often look for a one-third, one-half, or two-thirds retracement.

Assume that Eurodollar futures have experienced a rally from 92.00 to 93.00, measured from the lowest trough to the highest peak. Now, however, the market shows signs of reversing or retracing that 100-basis point movement. Look for support at the one-third retracement level (92.67), the one-half retracement level (92.50), and the two-thirds retracement level (92.33).

Other analysts disagree with respect to the one-third or 33 percent level and the two-thirds or 67 percent level. Some claim that it is more appropriate to identify the 38 percent (support at 92.62) and 62 percent (support at 92.38) retracement levels.

These alternate 38 percent and 62 percent levels are derived from the Fibonacci number series. The Fibonacci number series goes [1, 2, 3, 5, 8, 13, 21, 34, 55, 89, 144, . . .]. Note that each number is derived by adding together the prior two numbers.

This number series has some interesting and unique properties. For example, if you divide any number in the series by the prior number, the result will be remarkably consistent at about 1.618. (This only works well after the first few numbers in the series.)

Properties of Fibonacci Numbers

2/1 = 2.000	1/2 = 0.500
3/2 = 1.500	2/3 = 0.667
5/3 = 1.667	3/5 = 0.600
13/8 = 1.625	8/13 = 0.615
21/13 = 1.615	13/21 = 0.619
34/21 = 1.619	21/34 = 0.618
55/34 = 1.618	34/55 = 0.618
89/55 = 1.618	55/89 = 0.618
144/89 = 1.618	89/144 = 0.618

By dividing any number in the series by the next number, the result will be remarkably consistent at about 0.618. The reciprocal of 0.618 (1/0.618) is 1.618. The reciprocal of 1.618 (1/1.618) is 0.618.

More will be said about the remarkable properties of the Fibonacci number series later. The point is that traders often attribute significance to these numbers. The 62 percent retracement level is derived from the number 0.618. The 38 percent retracement level is simply 100 percent less the 62 percent figure.

Reversal Patterns

A reversal pattern is a formation identified on a bar chart, the initial stages of which may suggest that a reversal of a market trend is imminent. A *top* may occur at the completion of a sustained bull movement, signaling an imminent bear market. A *bottom* occurs at the completion of a sustained bear movement, signaling the beginning of a bull movement.

A *reversal* represents a formation on a chart which indicates the end of a sustained movement and the beginning of a new movement. A *top* indicates the conclusion of a bull movement and the inception of a bear movement. A *bottom* indicates the conclusion of a bear movement and the inception of a bull movement.

It is important to be able to distinguish a reversal from a consolidation pattern. A consolidation pattern is simply an area on the chart where the market takes a pause before it can continue to trend in the previously established direction. A reversal pattern indicates that the market is now ready to trade in a direction opposite the previously established direction.

The first early warning sign associated with a market reversal will be a penetration of a trendline. This suggests, of course, that the market has previously been trending either up or down. Of course, a simple penetration may or may not signal a reversal. It may simply indicate that the trend is moving at an unsustainable angle, and your trendlines require adjustment.

This section will explore five commonly referenced reversal patterns. Those five patterns include:

1. The head and shoulders,
2. Triple top or bottom,
3. Double top or bottom,
4. Rounded bottom, and
5. Spike or "V" top.

The *head and shoulders* (H&S) formation is the most widely recognized of the five reversal patterns named above. The H&S pattern is typified by three peaks: a "left shoulder" and a "right shoulder" coupled with a higher peak between known as the "head" (see Figure 3–6). Perhaps the best way

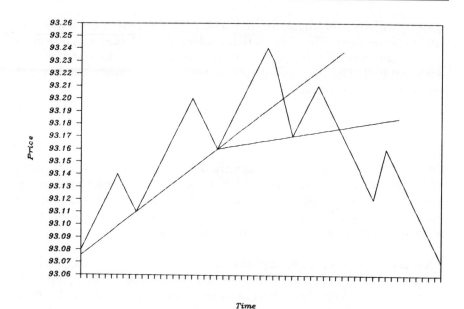

Figure 3–6   Head and shoulders top.

to describe the head and shoulders formation is to examine the chart closely, identifying early warning signs which may portend the coming reversal.

In the early stages of the H&S, there are generally no warning signs at all that a reversal might be on the horizon. Volume may in fact surge upwards on the bullish movement up to the left shoulder associated with a topping H&S.

Subsequently, one may see the market decline to the nape of the "neckline"—the trough between the left shoulder and head—on reduced volume. Still, there is no indication of a reversal because the market has simply returned to a support trendline as might normally be expected.

The next surge upwards to the head still provides no clear indication of a possible reversal. Sometimes, however, volume on this upward surge falls short of the volume on the prior upward surge to the left shoulder. The market then declines through the support level, down to the nape of the neckline—the trough between the head and the right shoulder.

Once the two troughs between the head and the right and left shoulders are formed, one may draw in a neckline. It is important to identify the slope of this neckline. The neckline associated with a true H&S formation tends to slope in the general direction in which the market was trending before entering the pattern. If the neckline slopes downwards in a topping

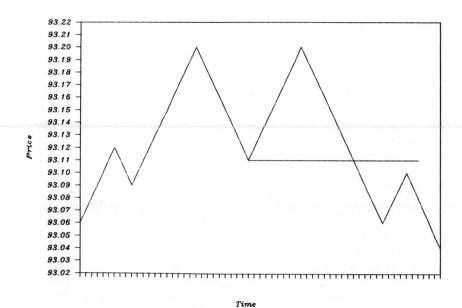

Figure 3-8   Double top.

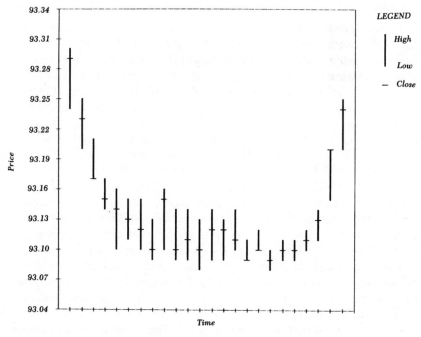

Figure 3-9   Rounding bottom.

41

Volume and volatility fall off while the market is in this pattern. While the market is trading in a rounding bottom, it is essentially being "lulled to sleep" over an extended period of time. Little or no fundamental information may be released during this period. Subsequently, the market break is accompanied by a burst of volume and a flurry of activity. This volume is said to be "stored up" during the lull. This break is often the result of new fundamental information which becomes known in the marketplace.

It is difficult to trade a rounding bottom because there is generally little indication with respect to when the market will break. Nor is there any indication with respect to the magnitude of that break.

A rounding pattern is much more common in the "traditional" futures markets (grains, livestock, metals) relative to the financial markets. This may be attributed to the fact that fundamental news which impacts upon the agricultural markets, for example, is not released with the same frequency as is news which impacts upon the financials.

Almost every day a news release regarding some fundamental measure of economic activity, inflation, or government fiscal or monetary policy hits the financial markets. But soybean crop reports, for example, are not made known with the same kind of frequency even in the growing season. In the winter months, many agricultural markets can become quite inactive. Thus the possibility of a rounding pattern with low volume and volatility over an extended period of time becomes quite possible.

If the rounded bottom is more typical of a traditional futures market than a financial futures market, a V *top formation* is more typical of a financial rather than a traditional market. In this and in other respects, the V or spike pattern is the antithesis of the rounding bottom.

A V or spike pattern more commonly occurs at a top than a bottom. It is characterized by high volatility over an extremely short period of time. Because the reversal occurs so sharply, it is often referred to as a V or, to be more precise, an inverted V formation (see Figure 3–10).

In fact, the pattern may begin and end within the course of a single day. This single day is sometimes referred to as the "key reversal day." A great deal of volume and volatility is realized on a key reversal day. A key reversal often results in a limit movement. Generally, the market will reach a new high on the key day followed by a sudden decline, often as a result of new fundamental news. The market may close at or near the low of the day which extends below the low for the previous day or two.

Like the rounded bottom, there is little or no warning before the reversal takes place, so it is difficult to trade profitably. Sometimes, however, early warning signs occur such as market gaps and high open interest.

Market gaps are common before and after key reversal days. A market gap is an area on the chart where no trading takes place. If you see the market gap upwards on light volume, this may portend a subsequent rever-

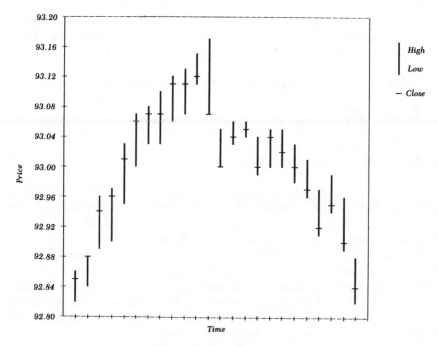

Figure 3–10   Spike or "V" top.

sal. Sometimes the market gaps down on heavy volume subsequent to a key reversal. In that case, the formation may be referred to as an "island reversal." More will be said about gaps later in this text.

Another sign of a possible reversal may be extremely high open interest. Growth in open interest in a volatile market may be unsustainable. In the long term, volume tends to rise, and open interest falls in a volatile market environment. The reason is intuitive: Opportunities are frequently available in a volatile market, and you need not hold positions overnight to take advantage of it.

When the market is trending upwards on high volatility with growing open interest, any "crack" in those long positions may result in a panic sell situation. If a significant number of the longs start to "take profits" by selling, others may follow, accelerating the decline.

Consolidation Patterns

A *consolidation pattern* represents an interruption of a trend. The market trades sideways for a while before it can continue in its bullish or bearish pattern.

A *consolidation* pattern occurs when the market trades in a neutral holding pattern for a limited period of time before resuming the direction in which it was trending prior to entering the pattern.

Common consolidation patterns include the following:

1. Pennants and flags,
2. Symmetrical, ascending, descending, or expanding triangles,
3. Wedge or diagonal triangles, and
4. Rectangle or sideways channels.

The *pennant* or *flag* is a very common consolidation pattern. It is essentially an indication of a market which has moved too far too fast. Market participants may be tempted to take some profits, to rethink their strategies, to "regroup" before continuing to trade aggressively.

A pennant differs from a flag in that the flag is more rectangular, while the pennant more closely resembles a triangular pattern (see Figure 3–11). Both patterns tend to slant or point away from the general market direction. If the market is generally bullish, for example, a flag or pennant will trend in a bearish direction. If the market is generally bearish, the flag or pennant will trend in a bullish direction.

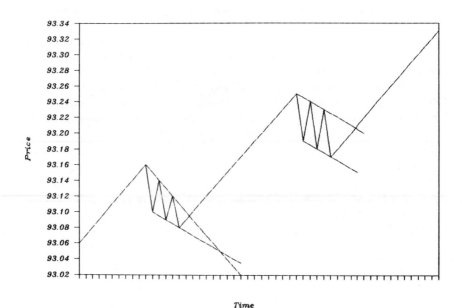

Figure 3–11   Pennant and flag.

This trend against the market direction tends to be short-lived. Flags and pennants are generally completed within two to three weeks or less from the time the "pullback" begins. Subsequently, these patterns are thought to be very "reliable" in the sense that they almost invariably result in a continuation of the prior market trend.

One old market saying goes "flags and pennants fly at half-mast." This suggests that flags and pennants may be observed about midway in a major market movement, but this way of thinking may be incompatible with Elliot wave theory.

Elliot wave theory suggests that the market may rachet up in a five-wave pattern—three "impulse" waves (waves 1, 3, and 5) with two intervening "corrective" waves (waves 2 and 4). If waves 2 and 4 take the form of a flag or a pennant, it is clear that these patterns cannot "fly at half-mast."

But what if the second wave b of the following three-step corrective phase (a, b, and c) takes the form of a flag or pennant? Under those circumstances, the flag or pennant may in fact "fly at half-mast."

Triangles are very similar in terms of their shape to pennants, yet they differ in a number of key respects. Foremost among these differences is that a triangle is generally thought of as a longer-term consolidation pattern, a pattern which may take several different yet similar forms.

A triangle is characterized by converging support and resistance levels which meet in the future at a point referred to as the "apex." But this triangle may take the shape of a symmetrical triangle, an ascending triangle, or a descending triangle.

A symmetrical triangle is characterized by an upward sloping support trendline coupled with a downward sloping resistance trendline (see Figure 3–12). An ascending triangle is characterized by a flat resistance trendline and an upwardly sloping support level (see Figure 3–13). Finally, a descending triangle is characterized by a flat support trendline and a downwardly sloping resistance level (see Figure 3–14).

Despite the somewhat different inclinations associated with these three kinds of triangles, they all share some common characteristics. Volume and volatility, for example, are expected to decline as you trade into any of these three triangular formations. Subsequently, the triangle is concluded with a sharp, sudden breakout as the market once again begins to trend.

However, the direction in which this breakout may occur is unknown. Triangles are generally thought of as consolidation patterns. As such, it is believed that triangles are most likely to result in a continuation of the trend which had been established prior to the formation of the triangle.

On the other hand, triangles sometimes result in a reversal rather than a continuation of the trend. Many analysts would attach a two-thirds probability to the possibility of a continuation with a one-third probability to the possibility of a subsequent reversal. Many analysts would attach slightly

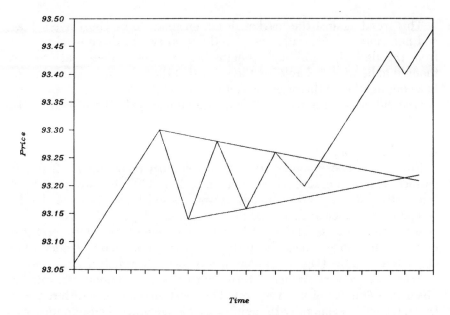

Figure 3–12　Symmetrical triangle.

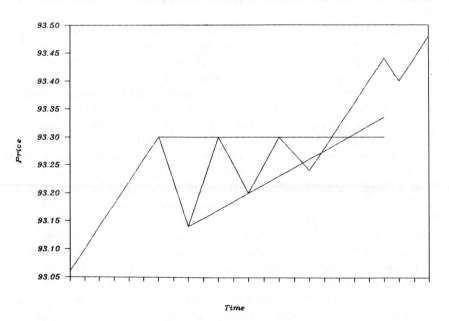

Figure 3–13　Ascending triangle.

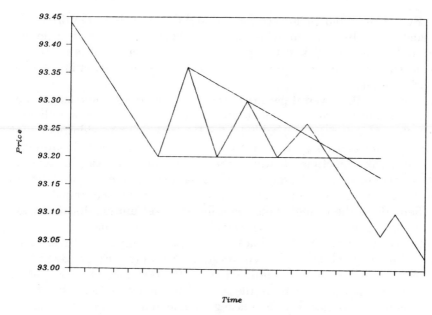

Figure 3–14 Descending triangle.

greater than two-thirds probability to an upward or downward break on the conclusion of an ascending or descending triangle, respectively.

Triangles are generally thought of as rather longer-term patterns. By this we mean that a triangle may continue for perhaps upwards of two to three weeks. What market conditions may portend a breakout? Technical analysts often measure a triangle horizontally from the beginning of the formation out to the apex (where the support and resistance trendlines converge). The breakout is believed to be likely to occur somewhere between the one-half way point and the three-quarters of the way point to the apex.

Elliot wave theory provides an even more complete description of the nature of a triangle. According to Elliot, a triangle will be composed of five waves. Let us refer to these waves as A, B, C, D, and E. Thus one might start anticipating a breakout as the market trends into the one-half to three-quarters way point to the apex area and as the market completes a 5th wave within the triangle.

Because the market is essentially neutral while trading in a triangle, many traders prefer to apply neutral option trading strategies (short straddles, short strangles). Unfortunately, it is only when three legs (A, B, and C) and four points are formed that one may identify a triangle. One cannot identify a triangle without four points to form converging support and resistance levels.

By the time four points are formed and the triangle is identified, the triangle may be close to achieving a breakout. It may be risky to sell straddles and strangles at this point, but when a breakout is imminent, many traders prefer to buy straddles and strangles in anticipation of a big market break.

Similar to the reversal patterns previously discussed, the triangle provides an indication with respect to the size of the movement upon a breakout. By measuring the vertical height of the triangle at its widest point (at the inception of leg A), you can estimate the minimum expected movement on the break. Sometimes, however, the market does not break out at all. If the market drifts past the three-quarters way point or the apex itself, many analysts believe that the market will continue to drift indeterminately.

Sometimes the triangle takes on a fourth, most unusual form, the expanding triangle. An expanding triangle looks like a symmetrical triangle with the exception that it is backwards, that is, support and resistance trendlines expand rather than converge to an apex (see Figure 3–15).

The expanding triangle is unlike most of the reversal and consolidation patterns considered thus far in the sense that it is accompanied by generally increasing rather than decreasing volume and volatility. This formation is extremely difficult to trade because it is characteristic of a market which is desperately searching without success for direction. There is no

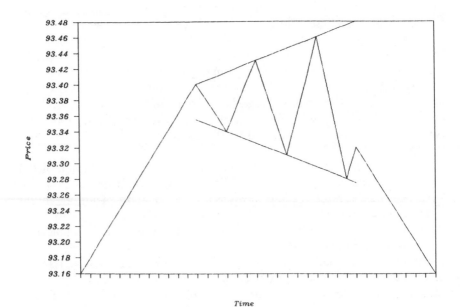

Figure 3–15 Expanding triangle.

really reliable way of identifying the prospects for an upward or a downward break.

The *wedge* strongly resembles a triangle in terms of its shape with one notable exception; the wedge generally slants against the general market trend quite sharply (see Figure 3–16). In most other aspects, it is quite like a triangle. It may be thought of as a longer-term formation taking upwards of two to three weeks to form. It tends to break out about one-half way to three-quarters way to the apex.

The *rectangle* may be thought of as a neutral trading range. Strong support and strong resistance are evident which means that the market generally drifts sideways for an extended period of time (see Figure 3–17). Generally increased trading activity occurs when the market is trading near either the support or resistance levels. These levels are used to establish new positions and take profits.

Price Gaps

A price *gap* represents an area on the chart where no trading activity occurs. Assume, for example, that today's high and low were at 93.36 and 93.28 in the Eurodollar futures market. Tomorrow the market opens

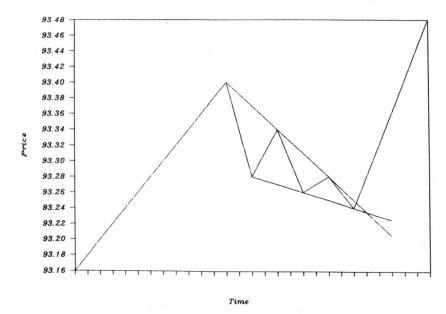

Figure 3–16   Descending bullish wedge.

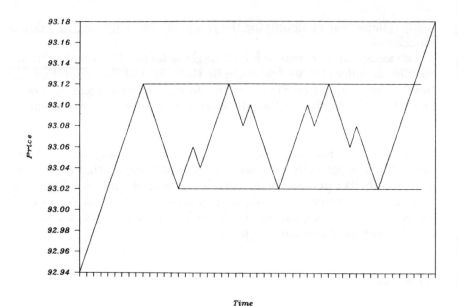

Figure 3–17   Rectangle.

at 93.25 and continues to trend downward. The area between 93.25 and 93.28 represents a price gap.

A *gap* represents an area on a chart characterized by an absence of any trading activity.

A gap may have a great deal of significance, or it may be essentially meaningless. One may identify two basic kinds of gaps, *pattern* and *nonpattern* gaps.

A nonpattern gap is sometimes referred to as a "common gap." This kind of gap may appear often in an illiquid or thinly traded market or when the market is drifting along in a rectangular pattern with no clear market direction. It is characterized by little interest and low volume.

From a predictive standpoint, the best advice is simply to discount a nonpattern gap. It usually provides little indication about the strength or weakness of a market trend. In fact, it may appear frequently in a basically trendless market. As such, a common gap is often "filled," that is, the market will subsequently trade within that area in which the gap was observed.

Pattern gaps are altogether different. A pattern gap is generally suggestive of subsequent market movements. Pattern gaps usually occur in very active, liquid markets, often when these active markets are experiencing a

impulse waves (waves 1, 3, and 5) may form, in particular, "extensions," "wedges," and "failures."

As a general rule, impulse waves tend to be of approximately equal size. (Size can be measured by the vertical height or price movement of a pattern and in terms of its horizontal width or duration.) This is the "rule of wave equality," but sometimes, even often, one of the impulse waves is larger in terms of its height and width than the other two approximately equal impulse waves.

This represents a wave "extension." Wave extensions tend to break down into a series of five smaller waves. Extensions are most likely to occur during the 3d impulse wave. This is intuitive to the extent that this wave may represent the technical trend-following phase of the market, that is, the wave which surges forth on the weight of a great deal of technical market participation.

Because wave 3 is generally the strongest and most likely to extend, Elliot suggests that while wave 3 is often the longest, it is never the shortest of the three impulse waves. Because wave 3 is so strong, the downward movement on the subsequent corrective wave 4 should not cover the same territory as did wave 1, that is, waves 1 and 4 do not overlap.

(In fact, Elliot's "depth of corrective waves" hypothesis suggests that corrections, particularly 4th wave corrections, tend to stop within the span of movement of the previous 4th wave movement of one lesser degree. In other words, a 4th wave correction of primary degree should cease before it hits the trough established by the 4th wave movement of intermediate degree within the 3d impulse wave.)

The wave which is least likely to extend is the 1st impulse wave. This is due to the fact that impulse wave number 1 generally represents the weakest impulse movement. The subsequent corrective wave number 2 may, in fact, give back almost all of the movement on impulse wave number 1.

Wave 5 is the second most likely or second least likely (depending upon your perspective) wave to extend (see Figure 3–21). Elliot developed some interesting guidelines which may be useful for forecasting how market movements may unfold subsequent to a 5th wave extension. In particular, a wave 5 extension is said to be *retraced twice!*

Assume you have reached a market top at the completion of the 5th wave of wave 5. The market is now expected to begin a three-wave corrective phase. The first corrective wave a is expected to fall or retrace to the beginning of the extension. The second corrective wave b is thereupon expected to advance to the previously established market top or beyond before falling off as wave c is established.

As such, the top of the 5th wave extension cannot represent the completion of the upswing as the market is likely to break down and then rally to

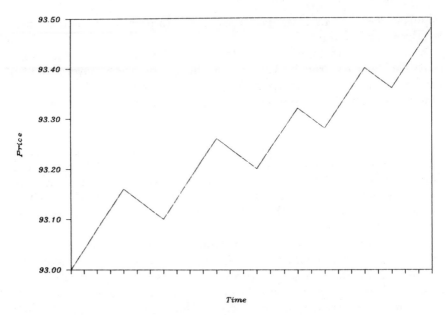

Figure 3–21 Fifth wave extension.

the same level or possibly to a new high. As discussed later, this lettered phase takes the form of an irregular correction.

An extended wave is of greater magnitude than the two nonextending waves. In particular, it may be expected to be about 1.618 times greater in vertical height than the nonextending waves. (The number 1.618 comes from the Fibonacci number series.)

A wedge or diagonal triangle may be mistaken for an extension because this triangle is generally played out in a series of five waves (see Figure 3–22). But unlike a 5th wave extension, this wedge may rise on reduced volume and volatility, that is, the market is becoming "exhausted." It has traveled a little too sharply and must display a slightly consolidative movement.

Similar to a triangular correction (discussed later), this wedge breaks down into a 3-3-3-3-3 pattern—a series of five waves which break down into three smaller waves each.

A "failure" represents an instance where the 5th impulse wave fails to clear the top of the 3d impulse wave (see Figure 3–23). Many analysts may mistake this formation for a lettered corrective phase. But the 4th corrective wave and the subsequent 5th wave failure may be distinguished from the beginning of an a-b-c corrective phase.

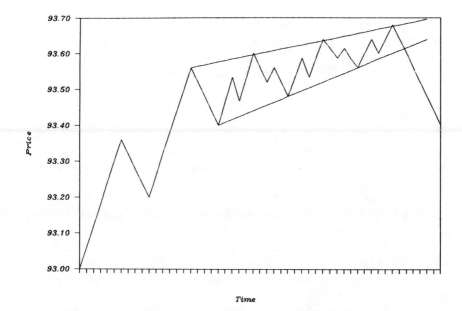

Figure 3–22   Diagonal triangle or wedge.

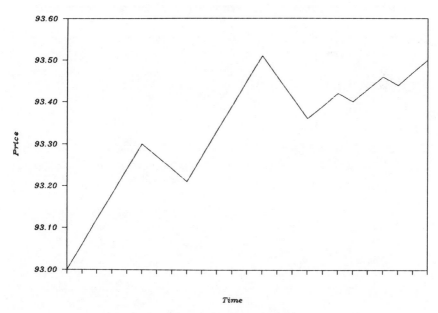

Figure 3–23   Fifth wave failure.

The distinction lies in the fact that this 5th impulse wave may break down into a series of five waves of smaller degree. It is, therefore, distinguished from wave b of an a-b-c correction in that wave b should break down into three, rather than five, smaller waves.

Corrective Waves

Just as impulse waves often take on alternate forms apart from the norm, the subsequent a-b-c lettered phase often takes on alternate forms as well. Let us illustrate the *normal* correction and its variations.

These variations may be referred to as "flats," "triangles," "double 3s," and "triple 3s." These issues are complicated further by the fact that there are several variations on the variations!

The normal a-b-c correction is sometimes referred to by its technical term, the zigzag. The normal zigzag is characterized in that its three waves break down into smaller waves with 5, 3, and 5 movements, respectively (see Figure 3–24).

Notice that wave b of the normal zigzag does not rally above the peak established at the beginning of wave a (or the top of the previous 5th wave). Elliot suggests that, as a general rule, the vertical distance travelled

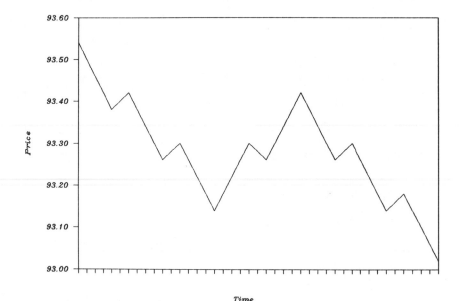

Time

Figure 3–24   Zigzag correction.

by wave b tends to be about 61.8 percent of the vertical distance of wave a. Waves a and c tend to be of about equal magnitude.

This means that the zigzag carries the market into an area well below the top established at the beginning of wave a. But other kinds of corrections such as the flats cannot be expected to carry the market into quite so low areas.

Whereas the zigzag is characterized as a 5-3-5 formation, the flat is characterized as a 3-3-5 formation (three waves which break down into smaller movements of 3, 3, and 5 waves, respectively).

This breakdown suggests strength in the previous market trend. Strength is indicated in the fact that the 1st wave breaks down into only three, rather than five, waves. The market's downward force during wave a is insufficient to create five waves.

In a normal flat, the subsequent upward wave b may fully retrace the movement of wave a; that is, the market may match its previous high established at the beginning of wave a or the conclusion of wave 5. Wave c thereupon drives the market to a point which is below the low established at the conclusion of wave a (see Figure 3–25).

In addition to the normal flat, there are three other types of flats: "irregular flat number 1," "irregular flat number 2," and the "running correction."

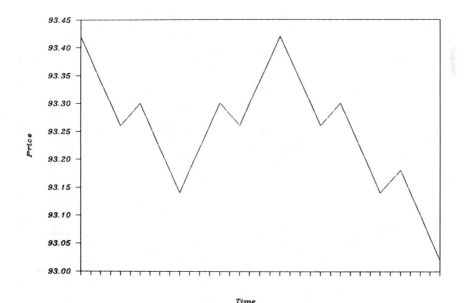

Figure 3–25   'Normal' flat correction.

Pursuant to irregular flat number 1, the market rallies not only to meet, but to exceed, the highs established at the beginning of wave a or the conclusion of wave 5. The subsequent 3d wave c falls below the low established at the conclusion of wave a (see Figure 3–26).

Irregular flat number 1 indicates great strength insofar as wave b rallies over the previously established highs. But it also indicates volatility as the market trades in successively wider ranges with each wave.

Irregular flat number 2 likewise shows strength but perhaps not such great strength as in irregular flat number 1. This is observed insofar as wave b meets but does not typically exceed the top established at the beginning of wave a. The subsequent 5th wave c pushes the market down, but not so far as to break the lows established at the bottom of wave a. In other words, irregular flat number 2 shows strength, but volatility is falling rather than rising (see Figure 3–27).

Finally, a "running correction" is indicative of very great strength in the market. This is indicated in the fact that a running correction positively carries the market into new higher ground. In fact, wave c often concludes at a price level in excess of the top established at the beginning of wave a or conclusion of wave 5 (see Figure 3–28).

In addition to zigzags and flats, corrective phases may take on the form of a triangle. Like the flat, a triangle can take on a number of forms (discussed in the context of traditional bar charting theory earlier). These

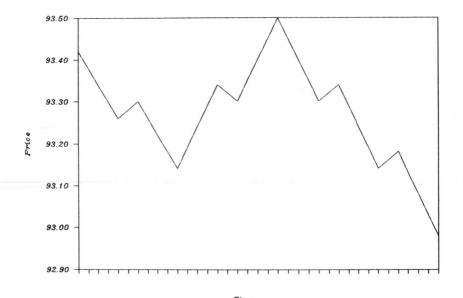

Figure 3–26   Irregular flat No. 1.

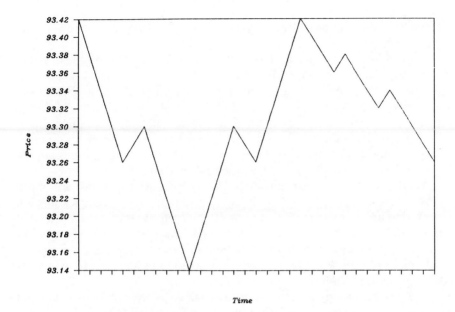

Figure 3–27   Irregular flat No. 2.

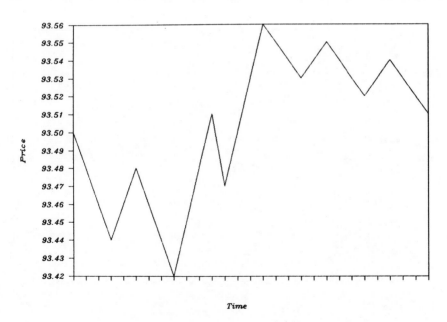

Figure 3–28   Running correction.

forms include the ascending, descending, symmetrical, and expanding triangles.

Elliot's interpretations of these triangles are quite similar to traditional interpretations discussed earlier, that is, triangles are continuation or corrective patterns. Ascending, descending, and symmetrical triangles generally tend to be accompanied by falling volatility and volume, while expanding triangles are accompanied by rising volatility and volume (see Figures 3–29, 3–30, 3–31, and 3–32). The break at the conclusion of an ascending, descending, or symmetrical triangle is expected to be roughly equivalent to the width of the triangle at its widest point.

Unlike traditional bar charting theory, Elliot's triangles are more closely defined in terms of their pattern. All of these triangles are expected to break down into five waves. (Let us refer to these five as waves a, b, c, d, and e.) These five waves in turn break down into three smaller waves. In the ascending, descending, and symmetrical triangles, the vertical height of each successive wave is expected to represent approximately 61.8 percent of the prior wave.

Finally, Elliot indicates that a three-stage corrective phase may take on a more complex or compound form—a "double 3" or "triple 3" (see Figures 3–33 and 3–34). These formations may be thought of as two or three zigzags and/or flats strung together. They are strung together by a three-step upswing referred to as x.

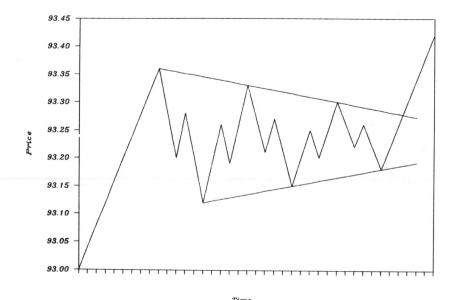

Figure 3-29   Symmetrical triangle.

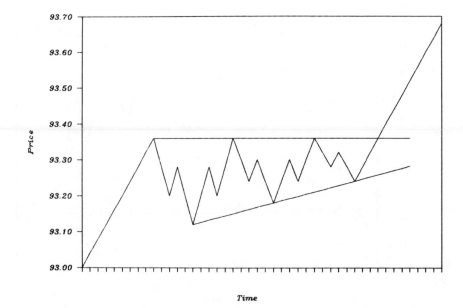

Figure 3–30　Ascending triangle.

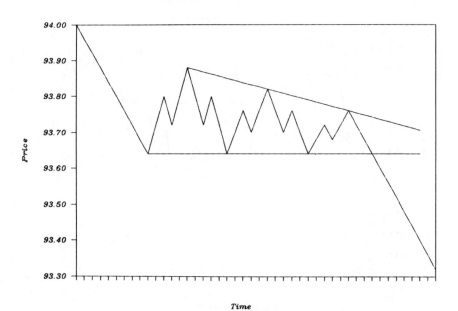

Figure 3–31　Descending triangle.

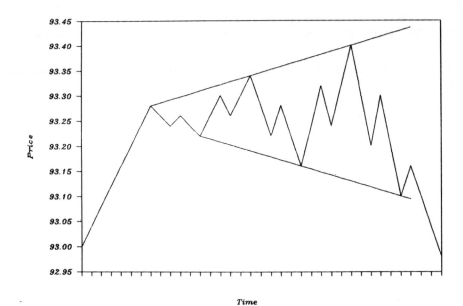

Figure 3–32   Expanding triangle.

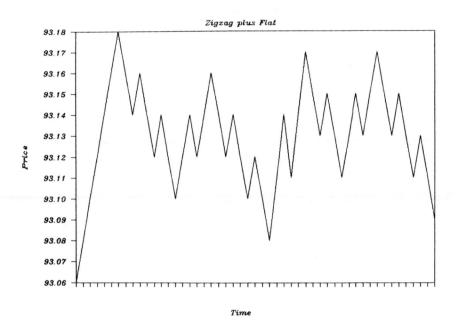

Figure 3–33   Double threes.

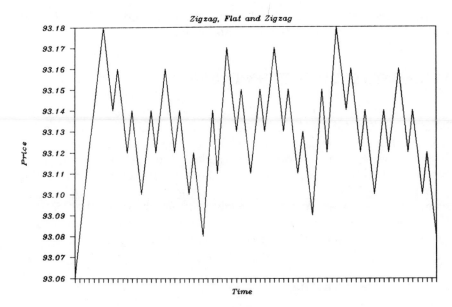

Figure 3–34   Triple threes.

These formations indicate that the market needs an extended period of time to correct itself. Insofar as this formation is mostly horizontal, a double 3 or triple 3 is a market which is searching for direction. Look for these patterns to be comprised of different types of corrective movements. For example, a double 3 may be comprised of a zigzag and some type of flat, or a triple 3 may be comprised of a zigzag and two different kinds of flats.

Elliot believed that patterns do not repeat themselves successively. If the last correction (in wave 2 of a five-step rally, for example) was a flat, expect the next correction (wave 4) to represent something other than a flat—such as a zigzag or triangle. This "rule of alternation" applies with equal respect to the 3s which make up a double 3 or triple 3 in the lettered phase of a market movement as well as to the corrective waves in the numbered phase of the market.

As suggested before, Elliot believed that the strength of a trend may be assessed, not so much by watching the trend itself, but by studying corrective patterns within the trend. The various corrective patterns previously discussed all give rise to an interpretation with respect to the strength of the trend within the market.

For example, a zigzag is indicative of normal strength in the market. The normal and the irregular flats indicate more strength in the market. The running correction is indicative of very great strength. Ascending, descending, and symmetrical triangles indicate more strength than does the zigzag, culminating in a swift but relatively short-lived breakout. Double and triple 3s show strength but of a tentative nature.

INTRADAY TRADING TECHNIQUES

Many analysts find that the charting techniques discussed previously can be extremely useful for the purposes of interday trading. On an intraday basis (within the same day), these techniques may be somewhat less useful.

Some analysts, for example, do not make use of intraday charts. If we believe that technical analysis works because it represents a self-fulfilling prophecy, it will be unwise to rely upon charting techniques which are not commonly referenced. As a result, analysts often rely upon other methods for purposes of intraday trading. Some methods discussed here include point and figure charting and "pivot point analysis."

Point and Figure Charting

Point and figure charting is a frequently referenced charting technique which may be used to plot price fluctuations on an interday or an intraday basis. For our purposes, however, we will restrict our consideration to intraday data.

Point and figure charts are characterized by a series of Xs and Os arranged in columns. The Xs represent price advances while Os represent price declines. Point and figure charts are considered useful because, if properly constructed, they "filter out" spurious price fluctuations. Because of the filtering mechanism intrinsic to the chart, it does not provide full information with respect to all (or at least small) fluctuations. Nor does it provide any information with respect to the time at which particular fluctuations took place.

Let us consider how one might construct a point and figure chart and how to interpret the chart. One begins a point and figure chart with a piece of graph paper showing a series of columns and rows. The next and most critical step is to identify one's "box size" and "reversal" criterion.

The box size refers to the number of ticks that is represented by each row. You may identify a box size from a single tick upwards. Assume that you plot T-bond futures prices; you might designate a two-tick box—each box represents $2/_{32}$ds or $62.50.

The reversal criterion refers to the number of boxes by which the market must reverse before a reversal is recognized and the chart changes from Xs to Os or vice versa. That means the reversal criterion provides the filtering mechanism by which one discounts relatively small breaks in the trend.

It is most common to designate a three-box reversal criterion. If the box size is designated as two ticks, this suggests that the market must reverse itself by a full six ticks before such reversal is recognized.

How does one construct a point and figure chart? Begin by placing a dot in the box corresponding to the first price observed. Assume that the market opens at 94–00 and begins to rally. As the market rallies in two-tick increments, fill in successively higher boxes, but only if the market rallies by a full two-tick box!

Thus if prices rise to 94–07, the highest box which is filled corresponds to 94–06. Only if the market rallies to 94–08 is the next highest box filled! Does a subsequent decline to 94–01 constitute a reversal? No! Only if prices fall a full six ticks or three boxes off the highest box filled in at 94–06 is a reversal recognized!

Now assume that the market falls all the way to 93–24. When the market hits 94–00, you move one column to the right and begin filling in Os down to 93–24. A subsequent rally back to 93–30 covers a full three boxes and, therefore, you move one column to the right and fill in a series of Xs up to 93–30.

Another reversal takes the market in our example down to 93–22, indicated by a column of Os, but the subsequent rally to 93–25 does not cover three full boxes. The market settles back to 93–22, but the rally to 94–05 constitutes a reversal. As soon as the market hits 93–28 on the way up, you move one column to the right and begin filling in Xs.

Constructing a Point and Figure Chart

| 94–00 | → | 94–07 | → | 94–01 | → | 94–06 | → | 93–24 | → |
| 93–30 | → | 93–22 | → | 93–25 | → | 93–22 | → | 94–05 | → |

94–08	
94–06	x
94–04	xo x
94–02	xo x
94–00	o x
93–30	ox x
93–28	oxox
93–26	oxox
93–24	o ox
93–22	o
93–20	

The simplest way of using a point and figure chart is to buy whenever you begin a new column of Xs; cover your longs and take a short position on a new column of Os. It is tremendously important to identify a workable box size and reversal criterion.

This kind of trading system will in fact work if the market exhibits clear trending tendencies. If the market is quite choppy and reverses frequently, however, the system will result in a series of losses, albeit relatively modest losses on any given trade.

While the point and figure chart is sometimes used as previously indicated, traders sometimes look for patterns in the charts just as you would look for patterns in a bar chart. Because this method filters out spurious information automatically, patterns sometimes stand out much more clearly in a point and figure chart than in a bar chart.

Consider some of the more commonly recognized patterns. You will note that many of these point and figure patterns are reminiscent of the bar chart patterns discussed earlier.

The patterns shown in Figure 3–35 are restricted to buy signals. Sell signals may be generated by similar formations. The only exception is to rotate these diagrams along a horizontal axis!

Once the market breaks, how far can it be expected to move? Count the number of columns over which the pattern formed. Look for the vertical market movement to equal the horizontal movement while the pattern formed.

Pivot Point Analysis

Pivot point analysis represents another technique which is frequently used on an intraday basis. This method allows one to identify potential levels of support or resistance. It relies on high, low, and closing price information from the preceding day. The central pivot may be calculated as the average of the high (H), low (L), and closing (C) price levels:

$$\text{Pivot} = (H + L + C)/3$$

Depending upon whether the market is above or below this pivot, it may act as either a support or resistance level. Other potential areas of support or resistance may be found with similar measures. In particular, one may calculate the "first support" and the "first resistance" levels or the "second support" and "second resistance" levels.

$$\text{1st Support} = (2 \times \text{Pivot}) - H$$

$$\text{1st Resistance} = (2 \times \text{Pivot}) - L$$

$$\text{2d Support} = \text{Pivot} - (H - L)$$

$$\text{2d Resistance} = \text{Pivot} + (H - L)$$

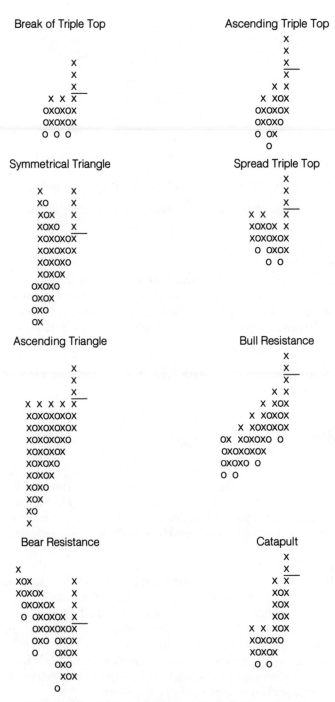

Break of Triple Top

```
          x
          x
          x
    x x  x‾
    oxoxox
    oxoxox
    o o o
```

Ascending Triple Top

```
              x
              x
              x
              x‾
           x x
           x xox
           oxoxox
           oxoxo
           o  ox
              o
```

Symmetrical Triangle

```
    x       x
    xo      x
    xox     x
    xoxo    x‾
    xoxoxox‾
    xoxoxox
    xoxoxo
    xoxox
    oxoxo
    oxox
    oxo
    ox
```

Spread Triple Top

```
              x
              x
              x
         x x  x‾
         xoxox x
         xoxoxox
         o oxox
           o o
```

Ascending Triangle

```
          x
          x
          x‾
    x x x x x‾
    xoxoxoxox
    xoxoxoxox
    xoxoxoxo
    xoxoxox
    xoxoxo
    xoxox
    xoxo
    xox
    xo
    x
```

Bull Resistance

```
              x
              x‾
              x
           x x
           x xox
           x xoxox
           x xoxoxox
      ox xoxoxo o
      oxoxoxox
      oxoxo o
      o o
```

Bear Resistance

```
    x
    xox        x
    xoxox      x
     oxoxox    x
    o oxoxox x‾
      oxoxoxox‾
      oxo oxox
      o   oxox
          oxo
           xox
          o
```

Catapult

```
              x
              x‾
           x x
           xox
           xox
           xox
      x x xox
      xoxoxo
      xoxox
      o o
```

Figure 3–35   Point and figure chart patterns (buy signals).

Example: On May 21, 1987, deutsche mark futures for delivery in June 1987 settled at 56.43 cents per mark. The low for the day was posted at 56.27, the high at 56.49. The pivot points may be calculated as follows:

2d Resistance = 56.62

1st Resistance = 56.52

Pivot Point = 56.40

1st Support = 56.30

2d Support = 56.18

Look for support or resistance on the following day at these levels on the next trading day.

TREND-FOLLOWING SYSTEMS

Many (if not most) technical trading methods represent *trend-following* systems to one extent or another. In other words, they do not attempt to predict the advent of a new trend, but rather are intended to identify the existence of a trend and recommend action on the expectation of a continuation of the same.

"Moving averages" represent some of the most common trend-following devices. Used in combination with "oscillators," they provide some very interesting and potentially useful technical tools.

Moving Averages

A moving average (MA) represents an average market price over a recent time period. Moving averages are constructed in order to identify the trend by filtering or "smoothing out" unusual or temporary price aberrations. Two issues which must be addressed include: How should one calculate a moving average and, once constructed, how might one interpret the statistic?

On the first pass, one might assume that there is a single, straightforward method of calculating a moving average. In actuality, however, there are several very different means by which one may construct an MA.

In order to calculate a moving average, one must decide exactly what statistic you wish to average. For example, you may elect to take an average of a series of market opening prices, highs, lows, or closes. Some analysts prefer to take an average based on the midpoint of the high/low range or on the pivot—the average of the high, low, and closing prices. Most analysts, however, use the close or settlement prices.

There are also several different ways of calculating a moving average. These means include: (1) a simple or arithmetic average, (2) a geometric average, (3) a weighted or linear weighted average, and (4) an exponentially weighted average. Let us consider each method in turn along with the advantages and disadvantages of each.

An arithmetic average simply refers to the kind of average with which we are all very familiar. Take the summation of a series of prices (P) divided by the number of observations (n).

$$MA = \sum_{i=0}^{n-1} P_i/n$$

Example: Consider the following data series and construct a simple average of the data:

i	Day	Price
0	Wednesday	92.10
1	Tuesday	92.00
2	Monday	91.90

$$MA = (92.10 + 92.00 + 91.90)/3$$
$$= 92.00$$

A geometric moving average means you take the nth root of the multiplicative sum of the numbers:

$$MA = \left[\prod_{i=0}^{n-1} P_i \right]^{1/n}$$

Example: Find the geometric average of the number series just illustrated.

$$MA = (92.10 \times 92.00 \times 91.90)^{1/3}$$
$$= 91.99$$

It is apparent that a geometric average tends to be "downwardly biased;" it consistently tends to understate the arithmetic average.

A weighted average is intended to accord greater emphasis to more recent, as opposed to less recent, observations. The rationale is simply that recent observations provide information which may be more relevant to forthcoming price movements than "stale" or old observations.

$$MA = \sum_{i=0}^{n-1} W_i P_i / \sum_{i=0}^{n-1} W_i$$

The weights (W) in a scheme such as that which is illustrated may be determined arbitrarily by the user.

Example: Arbitrarily establish weights of 10, 5, and 2 for the most recent and successively less recent observations.

i	Day	Price	Weight
0	Wednesday	92.10	10
1	Tuesday	92.00	5
2	Monday	91.90	2

Find the weighted moving average:

$$MA = [(10 \times 92.10) + (5 \times 92.00) + (2 \times 91.90)]/(10 + 5 + 2)$$
$$= 92.05$$

A criticism of this method is that our weights are being established in a strictly arbitrary manner. Some analysts prefer to identify weights on a linear basis. This means that you weight the most recent price with a number corresponding to the number of observations (n). The next most recent observation is given a weight of $n - 1$; the second most recent observation is given a weight of $n - 2$, and so forth.

Example: Find the linear moving average for the price series shown above. This means that you will weight these prices with 3, 2, and 1:

i	Day	Price	Weight
0	Wednesday	92.10	3
1	Tuesday	92.00	2
2	Monday	91.90	1

Find the linear weighted moving average:

$$MA = [(3 \times 92.10) + (2 \times 92.00) + (1 \times 91.90)]/(3 + 2 + 1)$$
$$= 92.03$$

Another weighting scheme is known as an exponentially weighted moving average. This method provides weights which are graduated on an exponential basis as shown here.

$$MA = \sum_{i=0}^{n-1} [(1 - a)^i \times P_i] / \sum_{i=0}^{n-1} (1 - a)^i$$

Where $0 < a < 1$

Example: Find the exponentially weighted moving average for the price series just shown. Set a equal to 0.5. This means that you will weight these prices with 1, 0.5, and 0.25, respectively.

i	Day	Price	$(1-0.5)^i$
0	Wednesday	92.10	1.00
1	Tuesday	92.00	0.50
2	Monday	91.90	0.25

Find the exponentially weighted moving average:

$$MA = [(1 \times 92.10) + (0.5 \times 92.00) + (0.25 \times 91.90)]/(1 + 0.5 + 0.25)$$
$$= 92.04$$

Once calculated, what do you do with a moving average? Let us explore three different systems which may be used to trigger buy or sell orders in the futures markets. These systems include: (1) a double crossover, (2) a triple crossover, and (3) a double crossover system with bands.

A double crossover system is quite straightforward. Simply calculate two moving averages: a "fast" moving average MA(f), incorporating a relatively small number of observations; and a "slow" moving average MA(s), incorporating a relatively large number of observations (see Figure 3–36).

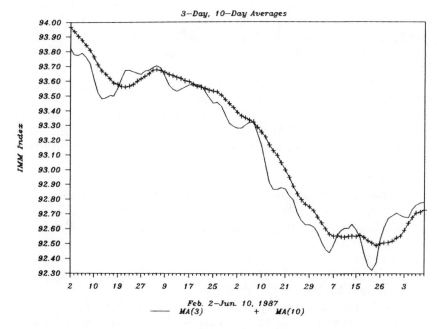

Figure 3–36   June 1987 Eurodollar moving averages.

A fast MA will be more reactive to recent market movements relative to a slow moving average which may tend to smooth out unusual or discrepant price movements. (The ultimate in fast moving averages is a one-day "mover.") How many observations should be used to construct a moving average? Enough observations should be used so that the average is "representative," but not so many as to incorporate old, stale data!

A better answer, however, is to calculate moving averages in such a way as to maximize your return given the trading systems you wish to employ! You will only know this answer through the process of simulation over a historical time period. Unfortunately, there is no guarantee that a particular system which produced good results over some past period will continue to produce profitable results.

This system may trigger a buy or sell upon a crossover. In other words, when the fast MA crosses up over the slow MA, this may trigger the placement of a buy order (covering any existing short positions at the same time). Should the fast MA cross down below the slow MA, put in a sell order, covering any existing long positions.

$$\text{IF } MA(f) > MA(s) \Rightarrow \text{Cover any shorts and buy.}$$

$$\text{IF } MA(f) < MA(s) \Rightarrow \text{Cover any longs and sell.}$$

This represents a trend-following system. If the market is trending, you may expect large profits. If the market is generally directionless or "choppy," you may expect to make a relatively large number of trades, many of which may result in small losses, meaning you will suffer from "whipsaws."

Losses tend to be cut short to the extent that a sudden reversal may result in a crossover. But when the market is trending, the fast moving average may remain on the upside or the downside of the slow MA for a lengthy period of time. Thus you tend to let your profits run! This is consistent with the old saying in the futures markets: "Let your profits run and cut your losses short."

The triple moving average is intended to provide the benefits of the double moving average system while minimizing losses as a result of whipsaw markets. It does so by attempting to identify buy and sell as well as neutral situations (where the best advice is to stay out of the futures market altogether).

As its name implies, this system utilizes three different moving averages: a "fast" average MA(f), an "intermediate" average MA(i), and a "slow" average MA(s) (see Figure 3–37).

When the fast mover breaks above both the intermediate and slow mover, buy futures. When the fast mover breaks below both the intermediate and

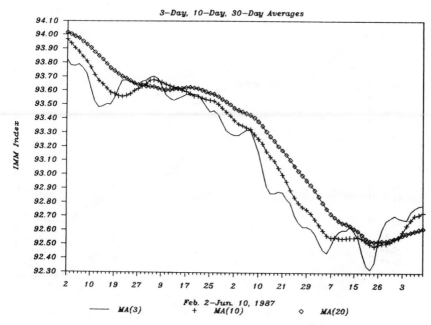

Figure 3–37   June 1987 Eurodollar moving averages.

the slow mover, sell futures. When the fast moving average is between the slow and intermediate averages, stay on the sidelines.

IF MA(f) > MA(i), MA(s) ⇒ Buy futures.

IF MA(f) < MA(i), MA(s) ⇒ Sell futures.

IF MA(f) is between MA(i) and MA(s) ⇒ Cover any longs or shorts.

Another way of attempting to minimize whipsaws and to take advantage of "true" trends is to utilize a variation of the double crossover system: a double crossover with "volatility bands" (see Figure 3–38).

This means you will compare a fast moving average to a slow moving average plus or minus some band. This band may be established at some fixed arbitrary amount; for instance, take the slow moving average plus or minus 1 point.

Example: A moving average based on the last 20 days in the bond futures market is at 94–24. Find an upper and lower band calculated as the 20-day MA plus or minus 1 point. Obviously, the upper band equals 95–24 while the lower band equals 93–24.

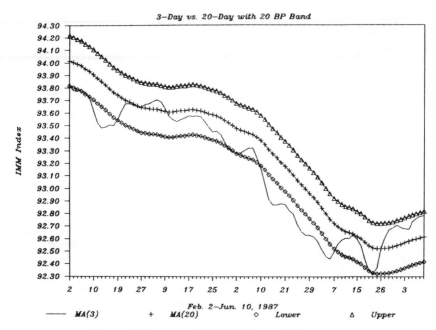

Figure 3–38   June 1987 Eurodollar moving averages.

Sometimes it is expressed as a percentage of the value of the slow moving average; for instance, take the slow moving average plus or minus 1 percent.

Example: A moving average based on the last 20 days in the deutsche mark futures market is at 55.80 cents per mark. Find an upper and lower band calculated as the 20-day MA plus or minus 1 percent. These levels equal 56.36 on the upper side and 55.24 on the lower side.

How can you use this system? The idea is to buy when the fast moving average crosses up over the upper band and to sell when the fast moving average crosses down below the lower band. Cover any longs or shorts and remain neutral if the fast moving average falls between the upper and lower bands.

IF MA(f) > MA(s) + band ⇒ Buy futures.

IF MA(f) < MA(s) − band ⇒ Sell futures.

IF MA(s) − band < MA(f) < MA(s) + band ⇒ Cover any longs or shorts.

Sometimes the system is used such that you cover any existing long position when the fast moving average crosses down below the slow moving average itself (rather than the slow moving average plus the band). You cover any existing short position when the fast moving average crosses up above the slow moving average (rather than the slow moving average less the band).

Which of these systems is best? Obviously, the answer to this question will vary from market to market. Moreover, different systems will produce different results over various time frames. The best answer is: Simulate results using historical data and employ the system which seems to produce the most profitable and stable results over time.

Oscillators

Moving averages are quite useful in determining the direction of the trend, but sometimes the trend moves "too far, too fast." If the market has rallied strongly, it may be "overbought." If the market has been declining sharply, it may be "oversold." In these cases, a consolidation, correction, or even a reversal becomes imminent. Oscillators represent statistics which may be used to identify these situations.

Oscillators may be used in conjunction with a way of thinking about the markets which is referred to as the school of "contrary opinion." The basic premise associated with contrary opinion is: When everyone is bullish, sell! The corollary is: When everyone is bearish, buy!

But this seems to contradict the idea that a trend, once in motion, tends to stay in motion. Consider two hypotheses which may explain the psychology of a trend in motion: market participants and the "strong hands" theory.

There are three basic kinds of traders in the market: longs, shorts, and uncommitted. Assume the market is trending upwards. In order to continue that trend, new participants must continue to enter the market on the long side. Likewise, new participants must continue to sell in order to sustain a bearish trend.

In either case, these new long or short positions will tend to drain the pool of uncommitted traders. When most or all of the uncommitted traders have committed themselves, there are no more traders to continue to push the market one way or the other. Finally, the bullish trend cannot be sustained and the market cracks, or the bearish trend halts and the market rallies.

Further, consider which side of the market has the stronger position in a bullish or bearish trend. Assume that 90 percent of all market participants are bullish and that only 10 percent of the participants are bearish. This suggests that for every nine traders who are long, only a single trader is short, that is, the shorts must have larger size positions than the longs.

Who has the stronger hand? If the shorts have been able to "fade" the market up so far, sustaining losses all the way up, they probably have the stronger hand. When the first of those longs decides to take his profit, the market cracks. Other longs, noticing that the market is falling, may start to take their profits as well. Soon open interest starts to fall dramatically, and the market falls quickly. Sometimes the market may decline quickly in a panic sell situation.

How can you statistically assess whether the market is in an overbought or oversold condition? Let's review a variety of statistics such as momentum, double moving averages, and the relative strength index.

Momentum refers simply to the change in the price of the instrument in question (P) over some arbitrary time period. Momentum may represent a 1-, 2-, 3-, 5-, 10-, 30-day lag, or any other period deemed appropriate.

$$\text{Momentum} = P_t - P_{t-1}$$

Example: Today's bond price is at 89–17. Yesterday the market was at 89–10. A one-day momentum may be calculated at positive seven ticks. Assume that the market was at 86–29 ten days ago. The ten-day momentum may be calculated at $2^{20}/_{32}$ds.

There is a tradeoff with respect to the lag. The longer the lag you select, the less the degree to which the statistic is unduly impacted upon by extraneous or spurious movements. The shorter the lag, the greater the degree to which the statistic is affected by fresh, current data.

Does momentum exceed zero or fall short of zero? That is, is the market trending upwards or downwards? If momentum is above zero and rising, the market advance is accelerating. If momentum is above zero but flat, the market is rising at a stable rate. If momentum is above zero but falling, the market is rising at a declining rate. Likewise, acceleration or deceleration may be observed in a falling market.

One of the unfortunate aspects about use of the momentum statistic is that it tends to be choppy, particularly when using a short lag (see Figure 3–39). Double moving averages tend to smooth out extraneous, choppy movements by comparing a fast moving average to a slow moving average (see Figure 3–40).

$$\text{Double MA} = \text{MA}(f) - \text{MA}(s)$$

Example: A three-day moving average of the bond futures price is quoted at 89–04. A 20-day moving average is quoted at 89–14. The 3/20 double moving average is quoted at negative 10 ticks.

The unfortunate aspect about the application of either a momentum or a double moving average statistic is that there is often difficulty in recognizing

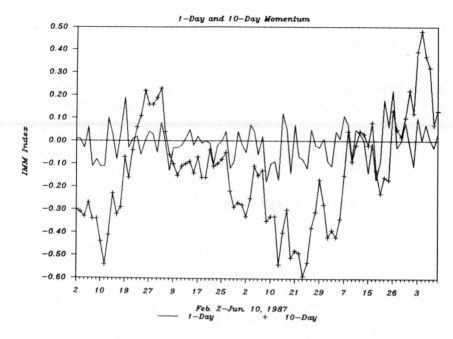

Figure 3–39   June 1987 Eurodollar momentum.

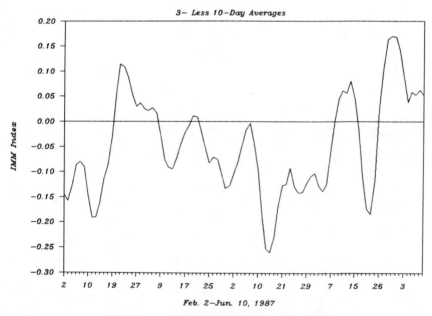

Figure 3–40   June 1987 Eurodollars—double MAs.

the "danger zone." How high must the statistic be in order to trigger an overbought signal? How low must the statistic be to trigger an oversold signal?

The relative strength index (RSI) was developed by a technician named Welles Wilder and is intended to provide a consistent overbought or oversold indicator (see Figure 3–41). The statistic must range between 0 and 100. Wilder's original work suggested that when the statistic meets or exceeds 70, an overbought condition is indicated, and the market may consolidate or reverse. If the statistic runs to 30 or below, an oversold condition is indicated.

$$RSI = 100 - [100/(1 + Up/Down)]$$

Where:

Up = Sum of price advances over past n days.

Down = Sum of price declines over past n days.

Example: Find a nine-day RSI for Eurodollar futures given the following data. This RSI of 54.54 is relatively close to 50.00. As such, neither an overbought nor oversold condition is indicated.

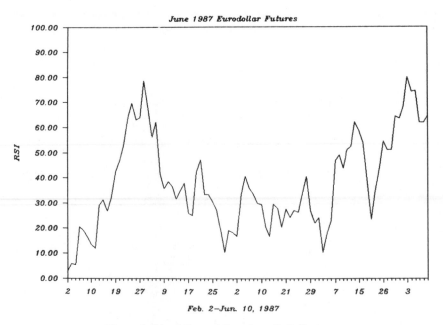

Figure 3–41   9-Day relative strength indicator.

	Price	Change
Most recent day	92.22	+ 0.02
	92.20	+ 0.10
	92.10	+ 0.04
	92.06	+ 0.17
	91.89	− 0.28
	92.17	− 0.01
	92.18	+ 0.15
	92.03	− 0.04
	92.07	− 0.07
	92.14	

$$\text{Up} = 0.02 + 0.10 + 0.04 + 0.17 + 0.15 = 0.48$$

$$\text{Down} = 0.28 + 0.01 + 0.04 + 0.07 = 0.40$$

$$\text{RSI} = 100 - [100/(1 + 0.48/0.40)] = 54.54$$

Often when using an RSI with relatively few observations, it may be best to liberalize one's definitions of what constitutes overbought and oversold conditions. Rather than 30 and 70, look for 25 and 75 or 20 and 80.

Often when the market is about to reverse, the RSI penetrates the danger levels significantly, backs off, and then penetrates the danger levels once again. This second penetration may or may not be as extreme as the first. It is often only after this second violation that the market reverses.

This is intuitive in the sense that the market often trades in a reversal formation—a sideways holding pattern—before reversing. The RSI may achieve an extreme level when initially entering the reversal pattern. Subsequently, the RSI may fall off those extreme levels and penetrate the danger levels again just prior to completing the reversal pattern.

QUESTIONS

1. Which statement is false regarding trendlines?
    (a) A support line is drawn to connect the bottom points of a price move.
    (b) A resistance line is drawn across the peaks of a trend.
    (c) Once broken, a resistance level becomes a support level.
    (d) A channel is an area above the resistance and below the support lines.
    (e) Most of the biggest profits occur on breakouts from trendlines that are never subsequently tested or pulled back.
2. The classic head and shoulders formation . . .
    (a) Is a major reversal indicator.
    (b) Has one head and one shoulder.
    (c) Can be used as a confirmation that the market is likely to continue trending in the same direction that it was before the head and shoulders formation appeared.

(d) The head of the formation looks much like a pennant or triangle formation.

(e) None of the above.

3. Which statement is false about gaps?
   (a) Are open areas on a chart by prices trading entirely above or below the prior trading range.
   (b) Occur relatively frequently in thinly traded markets.
   (c) Are usually caused by fundamental factors of supply and demand.
   (d) There are no well-defined trading rules for gaps.
   (e) If a breakaway gap is on low volume, you might expect a pullback.

4. Which statement is false about point and figure charts?
   (a) Point and figure charts may be used to plot intraday data.
   (b) Technicians frequently use the three-box reversal method.
   (c) The two important variables which must be defined to use a point and figure chart are the size of the box and the reversal criterion.
   (d) Point and figure charts can be read in much the same way as a bar chart.
   (e) The horizontal axis of a point and figure chart references time.

5. A buy signal may be triggered . . .
   (a) When a fast moving average crosses down under a slow moving average.
   (b) When the market price penetrates the upper band over a moving average.
   (c) When the moon is full.
   (d) When the relative strength indicator runs below 30.
   (e) When the RSI gives an overbought signal.

6. Calculate the first 12 numbers in the Fibonacci series. (Hint: the first four numbers are 1, 2, 3, 5.)

7. Identify the market of your choice. Calculate a fast and a slow moving average of your choice daily. When are buy signals generated? Sell signals? How much would you have made or lost by following this system trading 10 contract lots? How much commissions might be paid? How many transactions—winning and losing transactions?

8. Keep track of a 14-day relative strength index for the market of your choice. What does the index indicate, and how accurate was it?

4

Cost of Carry

Financial futures will tend to track the price of the instrument which is called for upon delivery of the contract. In the event that the contract provides an option to deliver any of a variety of different instruments, the contract will track the cheapest-to-deliver cash security.

Still, futures prices will typically trade apart from the price of the delivery instrument. That differential reflects *cost of carry*. This chapter discusses the concept of cost of carry in the context of fixed income, foreign currency, and stock index futures contracts.

A SIMPLE CARRY MODEL

One of the most critical questions asked by futures traders is: How can the contract be expected to price? Commodity futures pricing is often explained in terms of cost of carry or simply "carry" model. The carry model explains futures prices in terms of the spot market price adjusted by the cost of holding or carrying that commodity until futures contract maturity. Proponents of the anticipatory pricing model believe that the price of a futures contract represents the consensus opinion of futures market participants as to the value of the spot commodity market by the time the futures contract matures.

Some commodities may be more overtly affected by one or the other of these factors. Let us consider the way in which different financial futures are impacted by carry.

Indifference Analysis

To understand carry, consider a simple *indifference analysis.*

Which alternative is better: to buy a long-term bond today for $100 or to buy a futures contract which expires six months later at a price of $97, taking delivery of the same bond? To answer that question, we must look at the "basis" or the difference between cash and futures prices.

If you are an arbitrageur or a leveraged investor, you must borrow to finance the purchase of the cash bond. If you can finance this bond purchase at a 6 percent annual rate, it will cost you ½ percent per month to hold or "carry" the bond. For six months it will cost you $3.00.

Assume that the long-term bond yields 12 percent or 1 percent per month. You can earn $6.00 over the six months by carrying the bond. The net cost of buying the bond and holding it six months is $97.00.

Indifference Analysis

Now:	Buy cash	($100)
	Hold 6 mos	($3)
	Bond coupon	$6
		($97)
Six months later:	Buy futures, take delivery	($97)

The cost of either alternative is identical at $97.00. Therefore, you should be indifferent between these two alternatives.

Cost of carry futures pricing is enforced by arbitrageurs who step in quickly to capitalize on small pricing disparities.

> **Example:** If futures were at $98, arbitrageurs would sell the expensive futures and buy cash, securing a low-risk arbitrage profit. If futures were at $96, arbitrageurs would buy cheap futures and sell cash, again securing a low-risk arbitrage profit.

The investor in this example enjoys "positive carry." In other words, the bond threw off more coupon income than it cost to finance its purchase because long-term yields were higher than short-term yields. This is characteristic of a normal upwardly sloping yield curve.

Under these conditions, the price of fixed income futures which call for delivery during successively deferred months runs progressively lower. The basis, the cash security price less the futures price, grows successively larger. But sometimes short-term yields run higher than long-term yields.

When the yield curve becomes negatively sloped or inverted, the income generated from a long-term security will be less than financing costs (see Figure 4–1). This defines "negative carry."

Under these conditions, the price of fixed income futures in successively deferred months runs progressively higher. The basis will grow successively more negative in deferred months (see Figure 4–2).

Assume that short-term financing rates are at 8 percent, and the bond has a 6 percent coupon. At what price would you be indifferent between buying the cash bond (at $100) and buying futures which call for delivery of the same bond six months hence?

Indifference Analysis

Now:	Buy cash	($100)
	Hold 6 mos	($4)
	Bond coupon	$3
		($101)
Six months later:	Buy futures, take delivery	($101)

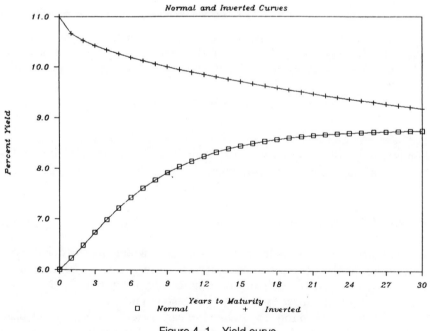

Figure 4–1   Yield curve.

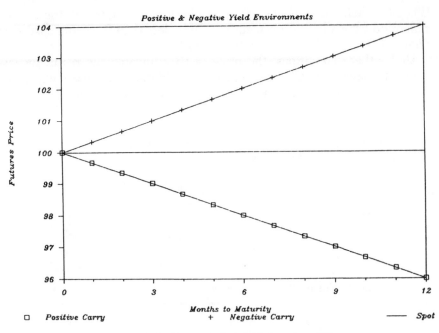

Figure 4–2   Futures prices in deferred months.

No matter whether positive or negative carry prevails, the expected price of a futures contract is reflected in short-term financing costs adjusted by any payouts associated with the carry of a particular cash item.

$$\text{Futures} = \text{Cash} + \text{Finance Charges} - \text{Payouts}$$

These payouts may be realized in the form of coupon payments for bonds, dividends for equities, or foreign short-term interest rates in the case of foreign exchange transactions.

Positive/Negative Carry

Futures prices track the value of the instrument which may be delivered in satisfaction of the contract upon contract maturity (or in the case of futures which permit the delivery of a multitude of alternate instruments, the price of the cheapest-to-deliver cash instrument).

The basis may be quoted as either the cash price less the futures price or vice versa, futures less cash. Practices vary from futures contract to futures contract, but it is typical to quote the basis such that it normally is calculated as a positive number. Therefore, in markets where positive carry normally prevails, the basis is often quoted as the cash price less the futures price. Where negative carry normally prevails, the basis is generally quoted as the futures price less the cash price.

Positive carry normally prevails in the fixed income futures markets. For example, long-term and intermediate-term yields associated with bonds and notes generally exceed short-term financing rates. Positive carry even prevails with short-term futures such as bills and Eurodollars. This is apparent when you compare 90-day yields with overnight yields.

As of this writing, positive carry prevailed in the British pound and Canadian dollar futures markets. These contracts are quoted in terms of U.S. dollars per foreign unit. Thus the applicable financing rate is the U.S. short-term rate. This makes sense because by taking U.S. dollars to buy foreign currency, you give up the opportunity to invest at the U.S. short-term rate. You get the opportunity to invest those foreign units at the prevailing foreign interest rate. If British and Canadian rates are higher than U.S. rates, this implies positive carry and successively rising futures prices.

Positive Carry Markets	*Negative Carry Markets*
Bonds, Notes, Bills, Euros, British pounds, Canadian dollars.	Stock index futures, Japanese yen, Swiss francs, deutsche marks.

Negative carry normally prevails in the stock index markets as well as a number of foreign currency contracts such as the Japanese yen, Swiss franc, and deutsche mark.

Stock index futures display negative carry because short-term rates typically exceed dividend yields. As of this writing, for example, short-term rates were in the $5\frac{1}{2}$ to 6 percent range. Dividend yields were closer to 3 to $3\frac{1}{2}$ percent.

The yen, franc, and mark contracts also display negative carry to the extent that rates in Japan, Switzerland, and West Germany currently run at lower levels relative to U.S. rates.

Cash/Futures Convergence

The magnitude of the basis depends on short-term financing rates, any payouts on the cash security, and the time remaining until delivery. But as the delivery month approaches, the basis generally narrows. It narrows because carry considerations have a diminishing impact over shorter and shorter time periods. During the delivery month, the basis between the cheapest cash security and the adjusted futures price should approach zero.

Returning to the example presented earlier, let us calculate the carry futures price for the bond in a positive carry environment over a three-month, rather than a six-month, time horizon.

Indifference Analysis

Now:	Buy cash	($100.00)
	Hold 3 mos	($1.50)
	Bond coupon	$3.00
		($98.50)
Three months later:	Buy futures, take delivery	($98.50)

Under the same conditions, the futures price over a six-month horizon was at $97.00. Over a three-month time horizon, the carry futures price is at $98.50. Over a two-month time horizon, the carry futures price should be at $99.00. Over a one-month time horizon, the carry futures price should be at $99.50.

The basis should approach zero because shorts may ultimately make delivery in satisfaction of the futures contract. Thus buying or selling futures during the delivery period is tantamount to buying or selling the cash security (or cheapest-to-deliver cash security) which may be tendered against the futures contract.

QUANTIFYING THE MODEL

The cost of carry model suggests that the futures price (F) equals the cash price (S) adjusted to reflect the cost of carrying the commodity until futures market maturity. Adjustments involve cash price plus any finance charges (r), less any payouts (d), and adjusted to reflect the time remaining until contract maturity (t).

(Payouts do not accrue on many physical commodities on which futures are based, namely, grain, livestock, and metals. Other charges, however, may accrue in addition to finance, namely, storage, spoilage, and insurance. These charges are treated as if they were finance charges.)

Simple Interest versus Continuous Compounding

Given an assumption of simple interest, that is, no interest on interest, the carry model may be quantified as follows:

$$F = S[1 + (r - d)t]$$

Example: Assume that the spot value of a security were at $100, short-term rates at 6 percent, coupon set at 12 percent, and the futures contract has six months (t = .5 years) to maturity. Find the expected futures price.

$$F = \$100[1 + (.06 - .12).5]$$
$$= \$97$$

The result in the previous example is identical to that developed in our simple indifference analysis. We have assumed a simple rate of interest without taking into account the potential effect of compounding of interest.

Using an assumption of continuous compounding, the model may be modified as follows:

$$F = Se^{(r - d)t}$$

Example: Calculate the futures price pursuant to the information presented in the previous example (cash price at $100, short-term rates at 6 percent, coupon at 12 percent, 6 months to contract maturity) assuming continuous compounding.

$$F = \$100e^{(.06 - .12).5}$$
$$= \$97.04$$

Continuous compounding has the effect of reducing the discount of futures to spot in a positive carry environment. It has the effect of increasing the premium of futures to spot in a negative carry environment. This impact may be observed by examining the following tables.

Carry Futures Prices, Simple Interest
1 Year Term, Spot = $100

Finance Rate	Payout Rate						
	2%	3%	4%	5%	6%	7%	8%
2%	$100.00	$ 99.00	$ 98.00	$ 97.00	$ 96.00	$ 95.00	$ 94.00
3%	101.00	100.00	99.00	98.00	97.00	96.00	95.00
4%	102.00	101.00	100.00	99.00	98.00	97.00	96.00
5%	103.00	102.00	101.00	100.00	99.00	98.00	97.00
6%	104.00	103.00	102.00	101.00	100.00	99.00	98.00
7%	105.00	104.00	103.00	102.00	101.00	100.00	99.00
8%	106.00	105.00	104.00	103.00	102.00	101.00	100.00

Carry Futures Prices, Continuous Compounding
1 Year Term, Spot = $100

Finance Rate	Payout Rate						
	2%	3%	4%	5%	6%	7%	8%
2%	$100.00	$ 99.00	$ 98.02	$ 97.04	$ 96.08	$ 95.12	$ 94.18
3%	101.01	100.00	99.00	98.02	97.04	96.08	95.12
4%	102.02	101.01	100.00	99.00	98.02	97.04	96.08
5%	103.05	102.02	101.01	100.00	99.00	98.02	97.04
6%	104.08	103.05	102.02	101.01	100.00	99.00	98.02
7%	105.13	104.08	103.05	102.02	101.01	100.00	99.00
8%	106.18	105.13	104.08	103.05	102.02	101.01	100.00

Enforcing Carry Pricing

Our model has been based so far upon a number of restrictive assumptions. A major assumption is that there are no restrictions on arbitrage activity. This assumption implies that one may buy or sell the underlying instrument at will without affecting market prices, that there is a zero bid/ask spread, that the underlying instrument is infinitely divisible, and that there are no restrictions on short sales. Obviously, many of these assumptions depart from reality.

Cost of carry is enforced only to the extent that arbitrageurs take advantage of situations where futures prices exceed or fall short of the carry price. When futures are overpriced relative to spot, arbitrageurs may:

1. Go short futures.
2. Borrow at the short-term rate r to finance the purchase of the underlying instrument, earning the payouts d accruing on the instrument over the term of the contract t.

By such action, an arbitrageur can lock in the original amount by which the futures price exceeded the carry price. When futures are underpriced relative to spot, arbitrageurs may:

1. Go long futures.
2. Short the underlying instrument, investing the proceeds at the short-term rate r, giving up the opportunity to receive any payouts d accruing on the instrument over the term of the contract t.

Later they may repurchase the underlying instrument at futures contract maturity. As a result, the arbitrageur may lock in the original amount by which futures fall short of carry. It may be impossible, however, to buy or sell the instrument underlying a futures contract in the context of stock index futures. Stock index futures are based not on the value of any particular stock, but on the value of an index, representing upwards to 1,700 plus stock in the case of the Value Line Composite Average.

Obviously, it is not feasible to trade in and out of upwards of 1,700 stocks at a time. In order to arbitrage stock index futures against the stock market, one must construct a stock portfolio, the movements of which may be expected to closely track movements of the stock index. Intuitively, it may appear necessary to construct a portfolio comprised of a high proportion of all the stocks included in the index, but often a less inclusive portfolio comprised of as few as 8 to 15 stocks may adequately track the index.

Presumably, an arbitrageur would prefer to limit the number of issues to a manageable number. However, as the portfolio is reduced to include fewer issues, it may lose its tracking reliability and cease to be an "arbitrageable" portfolio. As such, cash/futures arbitrage in the context of the stock index markets can become a costly and unmanageable proposition. As a result, index futures have been known to price at levels considerably apart from levels indicated by traditional futures pricing models.

Arbitrageurs will only engage in arbitrage activity when there is a prospect of recovering associated costs and realizing a reasonable return. Thus futures prices may drift within a range bounded by the carry price plus the costs of conducting arbitrage and the carry price less the costs of conducting arbitrage.

$$\left(\begin{matrix} \text{Carry} \\ \text{Price} \end{matrix} - \begin{matrix} \text{Arbitrage} \\ \text{Costs} \end{matrix} \right) \leq \begin{matrix} \text{Futures} \\ \text{Price} \end{matrix} \leq \left(\begin{matrix} \text{Carry} \\ \text{Price} \end{matrix} + \begin{matrix} \text{Arbitrage} \\ \text{Costs} \end{matrix} \right)$$

Because the costs of conducting this arbitrage appear to be greater than arbitrage costs in other futures markets, stock index futures prices often drift within a wide band over and under the carry price. Within that band, futures prices are dictated by the ebb and flow of buy and sell orders.

This drifting or "flutter" is driven fundamentally by the influx of buy and sell orders. Presumably, these orders express bullish or bearish sentiment of market participants. Many market observers have suggested that stock index futures prices closely conform to the anticipatory pricing model alluded to earlier. In other words, futures will trade close to the top of that arbitrage band when market participants are bullish; futures will trade close to the bottom of that band when market participants are bearish.

Discrete Payouts

Unlike bond interest, stock dividends do not accrue continuously but are paid at discrete intervals. Ex-dividend patterns tend to be seasonal—firms generally set ex-dividend dates in the second month of each calendar quarter, that is, February, May, August, and November. As such, it may be unreasonable to express these payouts as a percentage. Rather, the model must represent these payouts or dividends D as a discrete payment as follows:

$$F = Se^{rt} - D$$

Example: The spot value of a stock index is at 250.00. Short-term rates are at 6 percent and there are two months until futures contract maturity. Dividends accruing over the next two months total 1.50 index points. The futures contract value may be estimated at 251.01 or 1.01 points over the spot value.

$$F = 250e^{(0.06)(.1667)} - 1.5$$
$$= 251.01$$

This means that stock index futures may trade at relatively low premiums over spot just prior to an ex-dividend date and advance to larger premiums after an ex-dividend date. This effect may be particularly pronounced in the second month of each calendar quarter.

Example: Assume that the conditions described in the previous example are currently prevailing. (The stock index is at 250.00 and rates are at 6 percent with two months until contract maturity.) But assume that dividends accruing over the next two months total 3.50 index points. The futures contract value may be estimated at 249.01.

$$F = 250e^{(0.06)(.1667)} - 3.5$$
$$= 249.01$$

A final point: Dividends received currently are more valuable than deferred dividends. This point implies that the value of deferred dividends should be discounted. Considering this fact may be particularly important when one realizes that dividend payment dates often extend far past ex-dividend dates.

YIELD CURVE ANALYSIS

It was clear when we examined cost of carry in the context of the long- or intermediate-term Treasury futures markets that the shape of the yield curve wields a paramount influence in determining cost of carry. However, the shape of the yield curve, if closely studied, is even more revealing. In particular, the shape of the yield curve may be interpreted as an indicator of the direction in which the market as an aggregate believes interest rates may fluctuate.

Let us next examine several intuitive approaches to this proposition and conclude by looking at a quantitative approach to determining "implied forward rates."

The Shape of the Curve

There are three fundamental theories which attempt to explain the shape of the yield curve. In many ways, these three theories may be regarded as successively more sophisticated yet essentially complementary. These three theories may be identified as the (1) expectations hypothesis, (2) liquidity hypothesis, and (3) segmentation hypothesis.

Begin by assuming that the yield curve is flat; that is, investors normally express no particular preference for long- versus short-term securities. Hence long- and short-term securities have similar yields.

The expectations hypothesis alters our basic assumption with the supposition that fixed income market participants are basically rational. They will alter the composition of their portfolio to correspond to the anticipated direction of interest rates. For example, portfolio managers will shift their investments from the long-term to the short-term securities in anticipation of rising interest rates and falling fixed income security prices. This is due to the fact that longer-term securities tend to react more dramatically to shifting rates than do shorter-term securities.

(Note that by selling long-term securities and buying short-term securities, the portfolio manager assumes a defensive posture. The effects of this strategy are similar to those associated with a portfolio manager who hedges by selling futures against long-term security holdings.)

By shortening the average maturity of their holdings in a rising rate environment, investors will tend to bid up the price of short-term securities and drive down the price of long-term securities. As a result, short-term yields fall while long-term yields rise; the shape of the yield curve steepens!

On the other hand, portfolio managers will tend to lengthen the maturity of their portfolios in anticipation of falling rates by selling short-term securities and buying long-term securities. This activity will have the effect of bidding up the price of long-term securities and driving down the price of short-term securities. Thus long-term yields will fall while short-term yields rise; the yield curve flattens or inverts!

Yields expected to rise $\Rightarrow$ Yield curve steepens
Yields expected to fall $\Rightarrow$ Yield curve flattens

Therefore, the shape of the curve may be used as an indicator of the possible direction in which yields may fluctuate.

The liquidity hypothesis rejects the initial proposition just described. According to this theory, investors are *not* indifferent between long- and short-term securities even when yields are expected to remain stable.

All else being equal, investors will tend to prefer short-term securities over long-term securities. A long-term security means that the investor has his money tied up over a lengthy period of time. Short-term investments, on the other hand, may roll over frequently, providing the investor with augmented flexibility to alter the composition of the portfolio to correspond to breaking events.

In other words, short-term investments more strongly resemble cash. Given similar yields, it is better to own the more liquid and readily divestable security. Thus long-term securities must pay a "liquidity premium," so as a rule, long-term yields tend to exceed short-term yields even when yields are expected to remain relatively stable, that is, there is a natural upward bias to the yield curve.

The segmentation hypothesis attacks the second proposition associated with the expectations hypothesis, namely, that investors are capable of altering the structure of their portfolio quickly and efficiently in order to take advantage of anticipated yield fluctuations. While the portfolio may be altered to a limited degree in anticipation of yield curve shifts, investors are often constrained.

For example, regulatory requirements often restrict pension funds, requiring them to be invested in longer-term fixed income investments. Other restrictions may be self-imposed. Finally, bid/ask spreads in some segments of the fixed income markets may be prohibitive. As such, "kinks" are often observed in the fixed income markets.

While the liquidity and segmentation hypotheses attack certain aspects of the expectations hypothesis, they are all basically complementary. The latter two hypotheses may be thought of as refinements of the expectations hypothesis.

Implied Forward Rates

How might one quantify this valuable information implicit in the shape of the yield curve? To answer this question, consider the concept of an *implied forward rate* (IFR).

An implied forward rate answers this question: What short-term yield may be expected to prevail in the future? For example, what yield will be associated with a 180-day investment 90 days in the future?

An *implied forward rate* provides an indication about where short-term yields may be expected to be sometime in the future. For example, what do we expect a 180-day short-term investment to yield 90 days from today?

R(90)---- $d_1 = 90$ --- $> < $ ----IFR(180,90) ---- $d_3 = 180$ ---- $>$
R(270)----------------------- $d_2 = 270$ --------------------- $>$
```
   *------------- *----------------- *----------------- *
   0              90                180                270
                       Days until term
```

The 180-day implied forward rate 90 days in the future IFR(180,90) may be found as a function of the 90-day term rate R(90) and the 270-day term rate R(270). (Two hundred seventy days equals 90 plus 180.) Let us designate the number of days in each period as $d_1 = 90$ days, $d_2 = 270$ days, and $d_3 = 180$ days. The assumption is that an investor should be indifferent between investing for a nine-month term and investing at a three-month term, rolling the proceeds over into a six-month investment 90 days hence.

$$1 + R(d_2)\,(d_2/360) = [1 + R(d_1)\,(d_1/360)]\,[1 + IFR(d_3,d_1)\,(d_3/360)]$$

Solving the equation for IFR:

$$1 + IFR(d_3,d_1)(d_3/360) = \frac{[1 + R(d_2)(d_2/360)]}{[1 + R(d_1)(d_1/360)]}$$

$$IFR(d_3,d_1)\,(d_3/360) = \frac{[1 + R(d_2)(d_2/360)]}{[1 + R(d_1)(d_1/360)]} - 1$$

$$IFR(d_3,d_1) = \frac{[1 + R(d_2)(d_2/360)]}{(d_3/360)[1 + R(d_1)(d_1/360)]} - \frac{1}{(d_3/360)}$$

Example: Assume that the 90-day term rate equals 6.00 percent, the 270-day term rate equals 6.25 percent. What is the 180-day implied forward rate 90 days hence?

$$IFR(180,90) = \frac{1 + (0.0625)(270/360)}{(180/360)[1 + (0.06)(90/360)]} - \frac{1}{(180/360)}$$

$$= 0.0628 \text{ or } 6.28\%$$

Note that this implied forward rate exceeds both the 90-day and 270-day term rates. Thus the upward sloping yield curve is indicative of rising yields.

Example: Assume that the 90-day rate equals 7.00 percent and the 270-day rate equals 6.75 percent. Find the 180-day implied forward rate for 90 days hence.

$$\text{IFR}(180,90) = \frac{1 + (0.0675)(270/360)}{(180/360)[1 + (0.07)(90/360)]} - \frac{1}{(180/360)}$$

$$= 0.0651 \text{ or } 6.51\%$$

This implied forward rate falls short of both the 90-day and 270-day term rates, suggesting the possibility of falling yields.

Example: Assume that both the 90-day and 270-day term rates equal 6.50 percent. Find the 180-day implied forward rate for 90 days hence.

$$\text{IFR}(180,90) = \frac{1 + (0.065)(270/360)}{(180/360)[1 + (0.065)(90/360)]} - \frac{1}{(180/360)}$$

$$= 0.0634 \text{ or } 6.34\%$$

This analysis suggests that a flat yield curve is indicative of slightly falling rates! To understand, consider that the analysis is based on the expectation that investment in a 270-day term instrument should provide a yield equivalent to a 90-day term investment subsequently rolled over into a 180-day term investment.

These investments may be made in discount securities such as T-bills which do not provide for compounding. However, a compounding effect is implicit in the roll over from a 90-day to a 180-day investment.

Because some measure of the total return is realized after only 90 days, there are additional funds to invest in the 180-day instrument 90 days hence.

IFRs and Futures

Whereas our cost of carry analysis discussed in prior sections is often quite useful in identifying "normal" relationships in many futures markets, the IFR concept may be referenced as an indication of where short-term interest rate futures may be trading.

A T-bill or Eurodollar contract essentially represents a 91- or 90-day investment × days in the future. This is readily comparable to an IFR. In fact, by comparing IFRs to futures prices, you may identify arbitrage opportunities to the extent that IFRs basically represent where these short-term futures should be trading!

Example: It is December. Consider the following hypothetical interest rate structure in the Eurodollar (Euro) futures and cash markets:

Mar. Euro futures 94.74 (5.26)

Jun. Euro futures 94.78 (5.22)

Sep. Euro futures 94.75 (5.25)

3-month investment . . . . offer @ 5.54

6-month investment . . . . offer @ 5.63

9-month investment . . . . offer @ 5.63

Which is the best investment: (1) Buy the Euros maturing in June yielding 5.63 percent, (2) Buy the Euros maturing in March and buying March Euro futures, or (3) Buy Euros maturing in September and selling June Euro futures? Calculate the returns using the simple assumption that the three-month Euro has a 90-day (.25 years) term, the six-month Euro has a 180-day (.5 years) term, and the nine-month Euro has a 270-day (.75 years) term.

By buying the March Euros, you will earn 5.54 percent over the 90 days. Presumably, you will buy another 90-day Euro in March (at a price determined or locked in by virtue of the fact that you are long the March futures contract) earning a return of 5.26 percent in the subsequent 90-day period. The total return may be found by using the IFR equation as follows:

$$1 + R(.5) = [1 + .0554(.25)] [1 + .0526(.25)]$$
$$R = [[1 + .0554(.25)] [1 + .0526(.25)] - 1]/.5$$
$$= 5.44\%$$

The third alternative means that you buy Euros maturing in September earning 5.63 percent over 270 days. But by selling the June contract, you effectively commit to selling that Eurodollar investment 180 days hence when it has only 90 days to term. The return may also be found by using the IFR equation as follows:

$$[1 + R(.5)] [1 + .0522(.25)] = [1 + .0563(.75)]$$
$$[1 + R(.5)] = [1 + .0563(.75)]/[1 + .0522(.25)]$$
$$R = [[(1 + .0563(.75))/(1 + .0522(.25))] - 1]/.5$$
$$= 5.76\%$$

Therefore, the third alternative provides a greater return at 5.76 percent relative to the first alternative with a return equal to 5.63 percent and the second alternative with a return equal to 5.44 percent.

Short-term futures are driven into line with these implied forward rates because of the availability of arbitrage opportunities. In the foregoing example, an arbitrage might have been constructed by selling the six-month cash Euro, foregoing a return equal to 5.63 percent and by buying the nine-month cash Euro and selling the June futures contract, earning a return equal to 5.76 percent.

Instead, one might have bought the six-month Euro, earning a return equal to 5.63 percent and sold the three-month bill and the March futures contract, foregoing a return equal to 5.44 percent. In either case, the execution of these transactions would have the effect of driving the market into an equilibrium such that no arbitrage opportunities are available.

This analysis also brings to the fore the concept of a *strip*. A strip may be purchased or sold by buying or selling a series of futures maturing in successively deferred months, usually in combination with a current position in the cash market.

> A *strip* involves the purchase or sale of short-term interest rate futures in successively deferred months, usually in combination with the purchase or sale of the current cash short-term instrument.

In our example, we illustrated the first two components of a strip when we discussed the idea of buying the current three-month Euro and buying futures which call (nominally) for the delivery of a three-month Euro three months hence.

A strip, albeit a short strip, may be constructed by buying the three-month Euro, buying the March futures contract, and buying the June futures contract. When the current Eurodollar investment expires, one (effectively) takes delivery of another three-month Euro at a predetermined price by virtue of the fact that one may be long against the March contract. Subsequently, when that three-month instrument expires, one invests for another three months at a predetermined or locked-in price by virtue of the long June contract.

The value of this strip may be found with another variation of the IFR formula. This value may be compared against the prospect of simply investing Eurodollars for a nine-month period.

Example: Return to our previous example. Is it preferable to buy the nine-month Euro yielding 5.63 percent, or to buy the three-month Euro, buy March futures, and buy June futures?

$$
\begin{array}{lll}
\text{Mar. Euro futures} & \ldots\ldots 94.74 & (5.26) \\
\text{Jun. Euro futures} & \ldots\ldots 94.78 & (5.22) \\
\text{3-month Euros} & \ldots\ldots \text{offer} \quad @ \quad 5.54 &
\end{array}
$$

$$1 + R(.75) = [1 + .0554(.25)]\,[1 + .0526(.25)]\,[1 + .0522(.25)]$$
$$R = [[1 + .0554(.25)]\,[1 + .0526(.25)]\,[1 + .0522(.25)] - 1]/.75$$
$$= 5.41\%$$

This suggests that it is more attractive to simply buy the nine-month Euro.

QUESTIONS

1. (a) Assume that you could buy a cash bond right now for $100 with a 10 percent coupon when short-term financing rates are at 8 percent. At what price would you expect a futures contract which called for the delivery of that very same bond in six months to trade?
   (b) Where would a futures contract with only three months to maturity trade?
2. Cash/futures convergence . . .
   (a) Applies with respect to contracts which call for the physical delivery of the underlying instrument but not necessarily with respect to cash-settlement contracts.
   (b) Results in positive carry.
   (c) Is characteristic of an environment where short-term rates exceed long-term rates.
   (d) Works against the hedger who sells bond futures against a long cash position in a positive yield curve environment.
   (e) May be controlled by following the basis closely.
3. Should Japanese short-term interest rates run to higher levels than U.S. short-term rates . . .
   (a) Japanese yen futures on the CME should trade at successively higher and higher levels in successively deferred months.
   (b) Japanese yen futures on the CME should trade at successively lower and lower levels in successively deferred months.
   (c) The discount of futures to spot will diminish as contract maturity approaches.
   (d) It suggests that yen are overpriced relative to the dollar.
   (e) (b) and (c) above.
4. (a) Spot yen are valued at $.005500. U.S. short-term rates are at 6 percent, and Japanese rates are at 4 percent. Evaluate the forward price of yen 30 days hence using a simple rate compounding formula.
   (b) What is the 90-day forward price?
   (c) What are the 30- and 90-day forward prices using continuously compounding interest?

   Reminder: $F = S e^{(r-d)t}$

   Where: F = forward price
             S = spot price
             e = base of natural logarithm
             r = U.S. interest rate
             d = Japanese interest rate
             t = years in life of contract

   (d) What are the 30- and 90-day forward prices (using the continuous compounding assumption) represented in yen/dollar?
5. Which statement is true in the event that short-term rates rise and long-term rates fall?

   (a) The yield curve is steepening.
   (b) The bond basis is likely to widen.
   (c) The yield curve is inverted.
   (d) Hedgers who are long cash bonds and short bond futures will expe-
        rience a basis loss.
   (e) Arbitrageurs who are short the basis will experience a loss.
6. Long-term rates are falling but short-term rates are falling faster.
   Which statement is false with respect to bond futures?
   (a) Bond futures are generally advancing.
   (b) The spread between nearby and deferred futures will tend to widen.
   (c) Arbitrageurs will want to buy the basis.
   (d) Hedgers who are long cash and short bond futures will experience a
        loss.
   (e) The yield curve is steepening.
7. Arbitrageurs will sell the bond basis when . . .
   (a) Positive carry prevails.
   (b) Futures run at a discount to the cheapest-to-deliver bond.
   (c) They expect the yield curve to steepen.
   (d) The basis is converging at a slower rate than expected.
   (e) Futures are running at a discount to carry.
8. When yields are expected to decline . . .
   (a) Investors will buy short-term securities and sell long-term securities.
   (b) Short-term securities should be bid up in price.
   (c) This expectation may become apparent in the form of an inverted
        yield curve.
   (d) Investors generally prefer long-term over short-term securities.
   (e) (a) and (b) above.
9. The 180-day term rate equals 6.40 percent; the 270-day term rate
   equals 6.55 percent. Find the 90-day implied forward rate 180 days
   hence.
10. Assume that it is March. Consider the following interest rate structure:

Jun. Euro futures 93.88		(6.12)
Sep. Euro futures 93.95		(6.05)
Dec. Euro futures 93.88		(6.12)
3-month investment . . . offer	@	5.61
6-month investment . . . offer	@	6.18
9-month investment . . . offer	@	6.20

   Which is the best investment: (1) Buy the Euros maturing in September,
   (2) Buy the Euros maturing in June and buying June Euro futures, or (3)
   Buy Euros maturing in December and selling September Euro futures?
   Calculate the returns.

5

Discount and Interest Bearing Securities

U.S. Treasury securities are issued for many different maturities, with terms ranging from 3 months to 30 years. Marketable Treasury securities may be segmented into several categories: bills, notes and bonds, and STRIPS. The purpose of this chapter is to familiarize the reader with the characteristics, issuance, and pricing of these securities.

TREASURY AUCTION PROCEDURES

The Treasury Department periodically holds auctions in order to raise funds in support of U.S. government activities. These auctions typically occur in regular cycles in accordance with standardized procedures.

Bill Auctions

Treasury bills (T-bills) are short-term obligations of the U.S. Treasury with an original term to maturity of less than one year. The Treasury department regularly auctions T-bills with three specified maturities. These T-bill maturities are:

3 months = 13 weeks = 91 days

6 months = 26 weeks = 182 days

1 year = 52 weeks = 364 days

Three- and six-month bills are generally auctioned weekly on Mondays with settlement on the following Thursday. One-year bills are generally auctioned on a monthly basis.

The U.S. Treasury sells T-bills on an annual discount yield basis, that is, bills are sold at a discount yield which reflects the percentage discount from the bill's face value. The percentage discount is adjusted for the bill's term to maturity.

Participants in the auction may submit either a "competitive" or "noncompetitive" bid, stipulating the size of the bill position desired. The competitive bid must also state the minimum discount yield that the bidder is willing to accept. Bids are accepted at the twelve regional Federal Reserve Banks.

The distinction between a competitive and a noncompetitive bid is that noncompetitive bidders are guaranteed receipt of the quantity of T-bills requested at the average accepted auction discount yield, whereas competitive bidders are not assured that they will receive the quantity of T-bills for which they bid.

Noncompetitive bids are subtracted from the quantity of securities to be auctioned before competitive bids are accepted, thus diminishing the supply of competitively auctioned securities. The only caveat for noncompetitive tenders is that the total size of the bid cannot exceed $1 million.

All competitive bids must be submitted by 1:00 P.M. (New York time). These bids are then ranked from lowest to highest in terms of yield. The Treasury begins accepting bids from the lowest discount yield level and continues to accept higher bids until the preannounced quantity of bills has been auctioned successfully. When the auction results are finalized, the minimum, the maximum, and the average bid accepted are announced.

Typically, auctioned bills are settled (paid for) on the Thursday following the auction. This date is known as the "settlement date." Payment for Treasury securities on the settlement date must be made in same-day funds.

One indicator of the success of a Treasury auction is the auction "tail." The tail reflects the yield spread between the average accepted yield and the highest accepted yield. Conventional wisdom has it that a small tail indicates dealers have aggressively bid. A small tail is viewed, therefore, as a bullish indicator. A large tail is indicative of a sloppy auction and may indicate weak retail demand for a specific maturity Treasury instrument.

Note and Bond Auctions

U.S. Treasury notes and bonds are also auctioned regularly by the Treasury. Two-year notes are auctioned on a monthly basis. Notes are auctioned quarterly with a 3-, 4-, 5-, 7-, and 10-year term. Thirty-year bonds also go off on a quarterly basis.

The 3- and 10-year notes and 30-year T-bonds are generally auctioned in sequence on Tuesday, Wednesday, and Thursday, respectively, during the first full week of February, May, August, and November. These quarterly auction weeks are referred to as the "quarterly refundings."

The Treasury typically conducts a "mini-refunding" during the last full week of March, June, September, and December. Typically, the two-, four-, and seven-year notes are auctioned at these times. This auction period is known as a mini-refunding because the size of the issues is generally smaller than the issues auctioned during the quarterly refunding.

In years past, the Treasury auctioned 20-year bonds during the mini-refunding. This practice has been discontinued in favor of larger issues of 10-year notes and 30-year bonds.

It is during these quarterly periods that the Treasury auctions the largest quantity of U.S. government securities. A successful auction period often gives rise to a sustained rally in the Treasury security market, whereas a lackluster auction will frequently be followed by an erosion of Treasury security prices.

The Treasury department announces the size of the note and bond issues approximately one week prior to the specific auction. This announcement generally is made on a Wednesday at 4:30 P.M. EST. The debt market may develop a bullish or bearish tone when the actual size of a refunding exceeds or falls short of the anticipated size of the issuance, respectively.

The Treasury's STRIPS Program

STRIPS is the acronym for the U.S. Treasury's Separate Trading of Registered Interest and Principal of Securities program. The STRIPS program facilitates the marketing of *zero coupon* Treasury obligations. It does so because the Treasury assigns a separate CUSIP number to the corpus and coupon payments associated with the security. A CUSIP is a code which is necessary to identify a bond when transferring the security through the Fed wire system. In the absence of a CUSIP number, it is impossible to transfer securities through the Fed wire system.

Prior to the STRIPS program, zeros were created by brokerage firms under proprietary acronyms such as CATS and TIGRS. These instruments represent obligations collateralized by Treasury securities held in depositories designated by the originating institution. Unlike these proprietary products, STRIPS are backed directly by the U.S. government.

STRIPS fall into one of two categories, coupon or corpus strips. Coupon STRIPS may be thought of as individual securities created from the coupon annuity of a Treasury security. Corpus strips or zero coupon bonds are created from the principal component of a Treasury security.

Coupon STRIPS maturing on the same date share the same CUSIP number regardless of the specific coupon issue that the STRIP was originated from. The commonality of CUSIP numbers increases the liquidity of coupon STRIPS traded in the secondary market. Corpus STRIPS are also identified by CUSIP numbers, but they are strictly differentiated from coupon STRIPS, that is, coupon STRIPS and corpus STRIPS are not interchangeable. Notes and bonds can generally be reassembled after they have been stripped.

Even though STRIPS may be thought of as long-term instruments, they are traded on a yield rather than a price basis. The yield quote reflects the equivalent bond yield; that is, semiannual compounding is implicit in the yield quote.

Example: The price of a $1 million, 20-year zero coupon bond with a yield of 8.75 percent is equal to $180,360.

$$\text{Price} = \$1,000,000 \times 1.04375^{-40}$$
$$= \$180,360$$

Hence a 20-year maturity zero coupon bond yielding 8.75 percent is priced at slightly more than 18 percent of par.

TIME VALUE OF MONEY

Casual observers often associate the availability of cash resources as a significant asset, but experienced financial analysts know that there may be significant opportunity costs associated with holding sizable cash reserves. This opportunity cost reflects the possibility that these cash reserves may be applied to other, more productive pursuits, most notably, investment in fixed income securities.

The opportunity cost reflects the interest income foregone from holding cash equivalent assets (namely currency or checking account balances) in noninterest bearing form. In other words, there is a significant *time value* associated with money.

This section reviews the concept of time value, providing methods of measuring time value in the context of a variety of fixed income security markets. These concepts provide a foundation for pricing cash securities whether they represent interest bearing securities such as Treasury bonds or notes or discount securities such as bills.

Measuring Opportunity Costs

The opportunity cost may be assessed by reference to short-term risk-free interest rates corresponding to the length of a potential investing or holding period. Assume, for example, that an investor holds a $1 million cash balance for one year. The current annual risk-free interest rate is 6 percent, expressed as r. Assume that this 6 percent rate is a simple interest rate.

Simple interest accrues on a straightline basis throughout the investment period. There is no compounding during the investment period.

What is the investor's opportunity cost if he chooses to hold this cash balance in noninterest bearing form (cash)?

Future Value

If invested for one year at the annual simple interest rate, the future value (FV) of the investment would be:

$$FV = \text{Investment} \times (1 + r)$$

The quantity expressed in the parentheses $(1 + r)$ is generally referred to as a *future interest factor*. (FIF). This future interest factor reflects the proportionate amount by which an investment may grow over a one-year period under the assumption of simple interest.

Substituting $1 million for the investment value and 6 percent for the annual simple interest rate yields the following future value:

$$FV = \$1 \text{ million} \times (1 + 0.06)$$

$$= \$1,060,000$$

Hence the opportunity cost of holding a $1 million investment in a noninterest bearing account for one year would be equal to the forgone interest. If the annual risk-free interest rate is 6 percent, the opportunity cost could be assessed at $60,000.

Note that this opportunity cost calculation ignores the transaction costs of shifting into and out of a cash position. (These costs may be relatively minimal.) If there is an overriding need to maintain liquidity, the benefits received from maintaining an extremely liquid cash position may offset some or all of the opportunity costs of holding assets in interest bearing securities.

Semiannual Compounding

Assume that the term of a potential investment is one year but that interest is payable semiannually rather than annually. Payment of interest on a semiannual basis implies that one-half the annual interest rate is payable every six months.

If, for example, the annual interest rate is equal to 6 percent, interest equal to 3 percent of the face value of the investment is payable every six months. Does a semiannual interest payment structure have an effect on the opportunity cost of maintaining idle cash balances? The answer to this question is a definite yes! The payment of interest on a semiannual basis allows reinvestment of the interest payment for the remainder of the original investment period, that is, for the remaining six months of the original one-year period.

More frequent payment of interest creates a larger opportunity cost because interest may now be earned on the semiannual interest payment. The ability to earn interest on interest is generally referred to as the principal of *compound interest.*

> **Example:** The future interest factor commensurate with a one-year investment period at 6 percent annual interest was 1.06, indicating that a $1 million investment would grow to $1.06 million over one year's time. If one-half the annual interest is payable every six months, we must recalculate the future interest factor (FIF_2) to account for the payment of interest on interest.
>
> $$FIF_2 = (1 + r/2)^2$$
> $$= 1.03^2$$
> $$= 1.0609$$

Multiplying the $1 million original cash balance by the new future interest factor (1.0609) would result in a future investment value of $1,060,900. When interest is paid semiannually rather than annually, the opportunity cost has increased by $900 because we are now able to earn 3 percent on the $30,000 interest payment made after six months.

The semiannual compounding calculation assumes reinvestment of the semiannual interest payment at the original investment rate. This may be a typical condition for bank deposits, but you may wish to alter your reinvestment assumption in the context of coupon bearing debt instruments.

Effective Annual Yield

The future interest factor minus 1 is often referred to as the *effective annual yield* (EAY) on an investment. This effective annual yield is also referred to as the annual percentage rate (APR).

$$APR = FIF - 1$$

In the prior example, the impact of semiannual compounding was to increase the effective annual yield from 6 percent to 6.09 percent. The role of interest on interest plays a very important role in the analysis of trading opportunities.

The future interest factor can also be generalized to account for n compounding periods per year. The number of compounding periods can range from one to an infinite number of periods.

$$FIF_n = (1 + r/n)^n$$

$$= (1 + \text{Periodic Interest Rate})^n$$

The periodic interest rate is equal to the annual interest rate divided by n, the number of compounding periods per year.

Example: If we held a security that paid 6 percent annually, but paid in monthly installments (namely, a mortgage-backed security), what would the future interest factor and effective annual yield equal?

$$FIF_{12} = (1 + 0.06/12)^{12}$$

$$= (1.005)^{12}$$

$$= 1.0617$$

therefore,

$$APR = 6.17\%$$

Thus monthly compounding results in an advance in the effective annual yield of 17 basis points over annual compounding.

Continuous Compounding

As the number of compounding periods per year increases without limit, the future interest factor converges to a specific value. This is known as *continuous compounding* and is given in the following formula. If we allow n (the number of annual compounding periods) to approach infinity, the future interest factor (FIF_c) will be equal to:

$$FIF_c = (1 + r/n)^n$$

$$= e^r$$

where

$$e = 2.718281828 \text{ (base of the natural log)}$$

Example: The continuously compounded future interest factor may be computed as follows.

$$\text{FIF}_c = e^{0.06}$$
$$= 1.0618$$

Thus the APR is advanced by one basis point over the result achieved under a monthly compounding assumption.

360- versus 365-Day Rate Years

Short-term rates (also known as money market rates) are quoted on a 360-day year basis. Long-term rates (those applicable to notes and bonds) are quoted on a 365-day year basis. It is very important to be aware of the number of calendar days in a specific interest rate year. The actual yield on an investment based on a 360-day interest rate year vis-a-vis a 365-day interest rate year is approximately $365/360$ or 1.013889 times larger!

Example: Assume that you may invest idle funds at a 10 percent annual rate based on a 360-day interest rate year. What is the yield advantage of investing based on a 360-day year rather than a 365-day year? Remember that the 365-day year is approximately 1.013889 longer than a 360-day year.

$$\text{365-day yield} = \text{360-day yield} \times 1.013889$$
$$= 10\% \times 1.013889$$
$$= 10.139\%$$

As just demonstrated, a 10 percent rate payable on a 360-day basis provides a yield enhancement of approximately 14 basis points per annum when compared to a 10 percent rate payable on a 365-day basis.

Interest Rate Periods Less Than One Year

Assume that an investor holds a cash balance in a noninterest earning form for one week at a 6 percent annual rate. To convert the 6 percent annual rate to reflect a one-week holding period return (HPR), multiply the rate by the number of days in the holding period d (in this case d = 7) and divide by 360 (the number of days in the short-term half year):

$$HPR = r \times (d/360)$$
$$= (0.06) \times (7/360) = 0.001167$$
$$= 11.67 \text{ basis points}$$

Remember that the conversion from an annual rate to a holding period rate implies that interest is accruing at a pro rata amount per day, that is, there is no compounding occurring during the holding period. The annualized rate of return of 6 percent corresponds to a holding period rate of return of approximately 0.12 percent (actually 0.1167 percent) or 12 basis points (0.01 percent is equal to 1 basis point).

The FIF associated with the one-week holding period is calculated as follows:

$$FIF = 1 + [r \times (d/360)]$$
$$= 1 + [0.06 \times (7/360)]$$
$$= 1.001167$$

An example of the future value and the opportunity cost of a seven-day investment follows.

Example: The future value of $1 million invested at a 6 percent annual rate for one week is equal to:

$$FV = \$1,000,000 \times FIF$$
$$= \$1,000,000 \times 1.001167$$
$$= \$1,001,167$$

Hence the value of the cash balance invested at a 6 percent rate for seven days is equal to $1,001,167.

This is another way of saying that the opportunity cost for failure to invest the cash balance for one week is equal to the interest income that may have been earned during that time interval or:

$$\text{Opportunity Cost} = (\$1,000,000) \times (0.06) \times (7/360)$$
$$= (\$1,000,000) \times (0.001167)$$
$$= \$1,167$$

PRESENT AND FUTURE VALUES

The $1,001,167 with interest cash balance mentioned in the previous example is referred to as the *future value* of $1 million invested for seven days. Alternatively, the $1 million cash balance represents the *present value* of $1,001,167 discounted at a 6 percent rate for seven days. As such, present value factors are nothing more than the inverse or reciprocal operation of calculating future interest factors. The present or future value of an investment is a function of three factors:

1. The size of the cash flows of an investment,
2. The number of periods that an investment's cash flow stream will continue, and
3. The interest rate relevant for an investment's term to maturity and credit risk.

Remember that only U.S. Treasury securities are "credit-risk free." Other types of interest bearing securities are not credit-risk free, so that a risk premium, that is, a higher rate of interest, generally is demanded by market participants. The greater the perceived level of credit risk, the greater is the risk premium demanded.

Example: Determine the present value of a $1 million cash payment to be made one year from now. Assume that the relevant interest rate for a one-year period is 6 percent. Based upon the 6 percent interest rate, we know that the future interest factor is equal to 1.06. Remember that the present value interest factor (PVIF) is equal to the reciprocal of the future interest factor:

$$PVIF = 1/FIF$$
$$= FIF^{-1}$$

Substituting the 6 percent interest rate into the above equation gives us the following present value interest factor:

$$PVIF = FIF^{-1}$$
$$= 1.06^{-1}$$
$$= 0.94339623$$

Hence the present value (PV) of the $1 million payment to be received one year from now is equal to:

$$PV = PVIF \times Payment$$
$$= 0.94339623 \times \$1,000,000$$
$$= \$943,396$$

In many applications, present value interest factors are rounded to four decimal places. For the sake of accuracy, eight decimal places should be used when using PVIFs for calculation purposes.

The future value (FV) of the $1 million payment is equal to the present value of the payment $943,396 multiplied by the future interest factor (1.06):

$$FV = PV \times FIF$$
$$= \$943,396 \times 1.06$$
$$= \$1,000,000$$

Regardless of the frequency of compounding during an annual period, the effect of compound interest comes into play for fixed income instruments with longer than one year until maturity. The future interest factor formula can be adjusted to take account of annual compounding as follows:

$$FIF = (1 + r)^t$$

where

t = Years to maturity, *e.g.*, 1/2 year expressed as 0.5 years.

Example: Assume that 8 percent is the spot interest rate applicable for a $1 million, two-year investment. The FIF corresponding to this interest rate and time interval would be:

$$FIF = 1.08 \times 1.08$$
$$= 1.08^2$$
$$= 1.1664$$

The future value of the payment would be equal to:

$$FV = Payment \times FIF$$
$$= \$1,000,000 \times 1.1664$$
$$= \$1,166,400$$

The present value of $1 million to be received two years from today can be calculated by using the reciprocal of the future interest factor:

$$PV = FIF^{-1} \times \$1,000,000$$
$$= PVIF \times \$1,000,000$$
$$= 1.1664^{-1} \times \$1,000,000$$
$$= 0.857339 \times \$1,000,000$$
$$= \$857,339$$

The present value of a future cash flow can be calculated for any term to maturity using a generalization of the above formula; that is, the present value of $1 to be received t years from today can be calculated as follows:

$$PV = FIF^{-1}$$
$$= [1 + (r/n)]^{-tn}$$

where

n = Number of annual compounding periods.

Remember that t can take on any value ranging from $1/360$ (a one-day period) to infinity.

If the 8 percent interest rate mentioned in the prior example were paid semiannually rather than annually over the two-year investment period, what would the future value of the investment be?

Given a semiannual payment structure over a two-year period, we have an investment with four semiannual compounding periods, that is, two semiannual periods per year times two years is equal to four. The semiannual interest rate reflects a 4 percent payout; hence the equation for the future interest factor would be:

$$FIF = [1 + (r/n)]^{tn}$$
$$= 1.04^{2 \times 2}$$
$$= 1.16985856$$
$$FV = \$1,000,000 \times 1.16985856$$
$$= \$1,169,858.56$$

The effect of semiannual (rather than annual) compounding in this example is to increase the future value by $3,458.56.

Calculating Present Values for Zero Coupon Bonds

The present value of a $1 cash payment due in one year is analogous to the price of a one-year *zero coupon bond*.

A *zero coupon bond* is a fixed income security that is sold at a discount to its face value to reflect the current market yield to maturity. A zero coupon bond is the only fixed income security with a maturity greater than one year that eliminates reinvestment risk, that is, these securities offer a true yield to maturity.

Zero coupon bonds are quoted and traded on an equivalent bond-yield basis. Remember that calculating present values using the equivalent bond yield implicitly assumes semiannual discounting or compounding.

Example: Assume you have a firm offer to purchase a $1 million, five-year zero coupon bond at an equivalent bond yield of 7.5 percent. What is the current market price?

Note that the equivalent bond yield of 7.5 percent corresponds to a semiannual discount rate of 3.75 percent and that a five-year bond has 10 semiannual discount periods. The present value of this zero coupon security is equal to:

$$PV_{zero} = \text{Face Amount} \times [1 + (r/n)]^{-tn}$$
$$= \$1,000,000 \times [1 + (0.075/2)]^{-5 \times 2}$$
$$= \$692,020$$

A sum of $692,020 invested at a 7.5 percent equivalent bond yield, (compounded semiannually) will grow to $1 million in five years:

$$\$1,000,000 = \$692,020 \times [1 + (0.075/2)]^{5 \times 2}$$

ANNUITIES

Many investment securities generate a series of fixed payments at periodic intervals over time. The coupon and/or interest payments associated with T-bonds, T-notes, corporate bonds, and insurance company guaranteed investment contracts (GICs) all represent fixed payment streams that continue for a prespecified period of time. Cash flow streams of this type are referred to as *annuities*.

An *annuity* represents a fixed series of periodic payments made over a span of time.

The two major categories of annuities include ordinary annuities and annuities due. Both of these categories consist of a fixed series of periodic payments. The two types of annuities differ in that the first payment for an ordinary annuity occurs at the end of the first period, whereas the first payment for an annuity due occurs at the beginning of the first period.

The ordinary annuity is the more typical of the two annuity types, namely, bonds and notes. The best example of an annuity due is the cash flow stream arising from lottery winnings.

(Mortgage-backed securities are not included in the annuity class of fixed income instruments because the payment of interest and the amortization of principal are not fixed, that is, there may be significant variability of cash flows due to prepayments, defaults, and such.)

Pricing an Annuity

The Treasury auctions 10-year notes on a quarterly basis. There are 21 periodic cash flows associated with a newly issued 10-year note: 20 semi-annual interest payments and the corpus payment (principal repayment). The 20 semiannual interest payments represent a 20-period (10-year) annuity.

The current market value can be calculated as if the 20-component annuity represented a series of zero coupon bonds, each discounted at the current bond equivalent yield. The market price (present value) of this annuity is equal to the sum of the present values of the 20 zero coupon bonds. The market value of the corpus payment is equivalent to a 20-period zero coupon bond, discounted at the bond equivalent yield.

> **Example:** Assume that you have an offer to purchase $1 million par value of a 7 percent coupon, 10-year note. What is the present value of the coupon streams and corpus payment and the total cash flow stream, given that the current market yield (equivalent bond yield) is equal to 7 percent?
>
> The $1 million note will pay a $35,000 coupon every 6 months for the next 10 years. This is equivalent to a sequence of 20 $35,000 zero coupon bonds. The present value of the 20-coupon annuity is equal to:

$$PV = \text{Coupon} \times [1 + (r/n)]^{-1} + \text{Coupon} \times [1 + (r/n)]^{-2}$$
$$+ \text{Coupon} \times [1 + (r/n)]^{-3} + \ldots + \text{Coupon} \times [1 + (r/n)]^{-20}$$
$$= \$35,000[1 + (.07/2)]^{-1} + \$35,000[1 + (.07/2)]^{-2}$$
$$+ \$35,000[1 + (.07/2)]^{-3} + \ldots + \$35,000[1 + (.07/2)]^{-20}$$

The sum of the present values of the 20 zero coupon bonds can be written in a short form as:

$$PV_{\text{annuity}} = \sum_{i=1}^{tn} (\text{Coupon} \times [1 + (r/n)]^{-i})$$
$$= \$497,434$$

The present value of the corpus payment can be calculated as:

$$PV_{\text{corpus}} = \text{Face Amount} \times [1 + (r/n)]^{-tn}$$
$$= \$1,000,000 \times [1 + (.07/2)]^{-10 \times 2}$$
$$= \$502,566$$

The present value of a bond or note is equal to the present value of its coupon annuity and the corpus payment:

$$PV_{bond} = PV_{annuity} + PV_{corpus}$$
$$= \$497,434 + \$502,566$$
$$= \$1,000,000$$

The Effect of an Increase in Yield

In our previous example, we examined the pricing characteristics of a 7 percent coupon, 10-year T-note priced to yield 7 percent. If the market yield increases to 8 percent, the semiannual discount factor increases to 4 percent. What is the new market price of the coupon annuity, the corpus payment, and the T-note itself at the higher yield?

$$PV_{annuity} = \sum_{i=1}^{tn} (Coupon \times [1 + (r/n)]^{-i})$$
$$= \sum_{i=1}^{20} (\$35,000 \times [1 + (.08/2)]^{-i})$$
$$= \$475,661$$

$$PV_{corpus} = Face\ Amount \times [1 + (r/n)]^{-tn}$$
$$= \$1,000,000 \times [1 + (.08/2)]^{-10 \times 2}$$
$$= \$456,387$$

$$PV_{note} = PV_{annuity} + PV_{corpus}$$
$$= \$475,661 + \$456,387$$
$$= \$932,048$$

As may be seen in this example, the price of the 10-year note declines by \$67,952 (approximately 6.795 percent) when rates increase from 7 percent to 8 percent, that is, the price declined from \$1 million to \$932,048. Notice that the decline in the present value of the coupon annuity and the corpus payment are not proportional to their values at a 7 percent yield.

The percentage decline in the present value of the corpus payment is far larger than the decline in the present value of the coupon annuity. As the bond equivalent yield increases from 7 percent to 8 percent, the present value of the coupon annuity declines by 4.38 percent, whereas the present value of the corpus payment declines by 9.19 percent.

The relationship between the percentage change in the present value of the coupon annuity and the percentage change in the present value of the corpus payment, given a change in the equivalent bond yield (EBY), is a function of both the remaining term to maturity and the coupon rate of the fixed income debt instrument.

The Effect of a Decrease in Yield

Let us examine the impact of a 100-basis point decrease in interest rates from a 7 percent bond equivalent yield to a 6 percent bond equivalent yield. The present value of the coupon annuity, corpus payment, and total cash flow is as follows:

$$PV_{annuity} = \sum_{i=1}^{tn} (Coupon \times [1 + (r/n)]^{-i})$$

$$= \sum_{i=1}^{20} (\$35,000 \times [1 + (.06/2)]^{-i})$$

$$= \$520,712$$

$$PV_{corpus} = Face\ Amount \times [1 + (r/n)]^{-tn}$$

$$= \$1,000,000 \times [1 + (.06/2)]^{-10 \times 2}$$

$$= \$553,676$$

$$PV_{note} = PV_{annuity} + PV_{corpus}$$

$$= \$520,712 + \$553,676$$

$$= \$1,074,388$$

The price of the 7 percent note increases by \$74,387 (7.44 percent) when rates decline from 7 percent to 6 percent. The value of the corpus payment appreciates by \$51,110 (10.17 percent), while the coupon annuity increases in value by \$23,277 (4.68 percent).

Convexity

We have demonstrated that for equal changes in market yield (100 basis points), the price change corresponding to a decrease in yield is greater than the price decrease corresponding to an equivalent increase in yield. For greater changes in yield, the relative price disparity increases; that is, potential price increases exceed potential price decreases for an equal yield change. This is an example of a bond pricing property known as *convexity*. The convexity relationship is illustrated in the following table:

Convexity of a 7 Percent Coupon, 10-Year Maturity T-Note

Yield	Price	Price Change from 7 Percent (Percent of Par)	(Percent)
3%	134–10/32nds	34–10/32nds	34.31
4	124–17	24–17	24.53
5	115–19	15–19	15.59
6	107–14	7–14	7.44
7	100–00	0	0
8	93–07	(6–25)	(6.79)
9	87–00	(13–00)	(13.00)
10	81–10	(18–22)	(18.69)
11	76–03	(23–29)	(23.91)

The 7 percent T-note will price at par (100–00) to yield 7 percent. The price of this T-note will increase by 7.44 percent for a 100-basis point decline in yield, whereas the price will decrease by 6.79 percent for a 100-basis point increase in yield. This represents a percentage price change differential of 0.65 percent.

The price of the 7 percent coupon T-note will appreciate by 15.59 percent given a 200-basis point decline in yield from the 7 percent yield level, whereas the price will decrease by 13 percent given a 200-basis point increase in yield. This represents a 2.59 percent percentage price change differential biased towards the upside.

The percentage price change differential increases to 5.84 percent for a 300-basis point yield change and 10.40 percent for a 400-basis point change in yield from the initial level of 7 percent.

TREASURY BILL PRICES AND YIELDS

As stated previously, Treasury bills are auctioned and traded on an annual discount yield basis, that is, bills are sold at a price which reflects a discount from their face value (maturity value). The annual discount yield is used as a pricing convention to determine current market price. The annual discount yield must be adjusted to reflect the bill's term until maturity. Remember that bills are short-term money market instruments, so both yields and prices are quoted on a 360-day year basis.

Computing Yields

A formula for computing the periodic discount yield follows. Note that the annual discount yield represents a 360-day rate, regardless of a T-bill's term to maturity.

$$\text{Periodic yield} = \text{Annual yield} \times (d/360)$$

where

$$d = \text{Days in the discount period}$$

Example: A 91-day and a 364-day T-bill are sold at an annual discount yield of 6 percent. The periodic discount yield may be calculated as follows.

$$PY_{91} = 0.06 \times (91/360)$$
$$= 0.0152 \text{ or } 1.52\%$$
$$PY_{364} = 0.06 \times (364/360)$$
$$= 0.0607 \text{ or } 6.07\%$$

The periodic interest income earned from holding a T-bill is equal to the periodic discount yield multiplied by the face or par value of the bill.

$$\text{Interest Income} = \text{FV} \times \text{Periodic Yield}$$

The price of a bill is equal to the face value (100 percent of par) less the periodic discount yield.

$$\text{Price} = 100 - (100 \times \text{Periodic Yield})$$

or:

$$\text{Price} = \text{FV} - [\text{FV} \times \text{Annual Yield} \times (d/360)]$$

Example: The price of a $1 million face value unit of our 91-day and 364-day bills discussed above might be priced as follows.

$$\text{Price}_{91} = \$1,000,000 - [\$1,000,000 \times 0.06 \times (91/360)]$$
$$= \$984,833$$
$$\text{Price}_{364} = \$1,000,000 - [\$1,000,000 \times 0.06 \times (364/360)]$$
$$= \$939,333$$

The price of a bill is always less than the face value. Hence the annualized simple interest yield must be greater than the discount yield. The money market yield (MMY), also known as the simple interest rate, equals the periodic discount yield divided by the price of the bill, adjusted to reflect an annualized rate of return.

$$\text{Money Mkt Yield} = (\text{Periodic Yield/Price}) \times (360/d)$$

Example: The money market yield of our 91-day and 364-day bills may be calculated as follows.

$$MMY_{91} = (1.52\%/98.4833\%) \times (360/91)$$
$$= 6.11\%$$
$$MMY_{364} = (6.07\%/93.9333\%) \times (360/364)$$
$$= 6.39\%$$

Equivalent Bond Yield for Bills

Short-term interest rates are quoted on a 360-day year basis, whereas long-term interest rates are quoted on a 365-day year basis.

Interest on bonds and notes accrues on a simple interest basis and is paid out semiannually, whereas interest on short-term instruments accrues on a simple interest basis and is paid only at the maturity date of the instrument.

Yield quotes for a bond or note typically understate the true effective yield. The yield on an 8 percent bond trading at par may be quoted at 8 percent. Reinvesting the first coupon payment at an 8 percent rate for the remainder of the first year, the effective annual yield equals 8.16 percent. Thus the equivalent bond yield understates the true annual yield by 16 basis points as it does not incorporate interest on interest.

Most dealers will quote bills on a discount yield, a money market yield, or an equivalent bond yield basis. Quoting bills on an equivalent bond yield basis allows direct comparison of the yields on T-bills, T-notes, and T-bonds.

The money market yield for a bill with a term to maturity less than 183 days may be converted to an equivalent bond yield by the following calculation.

$$EBY = MMY \times (365/360)$$

Expanding:

$$EBY = \frac{\text{Annual Yield} \times (d/360)}{1 - [\text{Annual Yield} \times (d/360)]} \times (360/d) \times (365/360)$$

Rearranging:

$$EBY = [\text{Annual Yield} \times 365]/[360 - (d \times \text{Annual Yield})]$$

Thus the EBY for a bill with less than 183 days remaining to maturity is greater than the money market yield by a multiplicative factor of 1.0139 ($365/360$).

Example: The equivalent bond yield of our 91-day bill might be determined as follows.

$$EBY_{91} = [0.06 \times 365]/[360 - (91 \times 0.06)]$$
$$= 6.18\%$$

More Than 182 Days until Maturity

Remember that the equivalent bond yield understates the effective annual yield of a bond or note with more than one coupon period remaining until maturity. This is because the EBY ignores the possibility of coupon reinvestment (compound interest).

The money market yield for a T-bill with more than 182 days remaining until maturity can be construed to include an interest on interest component when compared to the equivalent bond yield of a semiannual coupon bearing security. Hence the money market yield for a T-bill with more than 182 days remaining until maturity must be adjusted downward to be directly comparable to a coupon security's EBY.

The EBY for T-bills with more than 182 days remaining until maturity can be calculated as follows:

$$EBY = \frac{(-d/365) + \sqrt{([d/365]^2 - [(2d/365) - 1][1 - (1/\text{Price})])}}{[(d/365) - 0.5]}$$

Example: Assume that you have recently purchased a one-year (364-day) T-bill at a 6 percent discount yield. Remember that the T-bill discount yield is based on a 360-day year. Find the equivalent bond yield.

$$EBY = \frac{(-364/365) + \sqrt{([364/365]^2 - [(2 \times 364/365) - 1][1 - (1/0.939333)])}}{[(364/365) - 0.5]}$$
$$= 6.37\%$$

YIELD MEASURES AND VOLATILITY PROPERTIES

Bonds and notes have demonstrated significant price and yield volatility since the late 1970s. The capacity to quantify price and yield volatility properties is exceptionally important. Fixed income traders used several standard methods to measure price and yield volatility properties of fixed income instruments.

Term to Maturity and Coupon Rate

Many bond market practitioners use rules of thumb to characterize bond price volatility. Two general rules are:

1. As the *term to maturity* of a specific bond issue increases, the price volatility of the bond also increases. If you anticipate that long-term rates will decline, buy the longest dated T-bond available. If you anticipate that rates will increase, the appropriate strategy would be to decrease the average maturity of your fixed income portfolio to minimize adverse price effects.
2. As the *coupon* of a specific bond issue increases (decreases), the percentage price volatility of the issue decreases (increases).

If you wish to capture the greatest percentage price volatility for a bullish (bearish) market scenario, your best strategy is to buy (sell) the longest-dated, lowest-coupon bond available. As of August 1986, this was the 7.25 percent issue of May, 2016.

A problem arises when the longest-maturity issue is not also the lowest-coupon issue. Under these circumstances, there is no direct answer to the question: What is the optimal bond issue to purchase in terms of maximizing profit potential from an interest rate fluctuation? The answer to that question is discussed in this section.

Several volatility measures may be used to quantify absolute or percentage price volatility as well as absolute yield volatility. The most frequently cited volatility measures include: (1) basis point value, (2) yield value of a thirty-second ($1/32$), and (3) Macauley and modified durations.

Basis Point Value

The *basis point value* (BPV) method is one of the most frequently cited measures of absolute price volatility. A BPV represents the absolute price change of a specific security given a one-basis point (0.01 percent) change in the security's yield.

The formula for calculating a BPV is given in the following equation:

$$BPV = d(\text{Bond Price})/d(\text{yield} = 0.01\%)$$

One method to measure BPV is to compare the price of the bond given a yield one-half basis point above and below current market yields. This is sometimes known as an "arc" BPV.

An alternative method is to take the derivative of the bond price with respect to the equivalent bond yield substituting a yield of one basis point in the equation. The derivative of the bond pricing equation with respect to the EBY is shown below.

$$d(\text{Bond Price})/d(\text{EBY}) = -0.5 \times \sum_{t=1}^{M} [t \times CF_t(1 + EBY/2)^{-t-1}]$$

where:

$$CF_t = \text{cash flow at time t}$$

If we multiply both sides of this equation by d(EBY) and substitute the value of one basis point (0.0001) for d(EBY) we arrive at the following equation for the BPV:

$$BPV = -0.5 \times 0.0001 \times \sum_{t=1}^{M} [t \times CF_t(1 + EBY/2)^{-t-1}]$$

The following table illustrates the basis point value associated with a variety of issues as of August 26, 1986. These BPVs are calculated assuming $100,000 par value for the bonds.

Basis Point Value, Selected Bonds, $100,000 par value
(08/26/86)

Issue	Price	Yield (%)	BPV ($)
7.625% 2002–07	102–00	7.41	92.47
8.750% 2003–08	110–08	7.67	101.74
9.125% 2004–09	113–30	7.67	105.72
12.750% 2005–10	148–05	7.85	133.53
14.000% 2006–11	161–22	7.86	147.06
10.375% 2007–12	126–13	7.81	123.53
12.000% 2008–13	142–21	7.88	137.58
13.250% 2009–14	156–21	7.86	151.31
12.500% 2009–14	148–17	7.89	145.01
11.750% 2009–14	143–24	7.68	144.02
11.250% 2015	141–25	7.65	156.06
10.625% 2015	134–25	7.63	149.18
9.875% 2015	125–10	7.69	139.89
9.250% 2016	119–24	7.57	136.39
7.250% 2016	101–00	7.17	123.35

The foregoing table illustrates that the BPV for the 7 1/4 percent bond of 2016 yielding 7.17 percent is equal to $123.35. This implies that if the yield of the 7 1/4 percent bond should fluctuate from 7.17 percent to 7.16 percent or 7.18 percent, then the price of a $100,000 face value unit would change by approximately $123.35 (just less than 4/32ds).

BPVs are positively related to the coupon rate and the term to maturity (or first call date). BPVs increase as the coupon of a bond increases or as the term to maturity of a bond increases. BPVs are inversely related to yield, that is, the lower the yield, the larger the BPV of the corresponding security.

BPVs measure absolute, not percentage, price volatility. For example, the 7 1/4 percent bond of 2016 had a BPV of $123.35, while the 10 3/8 percent bond of 2007–12 had a nearly identical BPV of $123.53. A key difference may be found, however, in the fact that the 7 1/4 percent issue was trading at 101–00 while the 10 3/8 percent issue was at 126–13.

A BPV of approximately $123 reflects a .122 percent price change for the 7 1/4 percent bond as opposed to a .097 percent price change for the 10 3/8 percent bond. Thus the 7 1/4 percent bond is more sensitive to changing yields on a percentage basis relative to the 10 3/8 percent.

The convexity associated with the price of a bond generally is reflected in its BPV. This means a BPV corresponding to a decrease in yield is greater than the BPV corresponding to an increase in yield. While the convexity of a bond is not pronounced over small yield changes, its effect is much more apparent over large changes in yield.

Example: Consider the BPV of the 7 1/4 percent issue of 2016 at yields 100 basis points higher or lower than the yield of 7.17 percent illustrated in the prior table.

Yield	Price	BPV
6.17%	114–21	$150.98
7.17%	101–00	$123.35
8.17%	89–25	$101.62

If yields increase 100 basis points from 7.17 percent to 8.17 percent, the BPV decreases by $21.73 per $100,000 face value unit. If yields fall 100 basis points from 7.17 percent to 6.17 percent, the BPV increases by $27.63 per $100,000 face value unit.

What is the basis point value of a short-term security such as a bill? Fortunately, the calculation is much simpler than that associated with a bond. In fact, the BPV of a bill or any other straight discount security is a simple linear function of its term and face value.

The BPV may be found by reference to our equation for the price of a bill:

$$\text{Price} = \text{FV} - [\text{FV} \times \text{Annual Yield} \times (d/360)]$$

By finding the price of the bill at current yield levels and comparing that result to its price at a yield level one basis point higher or lower, you may find the BPV of the bill.

Example: Find the BPV of a $1 million face value lot of bills currently yielding 5.50 percent with 90 days to maturity.

```
Yield @ 5.50%:
    Price = $1,000,000 - [$1,000,000 × 0.055 × 90/360]
          = $986,250
Yield @ 5.51%:
    Price = $1,000,000 - [$1,000,000 × 0.0551 × 90/360]
          = $986,225
Difference: $986,250 - $986,225 = $25.00
```

As a rule, the BPV of a $1 million face value 90-day bill equals $25.00. The BPV of a bill which varies in terms of face value or term from this standard reference is simply a linear multiple of $25.00. For example, the BPV of a $10 million face value 90-day bill equals $250.00. The BPV of a $1 million face value 180-day bill equals $50, a 270-day bill equals $75, and a 360-day bill equals $100.

Basis Point Values for Bills
(In Dollars)

	45-Days	90-Days	180-Days	270-Days	360-Days
$ 1 MM	12.50	25.00	50.00	75.00	100.00
$10 MM	125.00	250.00	500.00	750.00	1,000.00
$20 MM	250.00	500.00	1,000.00	1,500.00	2,000.00
$50 MM	625.00	1,250.00	2,500.00	3,750.00	5,000.00

Yield Value of a Thirty-Second (1/32d)

Some fixed income analysts prefer to measure bond volatility by reference to yield rather than price changes. The "yield value of a thirty-second"

(YV_{32}) is indicative of the expected change in the yield of a bond given a $^1/32d$ change in price.

The following ratio is generally used to denote the yield value of $^1/32$ relationship for a bond or note:

$$YV_{32} = d(Yield)/d(price = ^1/32d)$$

The YV_{32} bears an inverse relationship to the BPV. As yields decrease (increase), BPVs increase (decrease), while YVs decrease (increase).

Example: The BPV of the $7^1/4$ percent bond trading at a 7.17 percent yield was equal to $123.35 or $^{3.94}/32ds$. This implies that a price change of $^1/32d$ corresponds to a yield change of 0.0025 percent or approximately one-quarter basis point. At a yield of 8.17 percent the BPV declines to $101.62 reflecting a yield value of 0.0031 percent or approximately one-third basis point. At a yield of 6.17 percent the BPV advances to $150.98 reflecting a yield value of 0.0021 percent or approximately one-fifth basis point.

Yield	Price	BPV	YV$_{32}$
6.17%	114–21	$150.98	0.0021%
7.17%	101–00	$123.35	0.0025%
8.17%	89–25	$101.62	0.0031%

Hence as yields increase (decrease), YVs increase (decrease). Under the same conditions, BPVs decrease (increase), respectively. This implies a decrease (increase) in bond market price volatility, resulting in an inverse relationship between the yield value of $^1/32$ and the corresponding BPV.

YV_{32}	BPV
2.000 BPs	$15.62
1.000 BPs	$31.25
0.667 BPs	$46.87
0.500 BPs	$62.50
0.333 BPs	$93.75
0.250 BPs	$125.00
0.200 BPs	$156.25

Note also that as the yield of a specific issue changes, the yield value fluctuates in the same direction. As BPVs increase, YV_{32}s decrease. Hence a high YV_{32} implies low price volatility, whereas a low value for a YV_{32} implies high price volatility.

DURATION AND PRICE SENSITIVITY

In the late 1930s, a British actuary, Frederick Macauley, studied the sensitivity of bond prices to interest rate fluctuations. At the time, a bond's term was generally employed as an indicator of price sensitivity. Macauley noted, however, that the return associated with a fixed income security may be represented as a function not only of the return of principal at maturity, but also as a function of all the intervening coupon inflows.

Remember that a bond price is a function of its cash flows.

$$\text{Bond Price} = \sum_{t=1}^{M} [CF_t(1 + EBY/2)^{-t}]$$

The reciprocal of the factor in parentheses $(1 + EBY/2)^{-t}$, represents the periodic discount factor. Macauley devised a method for calculating the interest rate sensitivity of a bond, referencing the periodic discount factor as the interest rate sensitivity factor.

Macauley suggested using a measure of bond price sensitivity analogous to an economics concept known as "elasticity." Elasticity represents the expected percentage change in a dependent variable given a percentage change in an independent variable.

For example, the price elasticity of a demand curve measures the percentage change in the quantity of a good demanded, given a small percentage change in the price of the good. Holding all else equal, demand displays an inverse relationship with price changes, that is, as prices increase, demand decreases. Hence the price elasticity of demand may be represented as a negative number.

Macauley's Duration

Macauley measures price sensitivity as the percentage change in a specific bond's price, given a 1 percent change in the bond's discount factor. Macauley referred to this concept as the "duration" of the bond, commonly known today as *Macauley's duration*.

Denote Macauley's duration as McDur, the percentage change in the price of a bond as C(price), and the percentage change in a bond's discount factor as C(discount factor):

McDur = C(price)/C(discount factor)

$$= 0.5 \times \sum_{t=1}^{M} [t \times CF_t \times (1 + EBY/2)^{-t}/(\sum_{t=1}^{M} [CF_t(1 + EBY/2)^{-t}])$$

Unfortunately, this formula only works for bonds and notes on their issue date or on a subsequent coupon payment date. The following formula may be applied between coupon payment dates:

$$\text{McDur} = \frac{0.5 \times \sum_{t=1}^{M} [(t - 1 + a)\, CF_t (1 + EBY/2)^{-(t-1+a)}]}{\sum_{t=1}^{M} [CF_t (1 + EBY/2)^{-(t-1+a)}]}$$

where

a = fraction of half-year period remaining until next coupon payment

Macauley's duration may be thought of as the weighted average time until a bond's cash flows are received. As shown above, this number is stated in semiannual periods. To convert the semiannual duration measure to an annually stated duration measure, simply divide the semiannual duration by two.

$$\text{Macauley's Duration} = \text{McDur}/2$$

The weights in Macauley's duration formula are a function of the sum of the present values of a bond's cash flows (the price of the bond). Duration is a far superior indicator of a bond's relative price volatility than the simple term to maturity.

In general, the longer the term is extended, the higher the coupon or the lower the yield of a bond, the greater is its volatility as measured by duration. There are times, however, when an extension of a bond's maturity actually results in a shorter duration. The duration of a bond valued at par, at a premium to par, or at a modest discount to par increases as a function of its term. But the duration of a deep discount bond with a long maturity may actually decrease as a function of its term.

Duration of Zero Coupon Bonds

The duration of a zero coupon bond is readily identifiable. Substituting the cash flow structure of a zero coupon bond into the Macauley duration formula gives us the following equation for duration stated in semiannual periods:

$$\text{McDur} = 0.5 \times [M \times CF_M(1 + EBY/2)^{-M}]/[CF_M(1 + EBY/2)^{-M}]$$

where

M = number of semiannual periods until maturity

The Macauley duration of a zero coupon bond is equal to M/2 (the number of years until maturity). This also applies with respect to the duration of a discount security such as a Treasury bill.

Modified Duration

Macauley's duration can be used to rank bonds according to their relative percentage volatility. A more precise measure of relative percentage volatility may be found in the *modified duration.*

The modified duration (ModDur) concept can be calculated by taking the derivative of the bond pricing equation with respect to the equivalent bond yield.

$$d(\text{bond price})/d(\text{EBY}) = -0.5 \times \sum_{t=1}^{M} [t \times CF_t(1 + EBY/2)^{-t-1}]$$

Divide this equation by the bond price and multiply by d(EBY). Finally, multiply the equation by 100/100. After simplifying, we arrive at the following equation which describes the percentage change in a bond's price:

$$d(\text{bond price})/\text{bond price} = [-\text{McDur}/(1 + EBY/2)]\,[d(EBY)/100]$$

$$= -\text{ModDur} \times d(EBY)/100$$

where

$$\text{ModDur} = \text{McDur}/(1 + EBY/2)$$

A generalized formula for modified duration can be used for calculation purposes for any fixed income instrument.

$$\text{ModDur} = \text{McDur}/(1 + EBY/n)$$

where

n = the number of coupon payments paid annually

In the context of a term Eurodollars investment, the relevant number of semiannual periods n may be one (1). Interest is paid semiannually on U.S. Treasury bonds and notes and many corporate bonds, hence n = 2. Finally, most mortgages require monthly paydowns of principal and interest, hence n = 12.

Duration, Selected Bonds
(08/26/86)

Issue	Price	Yield (%)	BPV ($)	McDur	ModDur
7.625% 2002–07	102–00	7.41	92.47	9.38	9.05
8.750% 2003–08	110–08	7.67	101.74	9.37	9.03
9.125% 2004–09	113–30	7.67	105.72	9.42	9.08
12.750% 2005–10	148–05	7.85	133.53	9.15	8.80
14.000% 2006–11	161–22	7.86	147.06	9.23	8.88
10.375% 2007–12	126–13	7.81	123.53	9.93	9.55
12.000% 2008–13	142–21	7.88	137.58	10.00	9.62
13.250% 2009–14	156–21	7.86	151.31	9.81	9.44
12.500% 2009–14	148–17	7.89	145.01	10.12	9.74
11.750% 2009–14	143–24	7.68	144.02	10.17	9.79
11.250% 2015	141–25	7.65	156.06	11.18	10.77
10.625% 2015	134–25	7.63	149.18	11.46	11.04
9.875% 2015	125–10	7.69	139.89	11.34	10.92
9.250% 2016	119–24	7.57	136.39	11.79	11.36
7.250% 2016	101–00	7.17	123.35	12.40	11.97

Percentage Price Volatility

The percentage price volatility of a bond can be approximated by the use of the following formula:

$$\%age\ volatility = -\ ModDur \times d(yield)/100$$

where

$$d(yield) = change\ in\ yield\ measured\ in\ basis\ points$$

Example: On August 25, 1986, the 7 1/4 percent bond of 2016 was trading at 101–00 to yield 7.17 percent. The Macauley's duration was 12.40 years while the modified duration was 11.97 years. If the yield of the 7 1/4 percent bond changed by 100 basis points (1 percent), what is the percentage price volatility of the bond? Substituting the duration of the 7 1/4 percent bond into the above equation we have:

$$\%age\ volatility = -\ 11.97 \times 1\%/100 = -\ 11.97\%$$

This equation indicates that the price change corresponding to a 100-basis point (1%) change in yield for the 7 1/4 percent bond would be approximately equal to 11.97 percent. The word "approximately" is used in recognition of the convexity associated with the change in a bond price with respect to a change in its yield. The negative sign indicates that bond price changes and yield changes are inversely related.

The price change corresponding to a 100-basis point change in yield can be approximated directly by slightly rearranging the percentage price volatility formula as follows.

$$d(P) = - \text{modified duration} \times d(\text{yield}) \times \text{price}/100$$

$$= - 11.97 \times - 1\% \times (1.01/100)$$

$$= + 11.97 \text{ points or } 11 - {}^{31}/_{32ds}$$

Assuming that the yield of the $7\,{}^{1}/_{4}$ percent bond drops 100 basis points from 7.17 percent to 6.17 percent, its price would rise from 101–00 to 114–21. This reflects an advance of $13^{21}/_{32ds}$. If yields advanced from 7.17 percent to 8.17 percent, the price of the bond would fall from 101–00 to 89–25 or $11^{07}/_{32ds}$.

Notice that the price change associated with falling yields is larger than the price change associated with rising yields. This illustrates the convexity associated with bond prices.

Note also that the predicted price change based on our duration analysis differs from the actual price changes. Furthermore, the margin of prediction error is expected to increase as the change in yield increases. This is because modified duration measures the percentage change in price given an instantaneous or extremely small rate of change in yield.

QUESTIONS

1. Which of the following is false?
   (a) Thirty-year bonds are auctioned every three months during the quarterly refunding.
   (b) STRIPS are created by brokerage firms issuing zero coupon bonds against collateral in the form of Treasury securities.
   (c) Thirteen-week bills are auctioned every Monday and issued on Thursday.
   (d) Participants in the Treasury auction may submit a competitive or noncompetitive bid.
   (e) None of the above is false.
2. The present value of a bond or note . . .
   (a) Refers to the current price of the security.
   (b) Is the same as the future value of the bond or note.
   (c) Represents the discount summation of the annuity associated with the security.

(d) Is the discount summation of the annuity and corpus of the security.

(e) (a) and (d) above.

3. Short-term interest rates are typically calculated under the assumption that there are (fill in the blank) _____ days in a year. Long-term interest rates are typically calculated under the assumption that there are (fill in the blank) _____ days in a year.

4. Which statement is false?

    (a) An ordinary annuity means that payment is received at the conclusion of a period.

    (b) When you price an annuity, you add up the present value of all the payments.

    (c) The future value of $100,000 invested at a continuously compounding rate of 7 percent is more than the future value of $100,000 invested at a monthly compounding rate of 7 percent.

    (d) A zero coupon bond may be sold at a premium to par.

    (e) Treasury bonds and notes typically pay interest semiannually.

5. (a) Find the future value of $100,000 invested for two years at a simple rate of 7 percent.

    (b) Find the future value of $100,000 invested for two years at a semiannual compounding rate of 7 percent.

    (c) Find the future value of $100,000 invested for two years at a continuously compounding rate of 7 percent.

6. Which of the following is false?

    (a) The duration of a zero coupon bond is equal to its maturity.

    (b) Duration may be thought of as the weighted average maturity of a bond's discounted cash flows.

    (c) Duration may be used to measure the expected change in a bond price given a change in yield.

    (d) As yields rise, a bond's duration rises.

    (e) The duration of a bond is affected by coupon, maturity, and yield.

7. Find the price, money market yield, equivalent bond yield, and basis point value of a $10 million face value 180 bill with an annual discount yield of 6.25 percent.

8. The basis point value of a long-term bond equals $78.00. Find its yield value of a thirty-second.

6

Playing the Treasury Futures Basis

Perhaps the most fundamental question a financial futures trader may ask is: What do these interest rate futures reflect?

Futures based on fixed income instruments, such as Treasury bonds and notes, provide for the delivery of a variety of issues which can vary widely with respect to both coupon and maturity. Thus it is not always easy to tell where the price of a futures contract based on these instruments should be trading or what those prices mean. Understanding how Treasury futures markets key on Treasury securities markets and vice versa, that is, understanding *basis* relationships, is an essential requirement for serious interest rate futures speculators, hedgers, and arbitrageurs.

Bond and note futures prices correlate most closely with or track the cheapest-to-deliver cash security, so the first, most critical step to successful basis trading is identifying the cheapest-to-deliver cash instrument. Three methods may be used to make this identification. One may study the delivery experience, the basis itself, or implied repo rates.

THE DELIVERY EXPERIENCE

The T-bond futures contract traded at the Chicago Board of Trade (CBOT) calls for the delivery of $100,000 face value *nominally* 8 percent bonds. These bonds may be of any maturity as long as there are at least 15 years from the date of delivery to the earliest of the call or maturity date. The CBOT T-note futures contract calls for the delivery of $100,000 face value 6½- to 10-year *nominally* 8 percent notes.

While these contracts reference an 8 percent coupon, shorts may elect to make delivery of *any* bond or note which meets the maturity requirements regardless of coupon. At any given time, therefore, there may be upwards of 30 bonds and perhaps 15 notes which are "eligible for delivery."

Normally, a single issue or, at best, a handful of securities which are very similar in terms of coupon and maturity stands out as cheapest or most economic to deliver. Holders of short positions are well aware of exactly which issues are cheapest to deliver into the contract. Moreover, they may be expected to act accordingly. The simplest way to identify the cheapest-to-deliver cash security, therefore, is to examine which issues have been delivered against the futures contract in which you are interested.

For example, the 15,100 contracts which were satisfied by delivery in December 1985 deliveries were concentrated in relatively high-coupon, long-term securities as follows:

December 1985 Bond Deliveries	
11-1/4% −15	11
11-3/4% −14	2,281
12% −13	5,358
12-1/2% −14	7,269
13-1/4% −14	181
TOTAL	15,100

This was a typical delivery insofar as all of the bonds delivered were relatively homogenous. Occasionally, however, the issues which are tendered in satisfaction of futures contracts are scattered over a relatively wide range of coupons and maturities.

In December 1984, for example, a record 26,383 deliveries were made against the bond contract. This delivery was very atypical in that a wide variety of securities was represented.

December 1984 Bond Deliveries	
7-5/8% −07	4,705
7-7/8% −07	455
8-3/8% −08	8
8-3/4% −08	1,204
10-3/8% −12	13,213
12% −13	3,467
12-1/2% −14	3,330
TOTAL	26,383

Approximately 25 percent of these contracts was satisfied by delivery of relatively low-coupon, short-maturity securities with coupons in the 7 to 8 percent range. Another 25 percent was satisfied by delivery of relatively high-coupon, long-maturity securities such as the 12s and 12½s. Finally, about 50 percent of the delivery was satisfied with an intermediate-coupon, intermediate-term security—the 10⅜s.

March 1986 was a most unusual delivery month as well. An unusually high number of issues (a total of 19) was delivered in satisfaction of the bond contract. These issues ran the gamut between high-coupon and low-coupon, long-maturity and short-maturity securities. They covered bonds originally issued as 30-year securities and as 20-year securities.

March 1986 Bond Deliveries

7-5/8% –07	10
7-7/8% –07	10
8-3/4% –08	6
10% –10	647
10-3/8% –12	2,975
10-5/8% –12	4
10-3/4% –02/03	210
10-3/4% –05/03	2,045
10-3/4% –05	60
11-1/4% –15	7
11-3/4% –14	887
11-7/8% –03	4
12% –13	2,617
12-3/8% –04	45
12-1/2% –14	522
12-3/4% –10	659
13-1/4% –14	1,861
13-7/8% –11	403
14% –11	910
TOTAL	13,882

How do shorts decide which of the myriad eligible-for-delivery issues they will tender?

TRACKING THE BASIS

Identifying which securities have actually been delivered against a futures contract is a convenient way of tracking the cheapest-to-deliver issue, but it does not help when you are between delivery months. By tracking the *basis,* however, you can get a more precise idea of what is happening at all times during the year.

The basis subsumes the relationship between a cash security and a futures contract. As such, it is essential for basis speculators, hedgers, and cash/futures arbitrageurs to understand the basis. The key to understanding the basis is understanding the delivery process.

The Delivery Process

Bond and note futures call for the delivery of nominally 8 percent coupon instruments. This does not, however, imply that shorts must deliver 8 percent securities. Bond futures permit the delivery of *any* T-bond which does not mature and is not callable within 15 years from the date of delivery. Note futures permit the delivery of any T-note with 6 1/2 to 10 years from the date of delivery.

High-coupon securities are always worth more in absolute terms than low-coupon securities with comparable maturities and credit risk. This means that an adjustment must be made to the amount at which shorts invoice longs upon delivery to reflect the varying values for all of the diverse coupon and term securities which may be deliverable.

Bond and note futures employ the "conversion factor" invoicing system to reconcile these differences in value to the standard 8 percent coupon. Upon delivery of a note or bond, the "principal invoice amount" is calculated by multiplying the futures settlement price times $1,000 times the specific conversion factor for the security actually delivered.

$$\frac{\text{Principal}}{\text{Invoice Amount}} = \frac{\text{Conversion}}{\text{Factor}} \times \$1,000 \times \frac{\text{Futures}}{\text{Settlement}}$$

Conversion factors represent the price of the bond or note to be delivered if it were to yield 8 percent. Thus securities with coupons in excess of 8 percent have conversion factors greater than 1.0; securities with coupons under 8 percent will have conversion factors less than 1.0.

Conversion Factors

	Sep. '86	Dec. '86	Mar. '87	Jun. '87
7-5/8% 2/15/02 –07	0.9671	0.9676	nd	nd
8-3/4% 11/15/02 –08	1.0690	1.0683	1.0681	1.0673
9-1/8% 5/15/02 –09	1.1050	1.1041	1.1036	1.1026
12-3/4% 11/15/05 –10	1.4600	1.4570	1.4546	1.4516
14% 11/15/06 –11	1.5938	1.5903	1.5875	1.5840
10-3/8% 8/15/07 –12	1.2397	1.2383	1.2374	1.2360

Conversion Factors *(Continued)*

		Sep. '86	Dec. '86	Mar. '87	Jun. '87
12%	5/15/08 –13	1.4089	1.4074	1.4053	1.4037
13-1/4%	8/15/09 –14	1.5439	1.5414	1.5394	1.5368
12-1/2%	11/15/09 –14	1.4678	1.4662	1.4640	1.4623
11-3/4%	11/15/09 –14	1.3916	1.3898	1.3885	1.3866
11-1/4%	11/15/15	1.3645	1.3634	1.3628	1.3617
10-5/8%	8/15/15	1.2935	1.2930	1.2921	1.2916
9-7/8%	11/15/15	1.2103	1.2096	1.2093	1.2086
9-1/4%	2/15/16	1.1403	1.1402	1.1396	1.1395
7-1/4%	5/15/16	0.9155	0.9155	0.9159	0.9159

Example: On August 25, 1986, the 7 1/4s of 2016 were trading at $101^{00}/_{32ds}$. December 1986 bond futures were priced at $100^{01}/_{32ds}$, and the conversion factor for delivery of the 7 1/4s into the December contract was 0.9155. The principal invoice price may be computed as follows.

$$\text{Principal Invoice Amount} = \underset{(100-01)}{100.03125} \times \$1{,}000 \times 0.9155$$

$$= \$91{,}578.61$$

Example: On August 25, 1986, the 14s of 2006–11 were trading at $161^{22}/_{32ds}$, and Dec. bonds were at $100^{01}/_{32ds}$. The conversion factor for delivery of the 14 percent bond of 2006–11 into the December contract equals 1.5903. The principal invoice price may be computed as follows.

$$\text{Principal Invoice Amount} = \underset{(100-01)}{100.03125} \times \$1{,}000 \times 1.5903$$

$$= \$159{,}079.70$$

In addition, interest accrued since the last semiannual interest payment date is added to this principal invoice amount to equal the "total invoice amount."

$$\frac{\text{Total Invoice}}{\text{Amount}} = \frac{\text{Principal}}{\text{Invoice Amount}} + \frac{\text{Accrued}}{\text{Interest}}$$

Basis Definition

The basis for bond and note futures may formally be defined as the cash price less the "adjusted futures price" or the futures price multiplied by the conversion factor. This basis is typically expressed in 32ds—1 1/2 points equals $^{48}/_{32ds}$.

Adjusted Futures Price = Futures Price × Conversion Factor

Thus the adjusted futures price is analogous to the principal invoice amount. The only difference is that the principal invoice amount is generally expressed in terms of dollars per $100,000 face value unit. The adjusted futures price is generally expressed in terms of percent of par in decimal form or in 32ds.

The *basis* for bond and note futures is equal to the cash price less the adjusted futures price where that adjusted futures price equals the futures settlement price multiplied by the conversion factor of the cash security in question.

Example: On August 25, 1986, the 14s were cheaper to deliver than the 7 1/4s. This may be determined by comparing the cash price with the principal invoice price:

	Principal Invoice Price	Less	Cash Price		(Loss) Gain on Delivery
7-1/4%	$ 91,578.61	—	$101,000.00	=	($9,421.39)
14%	$159,079.70	—	$161,687.50	=	($2,607.80)

A loss of $9,421.39 is implied by delivery of the 7 1/4s. By contrast, a loss of $2,607.80 is implied by the delivery of the 14s, so the 14s are cheaper to deliver than the 7 1/4s. The basis may also be compared in terms of thirty-seconds.

Example: The basis for the 7 1/4s equals approximately $30 1/32ds$ or the cash price of $101 00/32ds$ less the approximate adjusted futures price of $91 19/32ds$.

$$Basis = 101.00000 - (100.03125 \times 0.9155)$$
$$[101\text{--}00] \qquad [100\text{--}01]$$
$$= 101.00000 - 91.57861$$
$$= 9.42139 \text{ or } 30 1.5/32ds$$

The basis for the 14s equals approximately $8 3/32ds$ or the cash price of $161 22/32ds$ less the approximate adjusted futures price of $159 02/32ds$ (see Figures 6–1, 6–2, 6–3, and 6–4).

$$Basis = 161.68750 - (100.03125 \times 1.5903)$$
$$[161\text{--}22] \qquad [100\text{--}01]$$
$$= 161.68750 - 159.07970$$
$$= 2.60780 \text{ or } 8 3.4/32ds$$

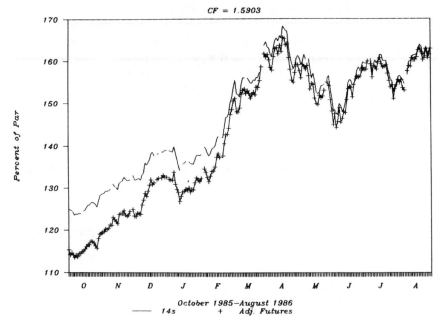

Figure 6-1   14s of 2011 vs. adjusted futures.

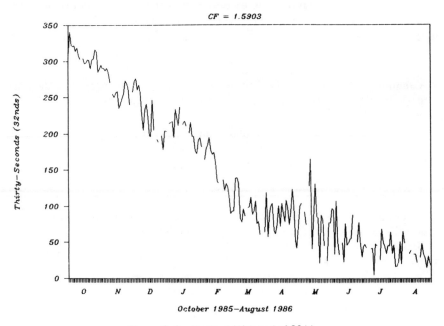

Figure 6-2   Basis: 14% bond of 2011.

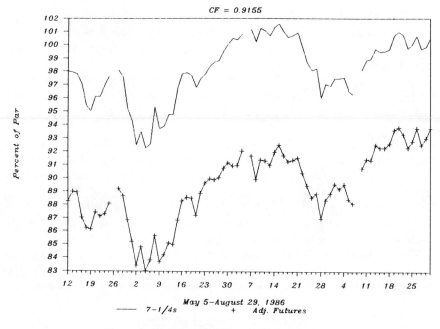

Figure 6–3   7 ¼s of 2016 vs. adjusted futures.

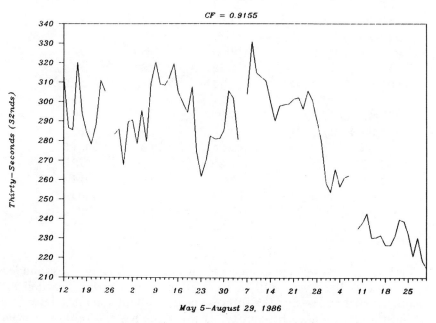

Figure 6–4   Basis: 7 ¼% bond of 2016.

While the 14s are cheaper to deliver than the 7 1/4s, the delivery of either issue looks like a losing proposition. In fact, the delivery of any of the eligible-for-delivery issues suggests a loss as all of these securities have a positive basis.

In general, the issue with the narrowest basis represents the cheapest-to-deliver instrument. Thus the 12 1/2s with a basis of $59.7/32ds$ appears to be marginally cheapest on August 25, 1986, followed closely by the 12s with a basis of $59.9/32ds$.

While all of these bases are positive, they tend to narrow as the delivery month approaches; therefore, cash and adjusted futures prices "converge" such that a negligible loss or gain is associated with the delivery of the cheapest cash security.

In a normal upward sloping yield curve environment where long-term yields exceed short-term yields, futures in successively deferred months will trade at successively lower and lower prices (see Figures 6–5 and 6–6).

This reflects the fact that the leveraged buyer of a long-term security enjoys positive carry. In other words, the amount earned by holding or carrying the long-term instrument exceeds the short-term financing cost.

Bond Basis (August 25, 1986)

	Price	Yield (%)	Basis
7-5/8% 2/15/02 –07	102–00	7.41	166.7/32nds
8-3/4% 11/15/02 –08	110–08	7.67	108.4
9-1/8% 5/15/02 –09	113–30	7.67	111.8
12-3/4% 11/15/05 –10	148–05	7.85	77.1
14% 11/15/06 –11	161–22	7.86	83.4
10-3/8% 8/15/07 –12	126–13	7.81	81.2
12% 5/15/08 –13	142–21	7.88	59.9
13-1/4% 8/15/09 –14	156–21	7.86	79.0
12-1/2% 11/15/09 –14	148–17	7.89	59.7
11-3/4% 11/15/09 –14	143–24	7.68	151.3
11-1/4% 11/15/15	141–25	7.65	172.8
10-5/8% 8/15/15	134–25	7.63	174.1
9-7/8% 11/15/15	125–10	7.69	138.1
9-1/4% 2/15/16	119–24	7.57	182.2
7-1/4% 5/15/16	101–00	7.17	301.5

Cash and futures converge because cost of carry becomes less and less significant as the term until delivery diminishes. During the delivery month, buying and selling the futures contract is tantamount to buying or selling the cheapest cash security, as the short has the option to make delivery at any time during the contract month.

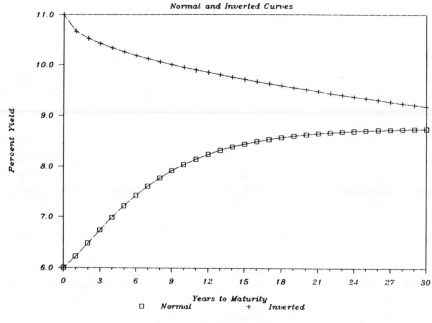

Figure 6–5   Yield curve.

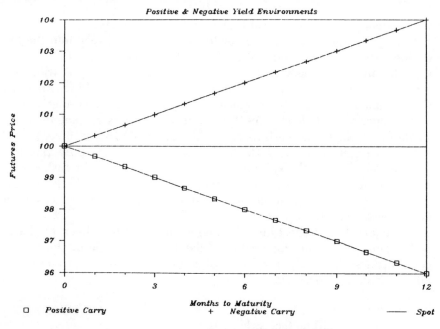

Figure 6–6   Futures prices in deferred months.

Wild Card Delivery Play

The threat, if not the actual practice, of delivery is said to drive cash and futures price "in-line"—to cause cash/futures convergence. But do cash and futures always converge completely? Certainly noncheapest securities cannot be expected to converge fully (even approximately), and there are certain "quirks" in the delivery process which normally prevent full convergence of even the cheapest deliverable issue.

In particular, there is a "wild card play" or "implied put option" associated with the delivery process. The wild card delivery play is a quasi-arbitrage made possible by timing differences associated with the futures and cash markets and with the conversion factor invoicing system itself.

The short has until 8:00 P.M. (Chicago time) to tender a notice of intention to deliver to the CBOT Clearing Corporation. This notice indicates intent to make delivery of bonds or notes two days later. The invoice price is based on the 2:00 P.M. settlement prices.

A great deal can occur between 2:00 and 8:00 P.M. If cash falls after 2:00, the short can go into the cash market, buy cheap securities to deliver versus the relatively high 2:00 P.M. settlement price. This implied put option has a value which is reflected in the basis.

Assume that the 14s are cheapest to deliver. A short can enter the delivery month with a "conversion factor weighted hedge." For example, he may carry a long position in $1 million face value of the 14s balanced with sixteen $100,000 face value short futures contracts.

Recall that the conversion factor for the 14s for delivery into the December 1986 contract equals 1.5903. This suggests that the 14s are roughly 160 percent as valuable as the 8 percent coupon upon which the futures contract is nominally based. And given similar yield fluctuations, the 14s can be expected to be approximately 160 percent as volatile.

A hedger should short 1.5903 units in the futures market for every single unit held in the cash market; this rounds to 16 contracts per $1 million face value cash. Thus the trader can afford to carry these positions into the delivery month, waiting for an opportunity when the cash market drops strongly *after* the 2:00 P.M. futures market closes. If the market declines, he will buy an additional $600,000 face value of the 14s in the falling cash market.

Subsequently, the short puts out a notice of intent to deliver, tendering the original $1 million face value of the 14s against ten of the futures contracts and the newly purchased $600,000 face value 14s against the tail of six futures contracts.

Step 1:

- Hold $1 million face value 14s.
- Sell 16 bond futures.

Step 2:

IF cash market falls sharply after 2:00 P.M. ⇒
- Buy $600,000 face value 14s in a declining market.
- Tender notice of intent to deliver by 8:00 P.M.

Step 3:

- Deliver original $1 million face value 14s against ten futures contracts.
- Deliver newly purchased tail of $600,000 face value 14s against six futures contracts.

The tail refers to the excess futures contracts and directly reflects the amount by which the conversion factor exceeds 1.0.

Profits are reflected in the differential between the principal invoice price fixed at the 2:00 P.M. close and the price at which he actually purchased the additional $600,000 face value 14s.

Of course, longs are aware that shorts enjoy this advantage as well as positive carry in a normally sloped yield curve environment. As a result, it is uncommon to witness full convergence early in the delivery period.

This is mitigated to the extent when low-coupon issues are cheapest to deliver. If, for example, the 7¼s with a conversion factor of 0.9155 were cheapest, there would be no tail to play. The greater the extent to which the cheapest's conversion factor exceeds 1.0, the greater is the tail, and the more the wild card play is worth to the short.

Last Seven Days

Most deliveries are not made until the end of the delivery period, often on the very last delivery day. No trading is allowed during the last seven business days of the month. However, a short may still carry his position and the obligation to make delivery into these last seven days.

Why would anyone want to carry a long cash/short futures position until the very last possible delivery day?

1. Assuming that the hedger owns the cheapest cash instrument and sells futures, a shift in the cheapest will work for the benefit of the hedger. (This may motivate a hedger to carry a position well into the delivery month but not necessarily into the last seven days.)
2. The short enjoys a timing advantage as to when he will make delivery, an important point if he is carrying a tail.
3. The hedger enjoys positive carry; that is, the coupon income accruing will exceed financing costs in a normal yield curve environment, and

4. The short may hope to cover a tail quickly if the market starts to bull up.

Despite all this, a long cash/short futures position with a tail carried into the last seven days may give rise to large losses if the market advances. There *is*, however, a strategy which may generate relatively risk-free profits during the last seven days. This strategy is similar to the "light-bar/heavy-bar" delivery play often used in the silver futures markets.

Silver futures contracts fix an invoice price based on the settlement price but allow shorts to defer, specifying the particular bar(s) to be delivered. If the market should subsequently bull up, the short will select bar(s) which weigh in at the light end of the tolerated weight range. If the market falls, the short delivers heavy bars. The delivery play works in a very analogous manner in the bond and note futures markets. High- and low-coupon issues may be thought of as analogous to heavy and light bars.

In order to execute a quasi-arbitrage in the bond or note markets, you must execute an intramarket spread. Specifically, you sell the expiring nearby contract and buy the first deferred contract in the ratio of the conversion factor of the cheapest to deliver. This strategy may yield a profit if the market rallies such that an issue with a lower conversion factor becomes economic to deliver or if the market declines such that an issue with a higher conversion factor becomes economic to deliver.

To illustrate, assume that the $7\frac{1}{4}$s of 2016 with a conversion factor of 0.9155 into the December 1986 contract are marginally cheapest to deliver, followed closely by the 14s. Our trader sells ten December 1986 and buys nine March 1987 contracts. In this case, the trader plays the market for a major decline.

If futures fall by one point, he loses $9,000 on the long March contracts. But the 14s with a conversion factor of 1.5903 should have declined by approximately 1.6 points or $16,000 for ten $100,000 lots.

If the $7\frac{1}{4}$s and 14s are both roughly cheapest to deliver, he may buy $1 million face value of the 14s and tender them against the ten December contracts for a profit of roughly $7,000. If the market advances by a point, he simply covers the ten nearby shorts with the $7\frac{1}{4}$s, offsetting the $9,000 gain in March futures with a comparable loss through the December delivery process.

- Short 10 December futures/long 9 March futures.

IF futures fall 1 point $\Rightarrow$

- Cover 10 Dec contracts with $1 million face value of 14s which decline $16,000.
- Sell 9 March contracts at $9,000 loss.
- Profit of $7,000.

IF futures rally 1 point ⟹

- Cover 10 Dec contracts with $1 million face value of 7 1/4s which advance about $9,000.
- Sell 9 March contracts at $9,000 profit.
- No profit/no loss.

If the 14s with a conversion factor of 1.5903 are cheapest, one may play for an advancing market. A trader may sell ten December contracts and buy sixteen March contracts.

If futures rally a point, the trader makes $16,000 on the long March futures. However, if the trader covers the December shorts with the 7 1/4s which may have advanced only about nine-tenths point for a loss of $9,000 on ten $100,000 lots, the trader may make $7,000. If futures decline by a point, he covers the ten nearby shorts with 14s, offsetting a $16,000 loss in March futures.

- Short 10 December futures/long 16 March futures.

IF futures fall 1 point ⟹

- Cover 10 Dec contracts with $1 million face value of 14s which decline $16,000.
- Sell 16 March contracts at $16,000 loss.
- No profit/no loss.

IF futures rally 1 point ⟹

- Cover 10 Dec contracts with $1 million face value of 7 1/4s which advance about $9,000.
- Sell 16 March contracts at $16,000 profit.
- Profit of $7,000.

Finally, the trader can play the market for either an advance or a decline if an intermediate-coupon issue is cheapest.

The high-coupon/low-coupon play works best when a number of issues varying widely with respect to coupon are near-cheapest to deliver and the market is very volatile. This was just the situation which occurred in December of 1984 when the 7 5/8s, the 10 3/8s, and the 12 1/2s all experienced heavy deliveries.

Figure 6–7 shows how the basis for these three issues (cash price less adjusted futures price fixed on the last day of trading, December 19th) declined considerably during the last seven days. This suggests that traders who played the high-coupon/low-coupon game for a falling market could have realized handsome profits.

Why Is One Issue Cheapest?

The conversion factor invoicing system is not perfect. Theoretically, the conversion factor invoicing system would render the delivery of all eligible-for-delivery bonds equally economic. However, a *single* issue usually stands out as cheapest or most economic to deliver. The biases in the invoicing system take two forms: (1) cash market biases and (2) coupon and maturity biases inherent in the mathematics of the conversion factor calculation.

Because the conversion factor invoicing system is based on a net present valuation formula, it cannot accommodate for peculiarities which affect cash bond prices. Some of these peculiarities are preferences for discount versus premium bonds, the changing shape of the yield curve, or, whether or not an issue falls under the Treasury's STRIPS program.

Delivery Biases

Cash market biases $\Rightarrow$

- Reinvestment risk.
- Tax considerations.
- Shape of the yield curve.
- STRIPS.

Conversion factor biases $\Rightarrow$

- Coupon Bias.
- Maturity Bias.

There is a persistent preference in the bond market for discount as opposed to premium bonds. This preference arises as a result of reinvestment risks.

To the extent that reinvestment income contributes heavily to the total return associated with a bond investment, fluctuating short-term rates can impact heavily upon the relative value of different bonds.

High-coupon bonds throwing off large-coupon streams are more heavily affected by reinvestment risk than low-coupon bonds where a larger proportion of the total return may be attributed to the accretion of the discount. Fluctuating short rates create uncertainty with respect to the total return. Uncertainties associated with high-coupon issues are reflected in the form of generally lower prices and higher yields. The yield spreads are magnified when rates are low or falling.

(In the past, tax considerations further induced a preference for low-coupon securities as opposed to high-coupon securities. This was due to the fact that the periodic coupon payments associated with a bond might be taxed at an ordinary tax rate, while any accretion of a discount or premium on a bond might qualify as a long-term capital profit or loss, subject to relatively lower effective tax rates. These tax considerations were important in the past. The tax code is always subject to change, and current regulations per this writing have significantly changed.)

The shape of the yield curve also affects which instruments are cheapest to deliver. In a normal or upwardly sloped yield curve environment where long-term yields exceed short-term yields, longer-term securities have higher yields and consequently reduced prices.

This factor may mean that the most recently issued 30-year securities may become cheapest to deliver. All of the bonds or notes deliverable against a contract are relatively homogeneous in terms of maturity. Thus this factor may not be extremely important in terms of identifying the cheapest-to-deliver security.

The ability of security dealers to strip certain issues affects whether they will become cheapest to deliver. Stripping refers to the practice of marketing separately the income inflows associated with a security. In particular, the stream of periodic coupon inflows may be separated from the corpus or the principal which is repaid at maturity of the security. Once stripped, these separate cash flows effectively become zero coupon bonds.

For several years, various brokerage companies offered zero coupon bonds under proprietary names such as CATS, TIGERS, and COUGARS. The firm would buy Treasury securities and issue certificates collateralized by these securities promising the pass-through of the appropriate income streams. Brokerage companies marketed these instruments because market conditions were such that the periodic coupon streams plus the corpus would command a greater cumulative value than the income streams taken as a bundle.

The U.S. Treasury noted this fact. As a result, in January 1985 they announced the introduction of the STRIPS. This program was effective beginning with the issuance of the 30- and 10-year securities in February 1985.

The STRIPS program assigned a separate CUSIP number to the corpus and coupon streams associated with a bond for identification when transferring the security through the Fed wire system. By adopting this practice, the Treasury made it possible for any trader with access to the wire to market the corpus and coupon payments separately.

Strippable bonds generally command a premium price relative to nonstrippable bonds. In early 1985, this premium was demonstrated quite convincingly in the marketplace as strippable bonds had yields which were between 10 to 15 basis points less than comparable nonstrippable bonds.

But beyond these cash market factors, there are some biases inherent in the way the conversion factor is calculated. In particular, there is an inherent, albeit slight, bias favoring the delivery of low-coupon, long-maturity securities when yields are in excess of the 8 percent contract standard. When yields are less than the 8 percent contract standard, the bias is towards the delivery of high-coupon, short-maturity securities.

IF yields > 8% ⟹

Bias towards delivery of low-coupon, long-maturity securities.

IF yields < 8% ⟹

Bias towards delivery of high-coupon, short-maturity securities.

When yields are close to the 8 percent contract standard, these biases do not manifest themselves. As of August 25th (as shown in the prior examples), yields were just under 8 percent as a result of a dramatic long-term decline in yields dating from mid-1984. As a result, conversion factor biases were not apparent.

The 12 1/2s and similar securities tended to be cheapest to deliver, that is, high-coupon securities with high reinvestment risks and correspondingly high yields. But when yields have been well in excess of 8 percent, conversion factor biases have been quite pronounced.

Consider that in the late 1970s and into the year 1984, yields were generally rising. As a result, the most recently issued 30-year security tended to be issued with a higher and higher coupon (coupons are set at levels comparable to prevailing yields).

That means recently issued bonds with long maturities tended to have relatively high coupon; less recently issued bonds with shorter terms to expiration tended to have lower coupons. As a result, there was no single group of bonds (bonds with long maturities *and* low coupons) which tended to dominate the delivery process. Rather there was a continual tug-of-war between bonds with low coupons though relatively short maturities and bonds with high coupons though relatively long maturities!

The determining factor tended to be the prevailing yield level. When yields were extremely high—over 10 3/4 percent to 11 1/4 percent—coupon bias became extremely strong. As a result, low-coupon issues even with relatively short maturities such as the 7 5/8s of 2002–07 and 8 3/4s of 2003–08 became cheapest.

For example, in the summer of 1983, yields were rising and prices dropping. In June 1983, deliveries were concentrated in long-maturity though high-coupon securities. The delivery process was dominated by the 14s of 2006–11, the 13 7/8s of 2006–11, and the 12 3/4s of 2005–10.

But by September 1983, the 7 5/8s of 2002–07, the 7 7/8s of 2002–07, the 8 3/4s of 2003–08, and the 9 1/8s of 2004–09 dominated the delivery process (low-coupon though relatively short-maturity instruments).

By December 1984, prices were rallying hard as yields declined, and as a result, coupon bias became less severe. Maturity bias became the more important of the two factors (see Figure 6–7).

Low-coupon albeit short-maturity issues dominated the delivery process in September 1984. In December 1984, deliveries were scattered widely between high-coupon/long-maturity issues such as the 12s of 2008–13 and 12½s of 2009–14, low-coupon/short-maturity issues such as the 8¾s of 2003–08, and an intermediate-term and coupon security such as the 10⅜s of 2007–12.

In addition to the shift between coupon and maturity biases, another factor was affecting the market going into December. It was widely believed that a major financial institution was accumulating large long positions in each successive delivery month throughout 1984.

Dating back to September 1983, low-coupon/short-maturity issues like the 8¾s and 7⅞s were cheapest. Because these securities were issued in the late 1970s, they had largely been "put away" in investors' portfolios until maturity. Shorts who wanted to make delivery of the cheapest security might not be able to acquire them in sufficient quantities. Thus they may be forced to deliver noncheapest securities. This factor also had an impact upon the collapse of the high-coupon/long-maturity basis in the fall of 1984.

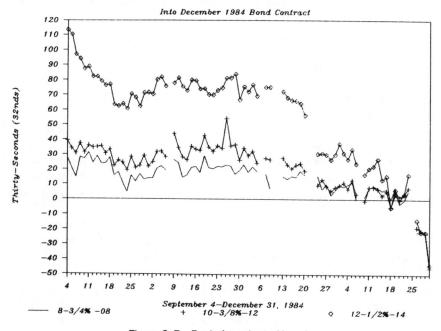

Figure 6-7   Basis for selected bonds.

By mid-1986, yields had fallen dramatically; therefore, more recently issued 30-year securities have historically low coupons. This means securities *are* available with both low coupons *and* long maturities.

It is exactly these kinds of securities which should dominate the delivery process *if* yields run well over 8 percent. But because yields were near 8 percent in mid-1986, conversion factor biases are not manifest. Rather, the cash market factors discussed above were driving the delivery process.

THE IMPLIED REPO RATE

Another way of identifying the cheapest-to-deliver security is to compare *implied repo rates* (IRR). The implied repo rate represents the expected percentage return associated with buying a cash security and selling futures with the intention of making delivery. The issue with the highest IRR is cheapest to deliver.

> An *implied repo rate* represents the expected return associated with the purchase of a cash security and the sale of futures with the expectation of eventually making delivery of the security into the futures market.

This return must be calculated, taking into account all cash flows associated with the series of transactions including accrued interest, coupon income, reinvestment of any coupon payments, and so forth.

Arbitrage Transaction

The implied repo rate is commonly used by arbitrageurs, basis traders, and hedgers. While it is not as easily referenced as deliveries against the futures contract or the basis, it provides a very accurate way of identifying the cheapest-to-deliver cash security.

An IRR of 8 percent suggests that a trader may earn 8 percent by shorting futures against the cash issue without considering the cost of financing. In other words, this trade will be profitable if the trader can finance the carry of the bond at a rate less than 8 percent.

An IRR of 4 percent suggests that a trader may earn 4 percent by shorting futures against the cash issue without considering financing costs. If financing costs are greater than 4 percent, buying the basis (buying cash and selling futures) is not an attractive proposition. Alternatively, *selling* the basis (selling cash and buying futures) may be quite attractive.

The implied repo rate may be calculated by comparing the net cash inflows associated with buying the basis with the investment. These figures are generally translated into an annualized amount over a 360-day year.

$$\text{Implied Repo Rate} = \frac{(\text{Net Credits} - \text{Net Investment})}{\text{Net Investment}} \times \frac{360}{\text{Days}}$$

Example: The 12$\frac{1}{2}$s of August 2009–14 are purchased on August 25, 1986, at 148^{17}/32ds for settlement on the 26th against the sale of December 1986 bond futures at 100^{01}/32ds. The implied repo rate over the 127-day holding period until December 31st (the last delivery day in December) equals 4.66 percent:

Net Investment:

Price of 12$\frac{1}{2}$s @ 148^{17}/32ds	=	148.5313
Accrued Interest	=	0.3736
TOTAL	=	148.9049

Net Credits:

December Futures @ 100^{01}/32ds times CF of 1.4662	=	146.6658
Accrued Interest @ 12/31/86	=	4.6875
Coupon Income	=	0
Reinvestment Income	=	0
Value of Implied Put @ 0.00	=	0
TOTAL	=	151.3533

$$\text{IRR} = \frac{(151.3533 - 148.9049)}{148.9049} \times \frac{360}{127}$$

$$= 4.66\%$$

This repo rate of 4.66 percent is low relative to short-term rates prevailing on August 2d, but bear in mind that this calculation is simplified in that it assumes full cash/futures convergence. The actual holding period return may be higher, approximating cash market repo rates.

Still, by comparing the implied repo rates associated with all the deliverable issues, you can identify the cheapest to deliver. The following table suggests that on August 25, 1986, the 12$\frac{1}{2}$s were marginally cheaper to deliver against December 1986 futures with an IRR of 4.66 percent, followed closely by the 12s with an IRR of 4.50 percent.

Note that the 12$\frac{1}{2}$s and the 12s share a virtually identical basis. This makes sense because both share very similar characteristics with respect to coupon and maturity. By relying upon the IRR calculation, you will determine that the 12$\frac{1}{2}$s are marginally cheaper.

In general, when two bonds show a very similar basis, the issue with the higher coupon will generally display the higher IRR. This is because the basis does not take into account accruing interest, which may offset much convergence loss.

Prior to the delivery month, it is best to rely upon the IRR. During the delivery month when the short may elect to make delivery at any instant, many traders tend to rely more heavily upon the basis to determine cheapest to deliver.

Implied Repo Rates

	Price	Yield (%)	Basis	IRR (%)
7-5/8%　2/15/02 –07	102–00	7.41	166.7	–7.15
8-3/4%　11/15/02 –08	110–08	7.67	108.4	–0.80
9-1/8%　5/15/02 –09	113–30	7.59	111.8	–0.71
12-3/4%　11/15/05 –10	148–05	7.85	77.1	3.85
14%　　11/15/06 –11	161–22	7.86	83.4	3.94
10-3/8%　8/15/07 –12	126–13	7.81	81.2	2.42
12%　　5/15/08 –13	142–21	7.88	59.9	4.50
13-1/4%　8/15/09 –14	156–21	7.86	79.0	3.86
12-1/2%　11/15/09 –14	148–17	7.89	59.7	4.66
11-3/4%　11/15/09 –14	143–24	7.68	151.3	–1.16
11-1/4%　11/15/15	141–25	7.65	172.8	–2.84
10-5/8%　8/15/15	134–25	7.63	174.1	–3.72
9-7/8%　11/15/15	125–10	7.69	138.1	–1.88
9-1/4%　2/15/16	119–24	7.57	182.2	–5.91
7-1/4%　5/15/16	101–00	7.17	301.5	–18.92

Delivery Plays

Full cash/futures convergence is unlikely to occur even for the cheapest-to-deliver security for reasons previously discussed, that is, the existence of delivery options on the part of the short. However, you *can* estimate the value of these delivery plays such as the implied put option. Presumably, the basis will converge to the point where it will reflect the value of this quasi-arbitrage. Using that estimate, you can calculate the implied repo rate on a slightly more accurate basis.

Example:　Assume that the implied put option is valued at $8/32ds$. The IRR may be calculated at 5.14 percent.

Net Investment:

Price of $12\frac{1}{2}$s @ $148^{17}/32ds$	= 148.5313
Accrued Interest	=　　0.3736
TOTAL	= 148.9049

Net Credits:

December Futures @ $100^{01}/32ds$ times CF of 1.4662	= 146.6658
Accrued Interest @ 12/31/86	=　　4.6875
Coupon Income	=　　　　0
Reinvestment Income	=　　　　0
Value of Implied Put @ 0.08	=　　0.2500
TOTAL	= 151.6033

$$IRR = \frac{(151.6033 - 148.9049)}{148.9049} \times \frac{360}{127}$$

$$= 5.14\%$$

Example: What if you were to estimate the value of the implied put option at $16/_{32ds}$? The IRR may be calculated at 5.61 percent.

Net Investment:

Price of 12 $1/_2$s @ 148$17/_{32ds}$	= 148.5313
Accrued Interest	= 0.3736
TOTAL	= 148.9049

Net Credits:

December Futures @ 100$01/_{32ds}$ times CF of 1.4662	= 146.6658
Accrued Interest @ 12/31/86	= 4.6875
Coupon Income	= 0
Reinvestment Income	= 0
Value of Implied Put @ 0.16	= 0.5000
TOTAL	= 151.8533

$$IRR = \frac{(151.8533 - 148.9049)}{148.9049} \times \frac{360}{127}$$

$$= 5.61\%$$

By taking into account the value of the implied put option or wild card delivery play, the implied repo rate increases into the range of prevailing short-term rates.

Why is it important for interest rate futures traders to be aware of changing cash/futures relationships? Clearly, "cash-and-carry" arbitrageurs attempting to take advantage of temporary cash/futures pricing aberrations must be aware of what is cheapest. In fact, the holding period return or implied repo rate is a way to measure the expected results of a cash/futures arbitrage.

Hedgers must also be aware of these cash/futures relationships. Hedgers should know that the most reliable hedge may be placed between futures and the cheapest to deliver. By shorting futures against long debt holdings, hedgers lock in, not the intermediate- or long-term yield, but a holding period return which approximates short-term repo rate yields.

Finally, speculators should be aware of these considerations because it is the price of the cheapest to deliver which essentially "drives" futures prices. Please note that the methods utilized in this chapter to identify the cheapest-to-deliver T-bond are equally applicable for identifying the cheapest-to-deliver T-note.

QUESTIONS

1. Which of the following does *not* represent a reasonable way of identifying the cheapest-to-deliver security against the bond futures contract?
   (a) Identifying which issues have been delivered against the contract.
   (b) Identifying all deliverable issues with a minimum of 15 years from the delivery date to the earliest of the call or maturity date.
   (c) Finding the deliverable security with the lowest basis.
   (d) Finding the deliverable security with the highest implied repo rate.
   (e) None of the above.

2. The conversion factor . . .
   (a) Represents the expected price of the cheapest-to-deliver-security.
   (b) Equals the principal invoice amount.
   (c) Represents the price of a given bond to yield 8 percent.
   (d) Can be calculated easily by hand.
   (e) Can be used to identify the expected relative movements of a given bond versus the 8 percent futures contract for a nonparallel yield movement.

3. Which statement is false?
   (a) The principal invoice amount reflects the futures settlement price multiplied by the applicable conversion factor.
   (b) The total invoice amount equals the principal invoice amount plus interest accrued since the last semiannual interest payment date.
   (c) The conversion factor is based on a net present valuation calculation.
   (d) The inverse of the conversion factor may be used as a hedge ratio for the cheapest-to-deliver security.
   (e) None of the above.

4. (a) On May 15, 1986, September 1986 bond futures were trading at 95–02 and the 7¼ percent long bond of May 2016 was trading at 97–01. What is the conversion factor for delivery into the September contract?
   (b) Calculate the basis.

5. Which statement is false?
   (a) The conversion factor invoicing system is biased towards the delivery of long-maturity, low-coupon securities when yields exceed 8 percent.
   (b) An inverted yield curve biases towards the delivery of short-maturity securities.
   (c) Traders who are long cash, short futures will tend to make delivery towards the end of the month in a negative yield curve environment.
   (d) Strippable securities tend to be bid up relative to nonstrippable securities.
   (e) Reinvestment risk cheapens low-coupon, relative to high-coupon, securities.

6. Assume that yields are well in excess of 8 percent. Given that yields begin to fall, which strategy is preferable?
   (a) Buy the basis for low-coupon and sell the basis for high-coupon securities.

(b) Buy bond and sell note futures.

(c) Go long cash and sell futures assuming that a concurrent upward movement is realized along the short-term end of the yield curve.

(d) Sell bond futures.

(e) Sell the low-coupon and buy the high-coupon basis.

7. Which statement is false? The wild card delivery play . . .

(a) Is also known as the implied put option.

(b) Is worthless unless the bond coupon exceeds 8 percent.

(c) Is occasioned by the fact that bond futures close at 2:00 P.M. (Chicago time) while the cash market may continue trading for at least another two hours.

(d) Is most profitable during the last seven days of the delivery month.

(e) Only works when the market breaks down after the futures close.

8. The implied repo rate . . .

(a) Reflects the percentage return one might earn by following a strategy of selling cash and buying futures.

(b) May only be calculated with the cheapest-to-deliver security.

(c) Of the cheapest to deliver is greater than the implied repo rate of all other deliverable securities.

(d) Can never be negative.

(e) None of the above.

9. Which statement is false?

(a) Full convergence can normally not be expected to occur even with the cheapest-to-deliver security.

(b) Traders will generally prefer to defer delivery until late in the month where the yield curve is positively sloped.

(c) Implied repo rates for bonds and notes tend to run at high levels relative to prevailing short-term interest rates.

(d) If two bonds have the same basis, the one with the higher coupon is generally cheaper to deliver.

(e) The implied repo rate should be compared to T-bill rates.

10. Find the basis and implied repo rates for a variety of securities deliverable against the bond and note futures contract. What securities are cheapest to deliver against the bond and note contracts? Why do these securities stand out as cheapest, and how do those securities compare to the on-the-run 30- and 10-year securities?

7

Financial Futures
Spread Relationships

Financial futures contracts offer significant opportunities to capitalize on anticipated market fluctuations. But many market participants find attractive opportunities trading, not the outright price of a financial instrument, but the differential between various financial "commodities" as reflected in financial futures prices.

The pricing relationships between different markets or different delivery months in the same contract are referred to as *spreads*. Spreads take two forms: *intramarket* or *intermarket* spreads.

An *intramarket spread* represents the price relationship between two contract months in the same contract market, that is, between a futures contract which calls for the delivery of bonds in March and one which calls for the delivery of bonds in June.

An *intermarket spread* represents the price relationship between futures contracts in two distinct contract markets, generally for the same month, that is, between a March note and a March bond futures contract.

Both of these spread relationships represent integral components of a futures trader's repertoire. Moreover, much can be learned by studying these relationships—information which has serious application in the context of other futures trading or risk-management applications apart from the obvious.

INTRAMARKET SPREADS

Intramarket spreads are driven by many of the same forces which impact upon basis relationships or the relationship between the instrument which may be delivered against the futures contract and the futures contract price itself. In other words, cost of carry considerations play a significant role in determining spread relationships between two delivery months.

Quoting the Spread

Intramarket spreads may be identified as either *bull* or *bear* spreads. A bull spread is identified as one in which the trader purchases a nearby and sells a deferred futures contract. A bear spread is thought of as one in which the trader sells a nearby and buys a deferred futures contract.

Bull spread ⇒ Buy nearby month/Sell deferred month

Bear spread ⇒ Sell nearby month/Buy deferred month

Sometimes spreads are quoted as the price of the nearby contract less the price of the deferred contract. This is typical in markets such as bonds and notes. In other markets, such as the stock index futures, the spread is typically quoted as the deferred month less the nearby month.

The way in which a spread is quoted depends upon whether positive or negative carry prevails, that is, whether futures in deferred months generally trade at a discount or a premium to nearby months. As a rule, the spread is quoted in such a way that it is represented as a positive rather than a negative number.

By quoting a spread as the nearby month less the deferred month in a market characterized by positive carry, the spread is quoted as a positive number. By quoting a spread as the deferred month less the nearby month in a market characterized by negative carry, the spread is likewise quoted as a positive number.

Positive carry ⇒ Nearby less deferred month

Negative carry ⇒ Deferred less nearby month

Thus care must be taken when identifying spreads as either bull or bear spreads. The execution of a bull spread in a positive carry market implies a belief that the spread will rally (the nearby month will trade to a higher premium relative to the deferred month, or the deferred month will trade to a larger discount to the nearby month). A bear spread implies a belief that the spread will decline.

The execution of a bull spread in a negative carry market implies a belief that the spread will decline (the nearby contract will rise relative to the deferred contract, or the deferred contract will fall relative to the nearby contract). A bear spread implies a belief that the spread will rally.

Futures and Cost of Carry

Let us review the factors which affect how futures contracts are priced. In particular, futures prices are affected to one extent or another by cost of carry. This means that the futures price may be represented as a function of the cash price adjusted by any finance charges associated with buying and holding the instrument on a leveraged basis and any payouts associated with holding that instrument, that is, any dividends, coupon payments, interest income.

$$\text{Futures} = \text{Cash} + \text{Finance Charges} - \text{Payouts}$$

In the case of bond and note futures, finance charges are normally identified by reference to prevailing repo rates. "Payouts" refers to interest accruing on the security. The following simple indifference analysis is used to illustrate how spreads move in the context of the bond and note futures markets. The same basic concepts are analogous in the context of other futures such as stock index, foreign currencies, or short-term interest rate instruments.

Example: It is now December. Assume that you are offered the opportunity to buy a cash bond today for $100^{00}/_{32ds}$ percent of par or to buy futures which call for the delivery of the same bond six months later in June at 99–00.

You are a leveraged buyer of bonds; short-term finance rates are at 6 percent, and the bond has an 8 percent coupon. Which alternative is better: Buy and hold the cash bond or buy futures, taking delivery of the same bond six months later?

Obviously, neither alternative is superior to the other insofar as both entail a net cost of 99–00. But what if you are offered the opportunity to buy the same bond and hold it for only three months until March? What futures price would make you indifferent between either alternative?

Indifference Analysis

	3 Mos	6 Mos
Buy cash	(100–00)	(100–00)
S-T finance @ 6%	(1–16)	(3–00)
L-T yield @ 8%	2–00	4–00
	(99–16)	(99–00)
Buy futures	(99–16)	(99–00)

In this example, the three-month futures contract should be priced at $99^{16}/_{32ds}$ or $^{16}/_{32ds}$ (one-half percent of par) greater than the price of the six-month futures contract at 99–00. Just as cost of carry considerations dictate the level of the basis or difference between cash and futures prices, cost of carry may likewise be instrumental in determining the level of the spread.

In the prior example, the bond market was characterized by positive carry; that is, the bond threw off more income than was paid in terms of finance charges. The spread may be quoted at $^{16}/_{32ds}$ or the nearby contract of 99–16 less the price of the deferred futures at 99–00.

How might cost of carry affect the spread in a contract calling for delivery of securities nine or twelve months hence?

Example: Under the circumstances just described, a nine- and a twelve-month contract may be priced at 98–16 and 98–00, respectively.

Intra-Market Spreads

Month	Price	Mar.	Jun.	Sep.	Dec.
Mar.	99–16	—			
Jun.	99–00	16/32nds	—		
Sep.	98–16	32/32nds	16/32nds	—	
Dec.	98–00	48/32nds	32/32nds	16/32nds	—

Thus the spread between any two contracts spanning three months equals $^{16}/_{32ds}$, the six-month spread equals $^{32}/_{32ds}$, and the nine-month spread equals $^{48}/_{32ds}$. The key to pricing these spreads is the shape of the yield curve, specifically, the fact that long-term yields exceed short-term yields by 200 basis points.

These cost of carry considerations become increasingly relevant as the span between two contracts grows larger. Nonetheless, this analysis suggests that the spread between any two months with a similar span such as the March/June and the June/September spreads, may be quite similar if not identical.

Shape of the Yield Curve

What might affect the level of these spreads? Obviously, if the cost of carry considerations which drove these spreads to the levels indicated above were to change, the spreads would likewise be altered.

The yield curve fluctuates along two dimensions: level and shape. A parallel shift in the yield curve suggests that both long- and short-term yields either advance or fall by an equivalent amount. A nonparallel shift in the yield curve suggests that the shape of the curve changes by either steepening or flattening.

Parallel shift ⟹

Long- and short-term rates advance or fall by equivalent amounts

Nonparallel shifts ⟹

Long- and short-term rates fluctuate by different amounts

Parallel shifts in the yield curve normally do not induce any fluctuations in the spread.

Example: Consider the possibility that short-term yields advance from 6 percent to 7 percent while long-term yields advance from 8 percent to 9 percent. As indicated earlier, the spread may be quoted, under the original circumstances, as $16/_{32}$ds, but when the yield curve steepens, the spread may widen. (Incidentally, the price of that 8 percent coupon bond will also be expected to decline in the face of rising yields. If the *current* yield of the 8 percent bond rises to 9 percent, the price of the bond may be expected to fall to about 88–28.)

	Indifference Analysis	
	3 Mos	6 Mos
Buy cash	(88–28)	(88–28)
S-T finance @ 7%	(1–18)	(3–03)
L-T yield @ 9%	2–00	4–00
	(88–14)	(87–31)
Buy futures	(88–14)	(87–31)

As suggested in the foregoing indifference analysis, the spread may now be trading at $15/_{32}$ds—virtually unchanged from the $16/_{32}$ds level indicated by our original analysis.

	Nearby	Deferred	Spread
Now:	Buy @ 99–16	Sell @ 99–00	16/32nds
Later:	Sell @ 88–14	Buy @ 87–31	15/32nds
Return:	(11–02)	11–01	1/32nds

If a trader had bought or sold this spread, there would have been virtually no profit or loss despite the fact that yield and price levels changed dramatically.

While parallel yield curve shifts may not induce fluctuations in the level of the spread, nonparallel shifts do have the potential to significantly impact the spread. Nonparallel yield curve shifts may take on a number of different forms. The yield curve may steepen when yield levels are generally rising or falling. This may occur when long-term yields are rising at a faster rate than short-term yields or when long-term yields are falling at a slower rate than short-term yields. In either case, the spread between long-term and short-term rates is widening.

Likewise, the yield curve may flatten when yields are generally rising or falling. This may occur when long-term yields are rising at a slower rate than short-term yields or when long-term yields are falling at a faster rate than short-term yields. In either case, the long-term/short-term yield spread is narrowing.

The expectations hypothesis which attempts to explain the shape of the yield curve suggests that the yield curve may be more likely to steepen when yield levels are rising. It also suggests that the curve is more likely to flatten when yield levels are falling.

This can be explained by the fact that fixed income portfolio managers may want to shift the composition of their portfolios from shorter-term to longer-term securities when yields are expected to fall or from longer-term to short-term securities when yields are expected to rise. By selling short-term and buying long-term securities in anticipation of falling yields, portfolio managers may cause the yield curve to flatten. By selling long-term and buying short-term securities when yields are expected to rise, portfolio managers may cause the curve to steepen.

When the yield curve is expected to steepen, a spreader may wish to buy the spread, that is, buy nearby and sell deferred futures. When the spread is expected to flatten, a spreader may wish to sell the spread, that is, sell nearby and buy deferred futures.

Yield curve steepens ⇒ Buy the spread

Yield curve flattens ⇒ Sell the spread

Example: Consider, for example, the possibility that short-term yields advance from 6 percent to 7 percent while long-term yields advance from 8 percent to 10 percent. As indicated earlier, the spread may be quoted, under the original circumstances, as $16/32$ds. But when the yield curve steepens, the spread may widen.

Indifference Analysis

	3 Mos	6 Mos
Buy cash	(80–00)	(80–00)
S-T finance @ 7%	(1–13)	(2–26)
L-T yield @ 10%	2–00	4–00
	(79–13)	(78–26)
Buy futures	(79–13)	(78–26)

According to the foregoing indifference analysis, the spread may widen out from $16/32$ds to $19/32$ds.

	Nearby	Deferred	Spread
Now:	Buy @ 99–16	Sell @ 99–00	16/32nds
Later:	Sell @ 79–13	Buy @ 78–26	19/32nds
Return:	(20–03)	20–06	3/32nds

Thus the spreader who bought the spread by buying nearby futures at 99–16 and selling deferred futures at 99–00 may have been able to close out the trade by selling nearby futures at 79–13 and buying back the deferred contract at 78–26 for a $3/32$ds profit.

Notice that very dramatic shifts in price level are indicated by this analysis. The spread moves only three ticks while prices moved approximately twenty points.

This is underscored by inspecting the actual relationship between the nearby and first deferred bond futures contract over a two-year period from January 1985 through December 1986 (see Figures 7–1 and 7–2). While bond futures traded in a range from near 65 upwards to near 105 (a full 40-point range), the nearby/first deferred spread ranged from $18/32$ds to $44/32$ds (only a $26/32$ds range).

Figure 7–1   Nearby (upper) vs. 1st deferred (lower) bonds.

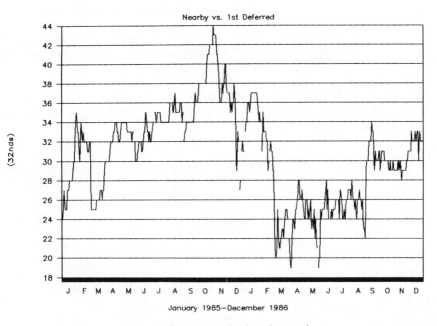

Figure 7–2   Intra-market bond spread.

Implied Forward Rates and Spreads

As previously indicated, the price of long-term interest rate futures may be modeled pursuant to cost of carry considerations, but short-term interest rate futures prices may best be understood by reference to implied forward rates. Implied forward rates provide an indication about where short short-term yields may be expected to be in the future. For example, what will 90-day investments yield 90 days in the future? This question may be answered by reference to our implied forward rate calculation.

$$1 + R(d_2)(d_2/360) = [1 + R(d_1)(d_1/360)] [1 + IFR(d_3, d_1)(d_3/360)]$$

The implicit assumption is that investors will expect similar returns by investing in a 180-day instrument or by investing in a current 90-day instrument, rolling that investment over into another 90-day instrument.

Example: Ninety-day investments are currently yielding 6.00 percent, while 180-day investments yield 6.25 percent. What will a 90-day instrument yield 90 days from now?

$$1 + (.0625)(180/360) = [1 + (.06)(90/360)] [1 + IFR(90,90)(90/360)]$$
$$IFR(90,90) = 6.40\%$$

Thus short-term interest rate futures which are based on a 90-day instrument to be delivered 90 days hence should be priced to yield 6.40 percent for a quote of 93.60 (100.00–6.40).

Using the same rationale, we may identify the possible price of a variety of other short-term interest rate futures pursuant to the following yield curve term structure.

	Spot Rate	Forward Yield	Futures Price	Spread
90-day	6.00%	6.40%	93.60	—
180-day	6.25%	6.79%	93.21	0.39
270-day	6.50%	7.15%	92.85	0.36
360-day	6.75%	—	—	—

What might happen if the yield curve steepens? In this example, the 90-day rate remains stable at 6 percent but the 180-, 270-, and 360-day rates advance to 6.30 percent, 6.60 percent, and 6.90 percent, respectively. This suggests that the spreads in successively deferred months may widen from 25 basis points to 35 or 34 basis points, respectively.

	Spot Rate	Forward Yield	Futures Price	Spread
90-day	6.00%	6.50%	93.50	—
180-day	6.30%	6.98%	93.02	0.48
270-day	6.60%	7.43%	92.57	0.45
360-day	6.90%	—	—	—

What happens if the yield curve flattens? In this example, the 90-day rate again remains pegged. But the 180-, 270-, and 360-day rates decline to 6.20 percent, 6.40 percent, and 6.60 percent, respectively. This suggests that the spreads in successively deferred months may narrow from 25 basis points to 19 or 20 basis points, respectively.

	Spot Rate	Forward Yield	Futures Price	Spread
90-day	6.00%	6.31%	93.69	—
180-day	6.20%	6.60%	93.40	0.29
270-day	6.40%	6.87%	93.13	0.27
360-day	6.60%	—	—	—

Thus it is clear that short-term interest rate spreads are affected by the shape of the yield curve. Again, a steepening curve suggests that these spreads will advance; a flattening curve suggests that these spreads will narrow.

Bond Spreads and Implied Repo Rates

Often, the cost of carry relationship between a bond or note futures contract and the cheapest-to-deliver security is summarized with a statistic known as the implied repo rate. The implied repo rate provides an indication about the expected short-term rate of return associated with the purchase of a cash security combined with the sale of a bond futures contract with the intention of delivering that security in satisfaction of the short futures position.

This return is calculated as a function of the cash inflows associated with this series of transactions compared to the net investment, annualized on a 360-day year.

Example: On March 4, 1987, the 12¾s of 2010 was cheapest to deliver. It had an implied repo rate of 4.41 percent for delivery into the June 1987 futures contract, calculated as follows.

Net Investment:

Price of $12\,^3/_4$s @ $149^{04}/_{32ds}$	= 149.1250
Accrued Interest	= 3.8391
TOTAL	= 152.9641

Net Credits:

June 1987 Futures @ $101^{12}/_{32ds}$ times CF of 1.4516	= 147.1560
Accrued Interest @ 6/30/87	= 1.5938
Coupon Income	= 6.3750
Reinvestment Income @ 6.00%	= 0.0489
TOTAL	= 155.1736

$$\text{IRR} = \frac{(155.1736 - 152.9641)}{152.9641} \times \frac{360}{118}$$

$$= 4.41\%$$

The implied repo rate calculated in the same manner against the deferred September 1987 futures contract was 4.35 percent.

A trader who buys the basis, that is, buys cash and sells futures, presumably will realize that implied repo rate over the life of this series of transactions. However, what if a trader buys the basis of a nearby bond futures contract and *sells* the basis of a deferred futures, that is, sells cash and buys futures?

Notice that if a trader both buys and sells the basis, no cash position remains. The trader is left with a short position in the nearby futures contract coupled with a long position in the deferred futures contract. In other words, the trader now holds a short intracontract futures spread!

What is the potential rate of return on this series of transactions? This return may be calculated if we plug the implied repo rates associated with the two futures contracts into an implied forward rate format.

Example: June, September, December, and March futures were quoted at 101–12, 100–14, 99–17, and 98–21, respectively. What were the intracontract spreads?

		Spread in 32nds			
Month	Price	6/87	9/87	12/87	3/88
6/87	101–12	—	—	—	—
9/87	100–14	30	—	—	—
12/87	99–17	59	29	—	—
3/88	98–21	87	57	28	—

On March 4, 1987, the $12\,^3/_4$s of 2010 was cheapest-to-deliver cash bond with an implied repo rate for delivery into the June 1987 futures contract of 4.41 percent. The IRR for delivery of the same bond into the September 1987,

December 1987, and March 1988 futures contracts was 4.35 percent, 4.37 percent, and 4.47 percent respectively. The last delivery day for these contracts falls 118, 210, 302, and 393 days subsequent to the current date.

The anticipated rate of return earned by selling June 1987 bond futures and buying September 1987 bond futures is illustrated in the following IFR equation.

$$1 + (.0435)(210/360) = [1 + (.0441)(118/360)] \, [1 + IFR(92,118)(92/360)]$$
$$IFR(92,118) = 4.22\%$$

Likewise, the implied forward rates may be approximated for other spreads as follows.

Month	IRR	"Cash & Carry" 6/87	9/87	12/87	3/88
6/87	4.41%	—	—	—	—
9/87	4.35%	4.22%	—	—	—
12/87	4.37%	4.28%	4.29%	—	—
3/88	4.47%	4.43%	4.49%	4.64%	—

The spreads quoted in terms of the implied forward rate may be referred to as a cash-and-carry return. To understand, consider the implications of buying or selling the June/September spread.

Selling June futures implies that you may also hold securities for delivery into the June contract, earning the implied repo rate of 4.41 percent indicated previously over the next 118 days. That means you are long the June basis.

By standing long for delivery in September, you will presumably take repossession of the same security. But the fact that you deliver the cash bond against June futures and buy September futures (effectively short the September basis), implies that you give up the opportunity to earn the implied repo rate between June and September.

To replicate the 4.35 percent implied repo rate over 210 days, a return of 4.22 percent is required over the 92 days from June to September, given a return of 4.41 percent over the first 118 days. Buying June futures implies that you may take delivery of securities 118 days later. If you sold the cheapest-to-deliver cash securities, this implies that you will take repossession of them in June; you sold the June basis, giving up the opportunity to earn 4.41 percent over the first 118 days.

Holding a short position in September futures in combination with a long cash position (as a result of taking delivery of bonds in June) means that you are effectively long the September basis, earning an implied repo rate between June and September.

Again, the 4.35 percent return over 210 days may be replicated by a return of 4.41 percent over the first 118 days and a subsequent return of 4.22 percent over the next 92 days.

These spreads may be enforced by cash-and-carry quasi-arbitrage operations. For example, if you can earn more than 4.22 percent over the 92 days between June and September, you may wish to sell the June/September spread, that is, effectively buy the June and sell the September basis. This means that by selling cash into the June futures contract, you believe you can reinvest those proceeds at a rate greater than 4.22 percent.

Cash and carry rate too low ⇒ Sell spread

Cash and carry rate too high ⇒ Buy spread

On the other hand, if you can borrow during the 92 days between June and September at a rate less than 4.22 percent, you may wish to buy the June/September spread, that is, effectively sell the June and buy the September basis. This means that by buying cash as a result of the long futures contract, you believe you can finance that purchase at a rate less than 4.22 percent.

It is not wise, however, to impute too much significance in these cash-and-carry returns. Remember that they are based on one's assessment of an implied repo rate. In the foregoing case, we assumed that full convergence would be realized between the cash and futures (the basis would converge fully to zero). Full convergence may or may not be likely. Further, we assume that the cheapest-to-deliver bond does not shift over the life of the spread.

Turtle

If you are satisfied that a bond spread is "too wide" (the cash-and-carry return is too low) or that the spread is "too narrow" (the cash-and-carry return is too high), you may take advantage by using a *turtle*.

A turtle spread involves the sale or purchase of an intramarket bond spread combined with the purchase or sale, respectively, of a bill futures contract. Because a turtle involves both bills and an intramarket bond spread, this may be regarded as a hybrid, a cross between an intramarket and an intermarket spread.

> A *turtle* entails the sale of an intracontract bond spread (sell nearby/buy deferred) and the purchase of a T-bill futures contract or the purchase of a bond spread (buy nearby/sell deferred) and the sale of a T-bill futures contract.

This spread may be motivated by examining the difference between the cash-and-carry return and the yield implicit in the quoted T-bill futures price. If the T-bill rate is higher than the cash-and-carry return, sell the bond spread and buy bills futures. If the T-bill rate is less than the cash-and-carry return, buy the bond spread and sell bill futures.

Example: On March 4, 1987, the June/September bond spread showed a cash-and-carry return of 4.22 percent. June 1987 bill futures were quoted at 94.58 for a discount yield of 5.42 (100.00–94.58). Assume that you sold nine June/September bond spreads at $^{30}/_{32ds}$ and bought one June bill at 94.58.

	Bonds			Bills		
$^3/_4$	Sell 9 spreads	@	$^{30}/_{32ds}$	Buy 1 futures	@	94.58
$^3/_{10}$	Buy 9 spreads	@	$^{28}/_{32ds}$	Sell 1 futures	@	94.42
			$562.50			($400.00)

Net Profit = $562.50 – $400.00

= $162.50

In this case, the trade might have been successful, but obviously, the bond spread moved by only the slimmest of margins. Your ability to get a favorable order fill will be critical to the failure or success of this strategy. Transaction costs will further limit and possibly overcome the profit potential.

The question arises: Why were nine bond spreads sold versus only one bill futures contract? The answer may be found by performing a "sensitivity analysis" of the cash-and-carry return.

We knew that the cash-and-carry return between June and September was 4.22 percent with a 30-tick spread. What if the June/September spread was quoted at 29 ticks or at 31 ticks? All else being held equal, a one-tick or $31.25 fluctuation would have an impact upon the implied repo rate and subsequently on the cash-and-carry return.

Example: If September futures were at 100–15 rather than 100–14, the September implied repo rate would be at 4.40 percent and the cash-and-carry return would be quoted at 4.33 percent. This represents an 11-basis point advance over 4.22 percent. If September futures were at 100–13 and the implied repo rate at 4.30 percent, the cash-and-carry return would be quoted at 4.11 percent. This is an 11-basis point decline.

Spread @ 31	Cash and carry = 4.11%
@ 30	= 4.22%
@ 29	= 4.33%

Thus a $31.25 movement in the bond spread induces an 11- or 12-basis point movement in the return. A single basis point movement may induce a change of only $2.84 in the return. We know, however, that a single basis point movement in the bill futures contract represents a $25 movement, a basis point value of $25.00.

In order to "match up" basis point values, you may need approximately nine bond spreads to every single bill contract:

$$\text{Turtle Ratio} = \text{BPV(bill)}/\text{BPV(bond spread)}$$
$$= \$25/\$2.84$$
$$= 8.8 \text{ or } 9 \text{ bond spreads}/1 \text{ bill}$$

INTERMARKET SPREADS

An intermarket spread often fluctuates much more dramatically than an intramarket spread. The reason is obvious: An intermarket spread involves two contracts which may vary in ways that are much more significant than simply the delivery month of the contract.

Or intention is to review the trading characteristics of a variety of the most popular intramarket spreads in the financial futures markets. We will consider the bill/bond spread, the Notes Over Bonds (NOB) spread, the T-bill/Eurodollar (TED) spread, the Value Line Composite Average/Standard & Poor's 500 spread, and, the Japanese yen/deutsche mark spread.

All of these spreads share some things in common; they all utilize similar yet different markets. For example, the NOB involves two intermediate- to long-term fixed income instruments. The TED involves two short-term fixed income instruments. The Value Line/S&P spread involves two stock index futures, while the yen/mark spread involves two foreign currencies. As we shall see, however, the differences are more dramatic than the similarities.

("*The* intermarket spread" is a reference to the Government National Mortgage Association (GNMA) CDR/T-bond futures spread. This reference evolved naturally because GNMAs and bonds were the first two interest rate futures contracts traded at the Chicago Board of Trade. Because there was only one intermarket financial spread available in 1977, it became known as *the* intermarket spread. Since 1982, the GNMA contract has been in a state of decline and no longer trades actively. As a result, this spread is no longer viable.)

Bill/Bond Spread

The spread between an intramarket bond spread and an outright bill futures contract was discussed earlier and is known as a turtle. What if you simply want to spread the outright bond price versus bills?

For example, you may believe that the yield curve between short- and long-term rates (represented by bill and bond futures, respectively) may change shape. It may steepen when bond yields rise faster or fall slower than bill yields, it may flatten or even invert as bond yields fall faster or rise slower than bill rates. You may wish to buy the bill/bond spread by buying bill futures and selling bond futures in anticipation of a steepening curve. Or you may wish to sell the bill/bond spread by selling bill futures and buying bond futures in anticipation of a flattening curve.

Yield curve steepens ⇒ Buy the bill/bond spread

Yield curve flattens ⇒ Sell the bill/bond spread

Notice that these are the exact same reasons that may motivate a trader to either buy or sell the intramarket bond spread. Most traders prefer the intramarket bond spread to the bill/bond spread. The reasons largely hinge upon (1) margining problems with a cross-exchange spread, (2) the relative ease of placing an intramarket bond spread, (3) quotation practices, and (4) identifying the correct spread ratio.

Bill futures are offered on the Chicago Mercantile Exchange while bonds are offered on the Chicago Board of Trade. As such, a trader may have to margin both sides fully rather than qualifying for a reduced spread margin, as is common with many spreads.

Another difficulty lies in the execution of the trade. Because the two contracts are offered on different exchanges, you will have to place two different orders—to "leg-into" the spread as best you can. By contrast, a bid and an ask may be quoted directly in the intramarket bond spread. The ability to execute the spread in one stroke reduces the risk of errors and execution skids.

The final problem revolves around the fact that bill and bond futures are quoted in very different ways. In particular, the $1 million face value bill futures contract is quoted in terms of the IMM index, that is, 100 less the bill discount yield. The $100,000 face value bond futures contract is quoted in percent of par in minimum increments of $1/32$d of a percentage point.

Thus contract sizes and quotation methods vary dramatically. There is no direct way of quoting the spread; traders normally reference the yield spread (the difference between long- and short-term yields prevailing in the cash market).

It is intuitive that the spread should be placed by taking on a bill and a bond position which are "equivalent" in terms of their respective movements in response to a fixed yield fluctuation. But how can this "yield equivalency" ratio be found?

Once again, the answer may be found by studying the responsiveness of the bill and bond futures contracts to a 1-basis point change in the yield of the deliverable item. The basis point value associated with a $1 million face value 90-day bill equals $25.00. The effective BPV for a $100,000 face value bond futures contract may be found by taking the BPV of the cheapest-to-deliver bond divided by its conversion factor.

Example: On March 4, 1987, the cheapest-to-deliver bond was the 12 3/4s of 2010. It had a BPV equal to $133.35 with a conversion factor of 1.4516 for delivery into the June 1987 futures contract. The bill/bond ratio of 3.67 may be derived as follows.

$$\text{Bill/Bond Ratio} = [\text{BPV(cd)}/\text{CF(cd)}]/\text{BPV(bill)}$$
$$= (\$133.35/1.4516)/\$25.00$$
$$= 3.67 \text{ bills/1 bond}$$

Some observers may find it remarkable that it requires almost four $1 million face value bills to match the price risks associated with a single $100,000 face value bond contract. But remember that the volatility of a fixed income instrument is heavily contingent upon maturity, among other variables.

Obviously, a 90-day bill has a much shorter maturity than a long-term bond. As a result, a single $100,000 face value bond futures may be three or four times as volatile as a single $1 million face value bill futures contract.

Notes Over Bonds Spread

The Notes Over Bonds spread is one of the most popular intermarket spreads available today. It is popular because it provides traders with a convenient way of taking advantage of either a parallel or a nonparallel shift in the yield curve.

You may trade in anticipation of a parallel shift in the yield curve by utilizing a one-for-one NOB spread, that is, trading a single note futures contract for every single bond futures contract traded. This is the most popular way of trading the NOB. This trade is quoted as the note futures price less the bond futures price (hence the term Notes Over Bonds). Normally, the spread is quoted in thirty-seconds (32ds). Each 32d is worth $31.25 based on the $100,000 face value contract size.

Example: June bond futures are quoted at 100–07 while June note futures are at 103–26. The NOB is quoted at 3 19/32ds or simply as 115/32ds.

It is quoted as the note price over the bond price because the shorter-term note contract will price at a premium to the longer-term bond contract when yields are in excess of the 8 percent contract standard. By quoting notes over bonds, the quote will typically represent a positive rather than a negative number.

The key to understanding how a parallel yield curve shift may be exploited using a one-for-one NOB spread is to understand the volatility associated with intermediate- and long-term fixed income instruments.

It is clear that the longer the term until maturity, the more responsive or volatile a security will be to yield fluctuations. The long-term (15 years or more to maturity) bond futures contract should react more violently to yield movements than will the intermediate-term (6 1/2 to 10 years to maturity) note futures contract. Given a parallel yield curve shift, you may expect bonds to move 18 ticks for every 10 ticks by which notes fluctuate. Thus there is a directional bias in the sense that bonds move generally faster than notes.

Therefore, if yields are expected to rise in a parallel fashion, the recommended strategy is to buy the NOB by buying one note and selling one bond. When yields rise, fixed income prices fall—but bond prices should fall faster than note prices. If notes fall by 10 ticks, bonds may fall by about 18 ticks. A profit of 8 ticks net or $250 per spread may ensue.

If yields are expected to fall in a parallel fashion, the recommended strategy is to sell the NOB by selling one note and buying one bond. When yields fall, prices rise—but bond prices should rise faster than note prices. If notes rise by 10 ticks, bonds may rally by 18 ticks. A profit of 8 ticks net or $250 per spread should ensue.

Yields rise ⇒ Buy the NOB

Yields fall ⇒ Sell the NOB

Figures 7–3 and 7–4 illustrate that as prices fall and yields rise, the NOB generally rallies. As prices decline and yields fall, the NOB generally declines.

How can you capitalize on a nonparallel shift in the yield curve using the NOB? If the yield curve steepens, this implies that bond yields rise faster or fall slower than note yields. As a result, you should buy the NOB by buying note and selling bond futures. If the curve flattens, this implies that bond yields will rise slower or fall faster than note yields. As a result, you should sell the NOB by selling note and buying bond futures.

Yield curve steepens ⇒ Buy the NOB

Yield curve flattens ⇒ Sell the NOB

But you must buy or sell the NOB in such a ratio that would neutralize the directional bias inherent in the spread. In other words, you should use

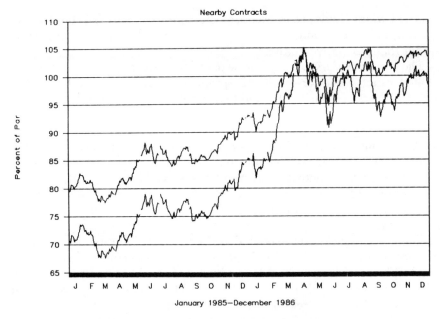

Figure 7–3 Note (upper) vs. bond (lower) futures.

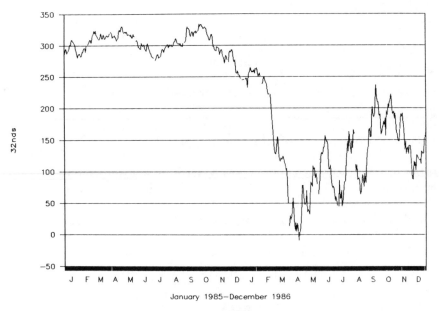

Figure 7–4 NOB spread.

a greater number of notes relative to bonds, so if a parallel curve shift is realized, profit and loss is neutralized.

Once again, the concept of a basis point value proves quite useful in identifying the appropriate ratio. Remember that a bond or note futures contract is tied to the cheapest-to-deliver security. As a general rule, the cheapest-to-deliver cash security price P(cd) may be *approximated* by the futures price P(f) multiplied by the conversion factor of the cheapest to deliver CF(cd).

$$P(cd) = P(f) \times CF(cd)$$

Applying some simple algebra, the price of the futures contract may be approximated by the price of the cheapest-to-deliver cash security divided by its conversion factor.

$$P(f) = P(cd)/CF(cd)$$

A change in the value of the note or bond futures price may be approximated by the change in the value of the cheapest to deliver divided by its conversion factor. We may operationalize the concept of "change in price" by reference to the basis point value of the cheapest-to-deliver cash security.

$$BPV(f) = BPV(cd)/CF(cd)$$

This concept may be applied to both the bond and note futures contracts.

$$BPV(bond) = BPV(cdbond)/CF(cdbond)$$

$$BPV(note) = BPV(cdnote)/CF(cdnote)$$

The ratio of notes to bonds needed to neutralize the directional bias inherent in the spread may be identified by taking the BPV associated with the bond futures contract divided by the BPV associated with the note futures contract.

$$\text{Note/Bond Ratio} = \frac{[BPV(cdbond)/CF(cdbond)]}{[BPV(cdnote)/CF(cdnote)]}$$

Example: On March 4, 1987, the cheapest-to-deliver bond was the 12 3/4s of 2010 with a conversion factor for delivery into the June 1987 futures contract of 1.4516. The cheapest-to-deliver note was the 11 3/4 percent of 1993 with a conversion factor of 1.1814. These securities had BPVs of $133.35 and $60.83, respectively. The appropriate bond note ratio equals 17.84, suggesting the use of 18 note futures for every 10 bond futures when trading the NOB to capitalize on a nonparallel yield curve shift.

$$\text{Note/Bond Ratio} = \frac{[\$133.35/1.4516]}{[\$60.83/1.1814]}$$

$$= 17.84 \text{ or } 18 \text{ notes/10 bonds}$$

T-Bill/Eurodollar Spread

The NOB spread is interesting in that it provides investors with the opportunity to speculate on the level and shape of the yield curve. It provides this opportunity because while Treasury bonds and notes are similar in many ways, they differ with respect to maturity and therefore, to price sensitivity.

The T-bill and Eurodollar futures contracts are also quite similar in many respects. Specifically, both are based on a 90-day instrument. Bills and Euros differ with respect to credit risk, however. Bills are obligations of the U.S. Treasury backed by the "full faith and credit" of the government. Euros represent private credit risks. The risk of default on a Eurodollar obligation is generally considered significantly higher than the risk of default on a T-bill.

Eurodollar yields are typically higher than bill yields. This means that Euro prices, quoted as 100 less the yield, are generally less than bill prices. The spread is typically quoted as the bill price less the Euro price, so the quote will represent a positive rather than a negative number. The spread is quoted in terms of basis points. Each basis point is equivalent to $25.00.

> **Example:** June bill futures are at 94.58 while June Eurodollar futures are at 93.73. The TED is quoted at 85 basis points or 0.85 full points.

The T-bill/Eurodollar spread is often used as a way of taking advantage of a phenomenon known as "flight to quality." If yields rise, investors may become nervous about holding low-quality securities. Investors may then buy bills and sell Euros (buy the TED), driving the spread to wider levels.

If yields fall, investors may become frustrated holding high-quality and consequently relatively low-yielding securities. As a result, they may become more anxious to buy lower-quality securities to enhance yield. Investors may then sell bills and buy Euros (sell the TED), driving the spread to narrower levels.

Yields rise $\Rightarrow$ Buy the TED

Yields fall $\Rightarrow$ Sell the TED

Figures 7–5 and 7–6 illustrate how the TED fell over the period from January 1985 through December 1986 as yields fell.

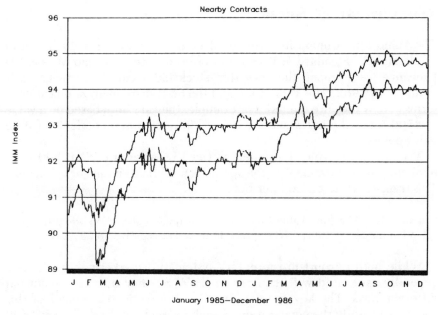

Figure 7–5   T-bill (upper) vs. euros (lower) futures.

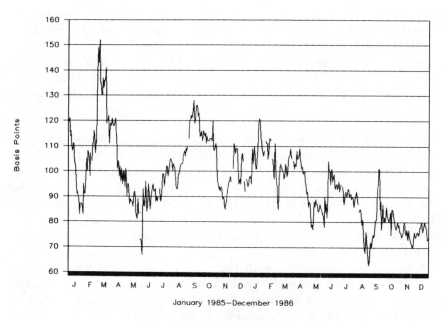

Figure 7–6   TED spread.

Value Line/S&P 500 Spread

The Value Line Composite Average offered at the Kansas City Board of Trade and the Standard & Poor's 500 offered at the Chicago Mercantile Exchange were among the very first stock index based contracts made available in 1982. The Value Line and the S&P share many similarities in terms of how they are quoted. For example, they are both based on a value of $500 times the index and are quoted in minimum increments of 0.05 index points.

The spread is typically quoted as the VLCA less the S&P 500. The minimum price movement in the spread is 0.05 index points or a "nickel." This translates into $25.00 per tick.

> **Example:**   The June Value Line contract is quoted at 264.45 while the June S&P is quoted at 290.70. The spread is quoted at negative 26.25.

While both purport to represent "systematic" market risk or the risk generally associated with equities in the U.S., they do so in somewhat different ways. The key to analyzing the prospective movement of this spread is to study the composition of each index. In general, the S&P 500 is considered a useful indicator of "blue-chip" stock activity. The VLCA is often considered a measure of "secondary stock" activity.

Because these indexes represent very different segments of the stock market, the Value Line/S&P 500 spread is a very interesting and heavily traded spread. In fact, this is probably the most popular of all intermarket stock index futures spreads.

The S&P 500 represents five hundred of the most active and heavily capitalized corporations in the United States, that is blue-chip stocks. The index is weighted by capitalization, so stock issued by highly capitalized corporations tends to exert a heavy influence upon the index as a whole.

The VLCA represents 1700 plus stocks and is typically thought of as an indicator of secondary or over-the-counter stock activity. This belief is not altogether supported by an examination of the index's composition. The VLCA references a wide variety of equities including most of the blue chips represented in the S&P 500 in addition to other New York Stock Exchange, American Stock Exchange, and over-the-counter National Association of Security Dealer's Automated Quotation system listed issues.

A peculiarity associated with the VLCA is that it is geometrically weighted. A geometric weighting tends to downwardly bias a stock index. A geometric average differs from a simple average of a weighted average in that you multiply the price of all n issues represented in the index and take the nth root.

Example: You own three different stock issues valued at $25, $35, and $45. Find the simple and geometric averages.

$$\text{Simple Average} = (\$25 + \$35 + \$45)/3 = \$35$$
$$\text{Geometric Average} = (\$25 \times \$35 \times \$45)^{1/3} = \$34.02$$

You can see that the geometric average falls slightly short of the simple average.

Example: Assume you purchase two stocks, stock A and stock B, both valued at $1.00. Stock A subsequently rallies to $2.00 while stock B falls to $0.50. Find the simple and geometric averages.

$$\begin{array}{ll} \text{Stock A} & \$1.00 \Rightarrow \$2.00 \\ \text{Stock B} & \$1.00 \Rightarrow \$0.50 \\ \text{Simple Average} & \$1.00 \Rightarrow \$1.25 \\ \text{Geometric Average} & \$1.00 \Rightarrow \$1.00 \end{array}$$

Even though this stock trader makes 50 cents or 25 cents on average, the geometric average suggests that there is no profit or loss on this trade. This means the VLCA may tend to lag market advances but may lead market declines.

How might you trade the VLCA/S&P 500 spread? The key is in understanding the relationship between blue-chip and secondary stocks.

When the stock market breaks up or down, the blue chips generally tend to react first. This may be due to the fact that large institutional traders tend to concentrate on the larger stock issues. As a result, the blue chips may rally harder than secondary stocks in the initial stages of a rally or fall harder than secondary stocks in the initial stages of a decline.

As a rally begins to be reflected in the secondary stocks, these volatile high-beta stocks tend to catch up with and outperform the blue-chips movement in a percentage sense. In the later stages of a rally, traders tend to become more pessimistic about the secondary stocks relative to the blue chips, and the secondaries fade.

Thus you may want to sell the Value Lines and buy the S&Ps in the earliest stages of an upwards market movement although in latter stages of a rally, you may wish to reverse the spread by buying the Value Lines and selling the S&Ps. As the rally loses strength, you may wish to sell the Value Line and buy the S&P.

As can be seen in Figures 7–7 and 7–8, the stock market has generally been rallying since early 1985; however, this rally traces its beginning to 1982. The fact that the Value Lines has been fading relative to the S&P is regarded by some as an indication of growing weakness in the long-term market advance.

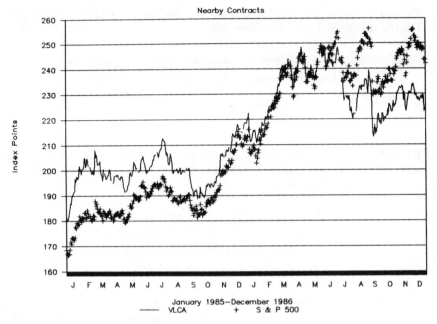

Figure 7-7   VLCA vs. S&P 500.

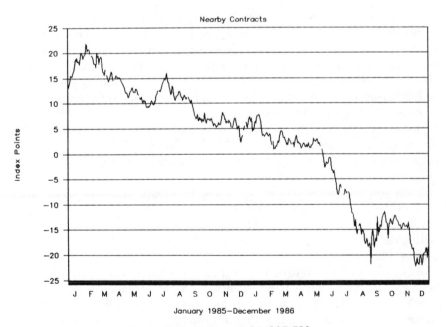

Figure 7-8   Spread: VLCA/S&P 500.

Yen/Mark Spread

The currency contracts offered at the Chicago Mercantile Exchange are dollar denominated contracts, uniformly quoted in terms of dollars per foreign unit (American terms). Currency market participants, however, are often interested in transactions known as "cross-rates," for example, trading Japanese yen versus the West German mark. You can effectively trade this cross-rate by spreading yen and mark futures contracts on the Chicago Mercantile Exchange.

The yen contract is quoted in cents per one hundred yen based on a 12.5 million yen contract size. For example, you may see a quote of 65.44 cents per hundred yen. A minimum price fluctuation of 0.01 cents per hundred yen translates into a movement of $12.50.

The mark contract is quoted in cents per mark based on a 125,000 mark contract size. For example, you may see a quote of 54.72 cents per mark. A minimum price fluctuation of 0.01 cents per mark likewise translates into a movement of $12.50.

The spread itself is quoted as the yen price (cents per 100 yen) less the mark price (cents per single mark). The minimum movement in the spread equals $12.50 assuming you spread a single yen versus a single mark futures contract.

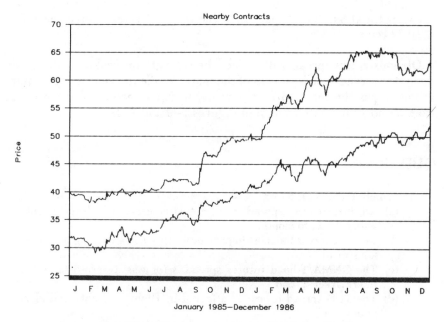

Figure 7-9   Yen (upper) vs. mark (lower) futures.

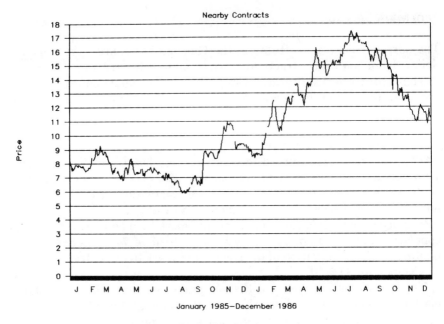

Figure 7–10   Yen/mark spread.

Example: June yen is at 65.44 cents per hundred yen while the June mark contract is at 54.72 cents per mark. The yen/mark spread may be quoted at 10.72 cents.

Obviously, this spread will reflect the strength or weakness of the yen versus the strength or weakness of the mark. While the yen had been quite strong versus the mark in recent years, it experienced a sharp reversal around mid-year 1986, as seen in Figures 7–9 and 7–10.

QUESTIONS

   1. Which statement is false?
      (a) An intracontract spread involves two contracts which differ only with respect to month.
      (b) Cost of carry is the most important factor when analyzing intermarket spreads.
      (c) The GNMA/T-bond futures spread is (or was) referred to as *the* intermarket spread.
      (d) The TED spread is heavily affected by flight to quality considerations.
      (e) The TED spread is quoted in terms of basis points.

2. September bonds are at 98–16; September notes are at 99–24. How would you quote the NOB?

3. Which statement is true about an intracontract bond spread?
   (a) The spread is quoted as a negative number in a positive yield curve environment.
   (b) The spread tends to widen when short-term rates rise as long-term rates remain stable.
   (c) You should buy the spread in a flattening yield curve environment.
   (d) The spread will narrow when the yield curve flattens.
   (e) None of the above.

4. The NOB is a good buy when . . .
   (a) Rates are falling.
   (b) The yield curve is flattening.
   (c) Long-term rates are falling relative to short-term rates.
   (d) The yield curve is steepening or rates are rising.
   (e) The sky is falling.

5. The TED spread is expected to narrow when . . .
   (a) The yield curve steepens.
   (b) Yields in general are falling.
   (c) Long-term rates decline relative to short-term rates.
   (d) The Fed tightens money supply.
   (e) Yields in general are rising.

6. Which is false about the S&P/Value Line (quoted as the VLCA less the S&P) spread?
   (a) This is the most popular intermarket stock index spread.
   (b) The S&P 500 is generally less volatile than the Value Line Composite Average.
   (c) The S&P 500 tends to be downwardly biased because it utilizes a geometric average of the 500 stock prices.
   (d) The spread tends to rise as a bull stock market trend begins to be expressed in the secondary stocks.
   (e) None of the above.

7. Start keeping track of an intramarket T-bond futures spread on a daily basis using closing prices. How has the spread moved? What did the yield curve do to cause that movement?

8. Using today's closing prices, find out the appropriate ratio in which to trade the NOB to neutralize a parallel shift in the yield curve. Do you think the yield curve will steepen, flatten, or remain stable? What is the appropriate NOB strategy?

9. Monitor the NOB on a daily basis using closing prices until the end of the course. Find out what is cheapest to deliver against the bond and note futures contracts. Follow the yield spread on these two issues. What happened to the spread and why?

10. Monitor the TED on a daily basis using closing market prices. What happened to the spread and why?

8

Hedging with Financial Futures

It is not uncommon for dealers and investors in a variety of financial instruments to find themselves with a cash market position which is incompatible with prevailing market conditions. For example, a fixed income security investor may have a portfolio composed primarily of long-term securities. But if interest rates are expected to rise, the value of this investment may decline significantly. Thus the investor is exposed to a grave risk of loss. An equity investor may be holding a conservative stock portfolio comprised of many low-beta stocks, but if the market is expected to rally, he will not be optimally poised to participate in the anticipated appreciation.

A foreign currency dealer's "book" of commitments to buy, security inventories, and commitments to sell may often become unbalanced, exposing the dealer to risk. For example, when commitments to buy foreign currency at a fixed price plus inventories of that currency exceed commitments to sell, the dealer is exposed to the risk of declining exchange rates. When commitments to sell exceed commitments to buy plus inventories, the dealer is exposed to the risk of advancing exchange rates.

Financial futures often prove a useful tool in balancing these exposures. A dealer or investor exposed to the risk of falling prices can hedge by going short futures. A dealer exposed to the risk of rising prices or an investor who wants to be poised to capitalize on this anticipation may find it expedient to go long futures.

This chapter is intended to present some of the techniques associated with hedging with financial futures. In particular, the critical question becomes: What is the relationship between the cash instrument or instruments to be hedged and the futures contract which is to be the subject of the hedge transaction?

CASH INSTRUMENT HEDGEABILITY

The viability of any prospective hedging program depends upon the strength of the relationship between the price of the instrument to be hedged and the hedge vehicle. The strength or weakness of this relationship determines whether or not the cash instrument is "hedgeable" using existing futures markets.

In some cases, the issue may be settled quite easily. For example, if you intend to hedge the U.S. dollar/deutsche mark exchange rate, there is generally little doubt that the DM futures contract will prove to be a reliable hedging vehicle.

Other cases are not quite as straightforward. Assume you want to hedge the risks associated with a cash Treasury bond using T-bond futures. If that bond may be identified as cheapest or near-cheapest to deliver, it is probable that the hedge may be quite effective. However, if the bond is *not* cheapest or if the bond is not even deliverable, the prospective effectiveness of the hedge may be marginally less effective. If you want to "cross-hedge" bonds with varying credit risks against the T-bond futures contract, the viability of the hedge is generally further reduced.

One way of assessing the viability of a prospective hedge is to identify the statistical correlation between cash and futures. If the correlation is high by whatever standard, the hedge may be pursued with some degree of confidence. If it is low, the hedge must be implemented with great caution and subsequent constant monitoring, if at all!

IDENTIFYING THE HEDGE RATIO

Assuming there is a reasonably high correlation between the cash instrument and the futures contract, the next step is to quantify the expected relationship between cash and futures. The question becomes: To what extent will the value of the cash instrument fluctuate given a particular fluctuation in the value of the futures contract?

This expectation defines what is known as the futures *hedge ratio.* This hedge ratio identifies the expected relationship between cash and futures price movements and may be used directly to identify how many futures must be sold (bought) to hedge a particular long (short) exposure in the cash market.

The futures *hedge ratio* defines the expected movement in the value of the cash instrument to be hedged given a particular movement in the value of the futures contract which is to serve as a hedge vehicle.

The simplest example may be found where movements in the value of the cash instrument are expected precisely to parallel movements in the value of the futures contract. The appropriate number of contracts or futures hedge ratio (HR) may be found by comparing the quantity to be hedged Q(h) with the futures contract size (CS).

$$HR = Q(h)/CS$$

This may occur, for example, when you are hedging a deutsche mark exposure with the deutsche mark futures contract. For example, you may have a 12.5 million deutsche mark exposure. You may hedge it with one hundred deutsche mark futures covering 125,000 marks each.

$$HR = 12,500,000/125,000$$

$$= 100 \text{ contracts}$$

Because the cash item to be hedged is the precise commodity which is called for on delivery, there is no reason to weight a hedge beyond matching quantities. But this is not true when, for example, you are considering the hedge of a fixed income security against any of the variety of interest rate futures products available. These securities may vary, not only with respect to the face value hedged, but also with respect to maturity, coupon, structure of the interest payments and principal repayment, and credit risks.

Conversion Factor Weighted Hedge

To illustrate a simple hedge strategy, let us begin with a simple scenario.

> **Example:**   It is August 25, 1986. A security dealer owns $10 million face value of the 12½ percent bond of 2009–14 (matures in the year 2014 but is callable in 2009). The bond is currently bid in the cash market at 148¹⁷/₃₂ds for a yield to call equal to 7.89 percent. The 12½s are currently cheapest to deliver against the December bond futures contract priced at 100–01. Given the conversion factor of 1.4662, the bond has a basis equal to 59.⁷/₃₂ds with an implied repo rate of 4.66 percent.

The dealer is uncertain about the direction in which interest rates may fluctuate. However, he is concerned that rates may drift higher in coming weeks, diminishing the price that the bonds will command if they are resold in the cash market. This forecast is not unlike many forecasts made by financial executives.

To alleviate this uncertainty, the dealer has decided to sell U.S. Treasury Bond futures.

Example: The dealer sells one hundred $100,000 face value bond futures contracts to "match" the $10 million face value 12½s. The dealer shorts these futures at the prevailing market price of $100^{01}/_{32ds}$.

Buy $10,000,000 12½% – 14 @ 148–17	$14,853,125
Accrued interest @ 8/26/86	$37,364
Sell 100 Dec. futures @ 100–01	—
Net Investment	$14,890,489

Assume that by November 28, 1986, the 12½s decline 10 points to 138–17 while futures decline to 93–23. What rate of return is realized?

Bond @ 11/28/86 @ 138–17	$13,853,125
Accrued interest	$356,658
Coupon income	$0
Reinvestment income	$0
Long futures @ 93–23 (cost of carry @ 2%) ...	$631,250
Net Credits	$14,841,033

$$\text{Return} = \frac{\$14,841,033 - \$14,890,489}{\$14,890,489} \times \frac{360}{94}$$

$$= -1.27\%$$

Compare the hedged return with the unhedged return:

	Return	
	Dollar	*Percent*
Hedged	– $49,457	– 1.27%
Unhedged	– $680,707	– 17.51%

This hedger was successful in limiting a potential loss of $680,707 to a relatively small loss of $49,457 by virtue of a sizable profit in the futures market. Still, this hedger could and should have done better!

Why did the hedge not perform better? The dealer neglected to consider that the risks associated with a 12½ percent Treasury bond differ from the risks associated with a bond futures contract based on an 8 percent standard or par grade. The relation between the cheapest-to-deliver cash security and a futures contract is subsumed in the invoicing process. In the case of bond and note futures, the principal invoice price is a product of the settlement futures price and the applicable conversion factor (CF). This is tantamount to saying that the cash price should approximate the futures price times the conversion factor.

The conversion factor for delivery of these 12½s into the December 1986 contract is 1.4662. This suggests that the 12½ percent bond is worth roughly 147 percent of a comparable 8 percent bond and, given similar yield shifts, is 147 percent as volatile as the 8 percent standard.

By weighting the hedge by the 1.4662 conversion factor, the dealer may implement a more effective hedge. To find the appropriate number of futures contracts with which to hedge, the dealer may use the following formula:

$$HR = [Q(h)/CS] \times CF$$

Applying this formula to our example:

$$HR = \frac{\$10,000,000}{\$100,000} \times 1.4662$$

$$= 146.62 \text{ or } 147 \text{ contracts}$$

Example: The dealer shorts 147 bond futures against the $10 million face value 12½s. What would happen if the cash market drops 10 points from 148–17 to 138–17?

Bond @ 11/28/86 @ 138–17	$13,853,125
Accrued interest	$356,658
Coupon income	$0
Reinvestment income	$0
Long futures @ 93–23 (cost of carry @ 2%) ...	$927,938
Net Credits	$15,137,721

$$\text{Return} = \frac{\$15,137,721 - \$14,890,489}{\$14,890,489} \times \frac{360}{94}$$

$$= 6.36\%$$

Compare the hedged return with the unhedged return:

	Return	
	Dollar	*Percent*
Hedged	$247,231	6.36%
Unhedged	– $680,707	– 17.51%

Note that the dealer was still unable to hedge 100 percent of the diminished principal value of the securities. The profit on the futures position of $927,938 fell short of the loss on the cash position of $10 million for a net shortfall of near $80 thousand. Nonetheless, he was able to hedge a much greater proportion of the loss using a conversion factor weighted hedge relative to the unweighted hedge.

What would happen if the market were to fall 10 points, 5 points, remain neutral, rally 5 points, or rally 10 points?

	Return	
	Hedged	*Unhedged*
Cash @ 138–17	6.36%	– 17.51%
@ 143–17	6.34%	– 4.65%
@ 148–17	6.32%	8.21%
@ 153–17	6.30%	21.07%
@ 158–17	6.17%	33.93%

Locking In a Short-Term Rate

Note that the simulated returns (in the 6.17–6.36 percent range) shown previously on a hedged basis fall short of the security's current yield of 8.21 percent. These simulated returns reflect not a long-term yield but rather a short-term yield.

This is intuitive when you consider the implications associated with the sale of futures against a long cash security. By selling futures, you enter into a commitment to make delivery of the securities by futures contract maturity. You effectively shorten the maturity of the cash security to coincide with the delivery period of the futures contract. You cannot expect to earn a long-term rate of return on a short-term instrument.

By hedging with futures, moreover, you lock in a specific rate of return with a relatively high probability; that is, the variance of potential returns is much reduced. But risk and reward must balance. High-risk investments tend to yield higher returns; low-risk investments yield relatively lower returns.

However, the central issue revolves around the shape of the yield. When the yield curve assumes its normal upwardly sloped shape, long-term yields exceed short-term yields. By effectively shortening the maturity of a long-term asset, you reduce the expected return from the current yield. If the yield curve were inverted and short-term yields exceeded long-term yields, shortening the maturity of the asset would result in an augmented return.

As discussed in the prior chapter, the shape of the yield curve determines whether futures in successively deferred months run at successively lower or higher levels—whether the basis (defined in the context of bond and note futures as the cash price less the futures price multiplied by the conversion factor) is positive or negative, respectively.

A hedger should be very concerned with the basis and the expected magnitude of cash/futures convergence. In this case, the basis was originally at

59. $7/32ds$ (148–17 less 100–01 times 1.4662), but over time, this basis may be expected to converge. This is even more likely since the $12\,1/2$s represented the cheapest-to-deliver cash security.

Convergence results in a loss to the hedger who is long cash/short futures in a positive yield curve environment (where the adjusted futures price falls short of the cash price, resulting in a positive basis). To understand, consider the possibility that cash prices will remain constant over the life of the hedge. This suggests that futures must rally to converge to cash. What if futures remained constant? This suggests that cash prices must decline to converge to futures. Either way, if you are long cash/short futures, a basis or convergence loss ensues.

The foregoing simulation applied the assumption that the basis converges at a 2 percent annual rate. This suggests an approximate 2 percent premium of long-term rates over short-term rates.

Example: In the examples discussed previously, cash prices declined 10 points from 148–17 to 138–17, accompanied by a $6^{10}/32ds$ decline in futures from 100–01 to 93–23 over the 94 days in the life of the hedge. This was calculated assuming that futures would parallel cash in the ratio of the conversion factor (1.4662) adjusted for 2 percent convergence:

$$C(f) = [F \times c \times (d/360)] - [C(c)/CF]$$

Where:

$$C(f) = \text{Change in futures price}$$
$$F = \text{Original futures price}$$
$$c = \text{Cost of carry}$$
$$d = \text{Days in life of hedge}$$
$$C(c) = \text{Change in cash price}$$
$$CF = \text{Conversion factor}$$

In the example discussed previously:

$$C(f) = [100\text{–}01 \times 2\% \times (94/360)] - [10/1.4662]$$
$$= -6.298 \text{ or } 6\ 10/32\text{ds}$$

The basis converged in our simulation from 59. $7/32ds$ to 35. $9/32ds$. But if carry in the example illustrated above were set equal to zero, this would suggest that futures would fall 6.820 points or $6^{26}/32ds$ to 93–07. This would place the basis at 59. $3/32ds$, that is, virtually unchanged. Thus the bond futures converged by $16/32ds$ or about $73,500 for 147 contracts. This $73,500 convergence loss effectively diminishes the net return on the hedge transaction.

In the absence of such convergence, the hedger would have realized a return of 8.25 percent, virtually identical to the return the unhedged bond holder would realize if cash prices remained stable rather than 6.36 percent. As such, the hedger realizes a short-term rather than a long-term rate of return!

How far could bond futures be expected to decline with what impact on the basis if the hedge were held an additional 33 days after November 28th until the last possible delivery day December 31st?

$$C(f) = [100\text{--}01 \times 2\% \times (127/360)] - [10/1.4662]$$

$$= -6.115 \text{ or } 6 \text{ } 04/32\text{ds}$$

This suggests that bond futures might fall to 93–29 for a basis equal to 27.$1/32$ds (138–17 less 93–17 times 1.4662). The implicit assumption in our analysis is that the basis will not fully converge in any event! This may be partially explained in that the short enjoys many advantages over the long during the delivery month in the form of the "implied put option" and other quasi-arbitrage opportunities available during the last seven days of the month (discussed in a prior chapter).

Still, the basis of 27.$1/32$ds seems quite wide for the cheapest-to-deliver bond hedged until the last delivery date. This suggests that a cost of carry higher than the 2 percent applied above may be applicable. We note, however, that the basis of even the cheapest-to-deliver cash security tends to track at a relatively wide level prior to the delivery month. (Thus the implied repo rate of the cheapest-to-deliver security tends to fall short of actual overnight or term repo return. The implied repo rate is discussed in detail in a prior chapter.)

Typically, this wide basis persists until well into the delivery period where convergence tends to accelerate. Given the assumption that the hedge is held until November 28th, pegging carry at 2 percent may not be unreasonable.

Anticipatory Hedge

The dealer in the prior example found himself net long debt securities; therefore, he was concerned about the possibility of rising rates and diminishing debt security values. The same dealer could just as easily have been net short cash securities; that is, his commitments to sell at a fixed price could exceed commitments to buy plus inventories. Under those circumstances, he may be concerned about the possibility of declining rates and rising prices.

What is the solution to these concerns? Implement an *anticipatory hedge* by going long futures. The dealer knows he will have to cover his short commitments in the near future. A long futures position will serve as a temporary substitute for those purchases, allowing the dealer to profit in an advancing bond market, offsetting possible losses on the short cash commitments.

Example: Our dealer has committed to sell $10 million face of the 12½s, currently trading at 148–17, and is concerned that prices will rise significantly before he can cover his short commitments. The dealer buys 147 bond futures at the prevailing price of 100–01.

Short $10,000,000 12½% – 14 @ 148–17	$14,853,125
Accrued interest @ 8/26/86	$37,364
Buy 147 Dec. futures @ 100–01	—
Initial Receipts	$14,890,489

Subsequently, the cash market rises to 158–17 while futures advance to 107–12. As a result, the dealer purchases the cash bonds at $1 million more than their original value. This is coupled with a $1,079,531 profit in the futures market.

Buy Bond @ 11/28/86 @ 158–17	$15,853,125
Accrued interest	$356,658
Coupon income	$0
Reinvestment income	$0
Short futures @ 107–12 (cost of carry @ 2%) ..	$-1,079,531
Net Payouts	$15,130,251

$$\text{Cost} = \frac{\$15,130,251 - \$14,890,489}{\$14,890,489} \times \frac{360}{94}$$

$$= 6.17\%$$

Compare the hedged cost of funds with the unhedged cost:

	Return	
	Dollar	*Percent*
Hedged	– $239,762	6.17%
Unhedged	– $1,319,293	33.93%

The foregoing analysis calculates the potential cost of funds associated with the initial short cash commitment. This means as long as the hedger can invest those funds at 6.17 percent or better over the 94-day time horizon, the short will be nicely covered.

On an unhedged basis, however, it is most unlikely that short-term funds can be invested to earn 33.93 percent or better. In dollar terms, the loss of $1.3 million on an unhedged basis may become quite distressing.

The long anticipatory hedge is similar but opposite to the short hedge described above. One significant difference, however, may be observed in the fact that by holding a short cash and long futures position, convergence actually works to the benefit of the hedger.

Basis Point Value Weighted Hedge

We have confined our discussion so far to the hedge of a cash instrument which represented the cheapest-to-deliver cash security. Far more common, however, is the situation where a risk-averse portfolio manager wants to hedge a security which is not cheapest, a security which varies in terms of coupon or maturity from the cheapest to deliver and which may, in fact, be completely *nondeliverable*!

The question is: How can you hedge such securities? Let us confine the discussion to consideration of the $7\frac{1}{4}$ percent bond maturing in 2016. On August 25, 1986, this security had a basis of $301.\,^{5}/_{32}$ds and an implied repo rate of -18.92 percent against the December 1986 futures contract. As such, it was far from cheapest. Since the $7\frac{1}{4}$ percent issue was not cheapest to deliver, a conversion factor weighted hedge is not in order. Rather, we shall illustrate what is known as a basis point value weighted hedge.

To understand the methodology associated with a BPV weighted hedge, consider the hedge objective: to balance as closely as possible the change in the value of the cash security to be hedged $Q(h) \times C(h)$ with the change in the price of the futures contract $CS \times C(f)$. To do this, you must weight the hedge, identifying an appropriate hedge ratio HR:

$$Q(h) \times C(h) = [CS \times C(f)] \times HR$$

(A basis point value represents the dollar change in the value of $100,000 face value securities in response to a 1-basis point or 0.01 percent change in yield. These figures may be determined on many hand-held calculators and are sometimes published in bond tables.)

Example: On August 25, 1986, the $7\frac{1}{4}$ percent issue of May 2016 traded at $101\,^{00}/_{32}$ds to yield 7.17 percent. The basis point value was $123.35 per $100,000 face value. This suggests that if the bond's yield rose or declined .01 percent, the price would decline or rise approximately $^{4}/_{32}$ds to $100\,^{28}/_{32}$ds or $101\,^{04}/_{32}$ds.

How can you use these basis point values? Let us return to our previous hedge objective statement. By applying some simple algebra, we may solve that equation for the hedge ratio:

$$HR = [Q(h) \times C(h)]/[CS \times C(f)]$$

Earlier, we indicated that futures prices most closely correlate with or track the price of the cheapest-to-deliver cash security. The relation between the change in the price of the cheapest-to-deliver cash security $C(cd)$ and the futures price is reflected in the conversion factor $CF(cd)$. Thus:

$$C(f) = C(cd)/CF(cd)$$

Substituting:

$$HR = [Q(h) \times C(h)]/(CS[C(cd)/CF(cd)])$$

Rearranging:

$$HR = [Q(h)/CS] \times CF(cd) \times [C(h)/C(cd)]$$

So far we have referred to the change in the cash or futures price rather loosely. However, the equation above may be made somewhat more relevant by substituting the basis point values for the cash security $BPV(h)$ to be hedged and the cheapest cash security $BPV(cd)$:

$$HR = [Q(h)/CS] \times CF(cd) \times [BPV(h)/BPV(cd)]$$

Note that the first two components of this equation are identical to what was derived earlier. The first task a prospective hedger must undertake is to identify the quantity to be hedged relative to the contract size. Secondly, the hedger must identify the conversion factor of the cheapest-to-deliver security.

Finally, the hedger must assess the expected change in the price of the hedged security relative to the change in the price of the cheapest-to-deliver-security.

Example: On August 25, 1986, the cheapest-to-deliver cash security against the bond futures contract was the $12\,^1\!/_2$ percent issue of August 2014. The basis point value of a $100,000 face value lot equaled $145.01 while the conversion factor for delivery of this bond into the December 1986 futures contract equaled 1.4662. The basis point value for $100,000 face value of the $7\,^1\!/_4$s equaled 123.35. Assume you want to hedge $10 million face value of the cash security. With this information, you can calculate the appropriate hedge ratio:

$$HR = [Q(h)/CS] \times CF(cd) \times [BPV(h)/BPV(cd)]$$
$$= [\$10,000,000/\$100,000] \times 1.4662 \times [\$123.35/\$145.01]$$
$$= 124.72 \text{ or } 125 \text{ contracts}$$

This suggests that one should hedge by shorting 125 bond futures.

Example: An institution sells 125 bond futures at 100–01 against $10 million face value 7 1/4 percent bonds of 2016, trading at 101–00.

Buy $10,000,000 7 1/4% – 16 @ 101–00	$10,100,000
Accrued interest @ 8/26/86	$202,921
Sell 125 Dec. futures @ 100–01	—
Net Investment	$10,302,921

The dealer shorts 125 bond futures against the $10 million face value 7 1/4s. What would happen if the cash market drops 10 points from 101–00 to 91–00 over the next 81 days until November 15, 1986?

Bond @ 11/15/86 @ 91–00	$9,100,000
Accrued interest	$0
Coupon income	$362,500
Reinvestment income	$0
Long futures @ 92–11 (cost of carry @ 1.4%)	$960,938
Net Credits	$10,423,438

$$\text{Return} = \frac{\$10,423,438 - \$10,302,921}{\$10,302,921} \times \frac{360}{81}$$

$$= 5.20\%$$

Compare the hedged return with the unhedged return:

	Return	
	Dollar	*Percent*
Hedged	$120,517	5.20%
Unhedged	– $840,421	– 36.25%

(This analysis applies the assumption that the BPV weighted hedge ratio provides an accurate assessment of the relative price movements between cash and futures.)

Note that the basis point value of a debt security changes over time and in response to fluctuating yields. In general, as the term to maturity winds down, the basis point value diminishes. As yields increase (decrease), BPVs decline (advance). Because basis point value is a dynamic concept, this suggests that hedgers must continually monitor their positions, adjusting when the hedge ratio calculated with reference to the basis point value changes.

Alternate Measures of Bond Volatility—Yield Value

The yield value of a 1/32d reflects the expected change in the yield of a bond given a 1/32d change in its price. The basis point value measures the expected price change of a bond given a 1-basis point change in its yield. The yield value of a $1/32d$ provides the expected change in the yield of a bond given a $1/32d$ change in price. As such, YV_{32} essentially represents the inverse of the BPV.

> **Example:** On August 25, 1986, the 7 1/4 percent issue of May 2016 traded at $101^{00}/32ds$ to yield 7.17 percent with a BPV of \$123.35 per \$100,000 face value or $3.^{94}/32ds$ at \$31.25 per $1/32d$. This suggests that a price change of $1/32d$ corresponds to a yield change of 0.0025 percent or approximately one-quarter basis point.

$$YV_{32} = 1/3.94 = 0.2533 \text{ basis points or } 0.0025\%$$

Given that the yield value of a $1/32d$ is simply an inverse function of the BPV, this suggests that you can simply invert the terms referring to BPVs in our hedge ratio formula provided above.

$$HR = [Q(h)/CS] \times CF(cd) \times [YV_{32}(cd)/YV_{32}(h)]$$

> **Example:** On August 25, 1986, the cheapest-to-deliver bond was the 12 1/2 percent issue of August 2014. The basis point value of a \$100,000 face value lot equaled \$145.01 for a YV_{32} of 0.2155 or 0.0022 percent. The conversion factor for delivery into the December 1986 futures contract equaled 1.4662. The yield value of the 7 1/4s equals 0.2533 basis points or 0.0025 percent. Find the hedge ratio for a \$10 million lot.

$$HR = [Q(h)/CS] \times CF(cd) \times [YV_{32}(cd)/YV_{32}(h)]$$
$$= [\$10,000,000/\$100,000] \times 1.4662 \times [0.2155/0.2533]$$
$$= 124.74 \text{ or } 125 \text{ contracts}$$

As expected, this is the same ratio derived using the BPV weighted method. Therefore, it is simply a matter of convenience and preference whether one employs the BPV weighted method or the YV_{32} weighted method.

Alternate Measures of Bond Volatility—Duration

A topic which has attracted a great deal of interest in recent years is duration. Duration refers to the average life of the cash flows associated with a security. With the exception of zero coupon bonds or other noninterest bearing items, the duration of a security is generally much less than its term to maturity.

Recall that Treasury bonds and notes entitle the holder to semiannual interest payments. These cash flows are received much in advance of the maturity date. Moreover, the present value of current coupon payments is greater than that of deferred coupon payments and, indeed, may be more than the present value of the final principal payment. Thus the duration of a security may be found by taking the summation of the product of the term and present value of each cash receipt divided by the price of the bond. This defines Macauley's duration.

Modified duration may be calculated as the Macauley's duration divided by one plus the bond's yield (adjusted by reference to the number of interest payments made annually). This statistic provides a useful measure of the expected percentage change in the price of a bond given a percentage change in its yield.

> **Example:** On August 25, 1986, the $7\frac{1}{4}$ percent issue of May 2016 traded at $101\,^{00}/_{32ds}$ to yield 7.17 percent with a Macauley's duration of 12.40 years and a modified duration of 11.97 years. This suggests that if the yield of the security were to advance or decline by 1 percent, its price would fall or rise, respectively, by approximately 11.97 percent.

How does an institution use the concept of duration to implement a hedging program? Duration measures percentage changes in debt prices relative to percentage changes in interest rates. The basis point value method provides a measure of the dollar change in debt prices relative to a 0.01 percent change in yield. As such, these concepts are quite analogous.

$$BPV(h) \text{ is analogous to } D(h) \times P(h)$$

where

$$D(h) = \text{modified duration of the hedged security}$$

$$P(h) = \text{price of the hedged security}$$

Substituting $D(h)P(h)$ for $BPV(h)$ and $D(cd)P(cd)$ for $BPV(cd)$, respectively, our BPV hedge ratio equation may be modified as follows:

$$HR = [Q(h)/CS] \times CF(cd) \times [D(h)P(h)/D(cd)P(cd)]$$

> **Example:** On August 25, 1986, the cheapest-to-deliver bond was the $12\frac{1}{2}$ percent issue of August 2014 trading at 148–17. The modified duration of this security equaled 9.74 years, while its conversion factor equaled 1.4662. The modified duration of the $7\frac{1}{4}$s trading at 101–00 equals 11.97 years. Find the hedge ratio for a $10 million lot.

$$HR = [Q(h)/CS] \times CF(cd) \times [D(h)P(h)/D(cd)P(cd)]$$

$$= [\$10{,}000{,}000/\$100{,}000] \times 1.4662 \times [11.97 \times 101.00/9.74 \times 148.53125]$$

$$= 122.53 \text{ or } 123 \text{ contracts}$$

Note that the hedge ratio of 123 contracts is quite similar to the hedge ratio of 125 contracts derived using the BPV or YV_{32} method.

Some analysts prefer to alter this equation slightly. Noting that the price of the futures contract P(f) should be roughly equal to the ratio of the price of the cheapest to deliver divided by its conversion factor P(f) = P(cd)/CF(cd), one may simplify the analysis as follows:

$$HR = [Q(h)/CS] \times [D(h)P(h)/D(cd)P(f)]$$

Example: On August 25, 1986, the December 1986 bond futures contract was trading at 100–01. Find the hedge ratio for a $10 million face value lot of the $7\frac{1}{4}$s.

$HR = [Q(h)/CS] \times [D(h)P(h)/D(cd)P(f)]$

$\quad = [\$10,000,000/\$100,000] \times [11.97 \times 101.00/9.74 \times 100.03125]$

$\quad = 124.09 \text{ or } 124 \text{ contracts}$

This modified formula results in a hedge ratio of 124 contracts—quite similar to the results derived using the BPV, YV_{32}, or the original duration weighted formula. However, this result is slightly higher than the other duration-based result.

This may be attributed to the fact that futures price typically falls short of the ratio of the price of the cheapest to deliver divided by its conversion factor. This is consistent with an upwardly sloped yield curve environment where long-term yields exceed short-term yields.

Yield-Adjusted Weighted Hedge

The hedge ratios discussed previously such as the BPV, yield value, or duration weighted methods do a good job defining the expected relationship between the hedged security and the futures contract. They do so by assessing the expected movements of securities with varying coupons, terms to maturity, and yields. However, these methods implicitly assume that comparable yield fluctuations will be realized between the hedged security and the cheapest-to-deliver instrument. This is quite obvious when you consider that the BPV measures the expected change in the price of a fixed income security given a 1-basis point change in yield.

But what happens when the yield curve is expected to flatten, that is, when long-term yields are expected to fall relative to short-term yields? What happens when the yield curve is expected to steepen, that is, when long-term yields are expected to rise relative to short-term yields? Under these circumstances, it is clear that the BPV weighted method will provide a less than completely accurate assessment of the relative movements of hedged security and futures contract; therefore, it makes sense to assess the expected relative yield movement of hedged security and cheapest to deliver.

If the yield of the hedged security is likely to be more volatile than the yield of the cheapest to deliver, use additional futures contracts. If the yield of the hedged security is likely to be less volatile, use fewer contracts.

$$HR = [Q(h)/CS] \times CF(cd) \times [BPV(h)/BPV(cd)] \times [CY(h)/CY(cd)]$$

where

$$CY(h) = \text{change in yield of hedged security}$$

$$CY(cd) = \text{change in yield of cheapest to deliver}$$

Example: Assume that the yield of the 7¼s of 2016 is expected to rise or fall by 11 basis points for every 10 basis points by which the cheapest to deliver 12½s of 2014 fluctuate. That means the yield curve between the 12½s and the slightly longer term 7¼s is expected to steepen if rates advance or decline if rates fall. Find the appropriate hedge ratio.

$$HR = [Q(h)/CS] \times CF(cd) \times [BPV(h)/BPV(cd)] \times [CY(h)/CY(cd)]$$
$$= [\$10,000,000/\$100,000] \times 1.4662 \times [\$123.35/\$145.01] \times [11/10]$$
$$= 137.19 \text{ or } 139 \text{ contracts}$$

Example: Assume that the yield of the 7¼s of 2016 is expected to rise or fall by 9 basis points for every 10 basis points by which the cheapest to deliver 12½s of 2014 fluctuate. That means the yield curve between the 12½s and the slightly longer term 7¼s is expected to flatten if rates rise or steepen if rates fall. Find the appropriate hedge ratio.

$$HR = [Q(h)/CS] \times CF(cd) \times [BPV(h)/BPV(cd)] \times [CY(h)/CY(cd)]$$
$$= [\$10,000,000/\$100,00] \times 1.4662 \times [\$123.35/\$145.01] \times [9/10]$$
$$= 112.25 \text{ or } 112 \text{ contracts.}$$

Our discussion so far has centered on ways in which one may hedge the risk associated with Treasury securities. However, the universe of securities in which one may invest is not limited to Treasuries. One may invest in other intermediate- to long-term obligations such as agency issues, corporate bonds, and Eurobonds.

Agencies and corporates are similar to Treasury notes and bonds in that they may be quoted in percent of par, generally pay semiannual interest, and provide for the return of the corpus on maturity. Eurobonds typically pay annual coupons. Further, these instruments are affected by the same general economic conditions which impact upon Treasuries.

Treasury obligations are generally considered free of credit risk or the risk that the issuer will default on the debt obligation. Therefore, Treasuries tend to demonstrate lower (after-tax) yields than comparable securities issued by corporations, states, or municipalities.

Borrowing from equity analysis, one might group debt security risk into two elements: general market risk and issue-specific credit risk. Because Treasury obligations are considered free of credit risk, they can be considered barometers of general market interest rate risk.

Non-Treasury debt securities are affected by general market risk, but they also are affected by credit risk. As a result, futures based on Treasuries may be used to hedge the general market risk associated with a non-Treasury security. The difficulty is to assess this credit risk.

Yield-adjusted hedge ratios are often referred to under these circumstances. The risk or adjustment factor $CY(h)/CY(cd)$ may be derived using a statistical regression. The slope or beta derived from a regression of the yields of the cash security to be hedged $Y(h)$ against the yields on the security which is cheapest to deliver $Y(cd)$ against the subject futures contract is indicative of this relationship. The results of this regression include the intercept term a, the slope or beta b, and an error term e.

$$Y(h) = a + b[Y(cd)] + e$$

An even more direct approach is to regress the changes in the yield of the hedged security $CY(h)$ against changes in the yield of the cheapest to deliver $CY(cd)$.

$$CY(h) = a + b[CY(cd)] + e$$

Unfortunately, this method is often difficult to apply in practice. For example, the price and yield histories of recently issued securities are (by definition) limited. But often after a bond has established a long history, it may be thinly traded. Hence it is not uncommon to "download" yield histories from publicly available data bases replete with "observation not available" (NAs).

One commonly used method for avoiding these problems is to substitute a regression of the yields implied by a bond index against the cheapest-to-deliver security for a regression of the actual bond yield against the cheapest. For example, various bond indexes are available which record the yield on portfolios of long-term Aaa, Aa, A, and Baa rated corporates.

Presumably, as the bond rating declines and credit risk rises, the risk factor rises proportionately. Thus you may employ higher and higher ratios when hedging bonds with similar coupon and term structures but with progressively lower credit ratings.

As the credit risk diverges farther and farther from that associated with Treasuries, the efficacy of the hedge generally suffers. This may be assessed by examining the "R-squared" associated with the regression results (a measure of correlation between the yield on the hedged security and the yield on the cheapest-to-deliver security).

HEDGING SHORT-TERM INTEREST RATE RISK

Our discussion so far has dealt exclusively with hedging problems associated with intermediate- to long-term fixed income securities. Let us consider some of the unique problems associated with hedging short-term interest rate instruments.

Some of the concepts are analogous. For example, the movement of a short-term interest rate instrument may be measured relative to some standard. The most notable standard is the expected movement in a Eurodollar or T-bill futures contract as offered on the Chicago Mercantile Exchange.

Other concepts are not quite so similar. Short-term investments or liabilities, by their very nature, roll over frequently. As such, techniques known as strips and stacks are referred to exclusively in the context of short-term interest rate futures applications.

Basis Point Value

Earlier we discussed the idea of comparing the basis point value of a long-term security to be hedged relative to the basis point value of the cheapest-to-deliver security in order to identify a reasonable hedge ratio. Likewise, we might apply this analysis to the short-term interest rate markets.

The analysis is simplified in the context of the short-term interest rate security markets to the extent that the T-bill and Eurodollar contracts are based on a single issue or standard, rather than referencing a "market basket" of various issues. Thus the question becomes: What is the BPV of the futures contract(s) and how does that compare to the BPV of the short-term asset or liability to be hedged?

In an earlier chapter, we discussed how one might identify the BPV associated with a short-term instrument such as a T-bill. In particular, we noted that these BPVs are a linear function of the face value of the issue and the number of days until maturity.

The minimum tick size in the T-bill and Eurodollar futures contracts equals one basis point 0.01 percent or $25.00. It is easy to identify a standard against which other short-term securities may be measured: the $1 million face value 90-day security upon which bill and ED futures are based with a BPV equal to $25.00.

The BPV of a 45-day $1 million face value security equals one-half that of the futures contract: $12.50. The BPVs associated with a 180-day, 270-day, or 360-day bill may also be found as a simple linear function at $50, $75, and $100, respectively.

The BPV of a one-half million dollar face value 90-day security equals $12.50 or one-half that of the futures contract. Two million dollar, $3 million, and $4 million face value 90-day securities have BPVs equal to $50, $75, and $100, respectively.

As a simple rule:

$$BPV = (Q(h)/\$1,000,000) \times (d/90) \times \$25$$

Where Q(h) equals the face value or the quantity to be hedged, d equals the number of days until expiration. The number of contracts needed to hedge may be found by comparing this number to the $25 BPV associated with the bill or Eurodollar contracts or by using the previous formula, but without multiplying by $25.

Example: Find the BPV and the number of contracts needed to hedge the following short-term instruments:

Q(h)	d	BPV	Contracts
$10,000,000	120	$ 333.33	13.3
$50,000,000	30	$ 416.67	16.7
$35,000,000	270	$2,625.00	105.0
$76,000,000	70	$1,477.78	59.1

What if one were to hedge a $30 million 90-day floating rate loan adjusted daily based on LIBOR rates against the risk of rising rates? Initially, it is clear that the BPV equals $750 which suggests that one should hedge by selling 30 Eurodollar futures. Unfortunately, the BPV will change as the investment runs closer and closer to term.

By the time there are 87 days until expiration, the BPV declines to $725, suggesting the use of only 29 contracts. By the time there are 60 days to term, the BPV falls off to $500, suggesting the use of 20 contracts; by the time there are 30 days to term, the BPV falls off to $250, suggesting the use of only 10 contracts.

Example: Our analysis suggests that the number of contracts required falls off by one every three days. This suggests that the hedger must continually reduce the number of short contracts by buying one contract back every three days in order to maintain the appropriate hedge ratio.

Days to Term	Action	Net Short	BPV
90	Sell 30 cnts	30 cnts	$750
87	Buy back 1 cnt	29 cnts	$725
84	Buy back 1 cnt	28 cnts	$700
.	.	.	.
.	.	.	.
60	Buy back 1 cnt	20 cnts	$500
.	.	.	.
.	.	.	.
30	Buy back 1 cnt	10 cnts	$250
.	.	.	.
.	.	.	.
6	Buy back 1 cnt	2 cnts	$50
3	Buy back 1 cnt	1 cnt	$25
0	Buy back 1 cnt	Net flat	$0

Consider the rationale behind this continual adjustment. If by the time there are 60 days left in the life of the hedge, LIBOR rates increase by 10 basis points, this implies that the hedger will pay an additional $5,000 over the next 60 days in interest expense.

$$\text{Added interest expense} = (60/360) \times (\$30\text{MM}) \times 0.001$$

$$= \$5,000$$

If the borrower is short 20 contracts, he will be compensated for the increased borrowing expense because 10 ticks at $25 per tick for 20 contracts equals $5,000.

If by the time there are only six days left, the rate falls by 10 basis points, this implies that the borrower will save $500 over the remaining six days, but he will lose $500 insofar as he held a short position in two contracts. Thus the borrower is hedged from the ill effects of rate advances and prevented from enjoying the benefits of declining rates.

Strip Hedge

The foregoing analysis was limited to a 90-day scenario. How could short-term interest rate futures be used in a situation involving a longer term loan? How could they be used in a loan which is expected to be rolled over at periodic intervals?

The answer may be found in the use of a *strip hedge*. You may buy or sell a strip by buying or selling short-term interest rate futures in each of a series of successive contract months. (In an earlier chapter, we discussed how implied forward rate calculations may be used to help identify the theoretical value of a bill or Euro futures contract.) By using a strip, you create a situation where the hedge will liquidate itself as the BPV of the loan declines.

> **Example:** Assume that it is December 1986. Also assume you have taken out a $10 million 18-month LIBOR-based floating rate loan extending out to June 1988, the rate on which is reset periodically every three months. (This conveniently coincides with the maturity of each successive Eurodollar futures contract).
>
> The rate paid over the first three months is already established and need not be hedged. Hence the hedger has risk over a 15-month period beginning in March 1987 and extending to June 1987. The BPV of a 15-month, $10 million face value loan equals $1,250, suggesting the use of 50 futures.

A strip hedge may be created by selling 10 futures in the five successive cycle months for a total of 50 contracts.

Initial Transaction	*BPV*
Sell 10 Mar. '87 futures	$250
Sell 10 Jun. '87 futures	$250
Sell 10 Sep. '87 futures	$250
Sell 10 Dec. '87 futures	$250
Sell <u>10</u> Mar. '88 futures	<u>$250</u>
<u>50</u>	<u>$1,250</u>

What will happen as the loan term draws near?

Date	Action	Net Short	BPV
Mar. '87	10 Mar. '87 cnts mature	40 cnts	$1,000
Jun. '87	10 Jun. '87 cnts mature	30 cnts	$750
Sep. '87	10 Sep. '87 cnts mature	20 cnts	$500
Dec. '87	10 Dec. '87 cnts mature	10 cnts	$250
Mar. '88	10 Mar. '88 cnts mature	Net flat	$0

Because this hedge unwinds itself as time marches on, it always covers the risk exposure, as measured by the BPV, of the subject loan. For example, if rates increase 10 basis points by June 1987, this implies added interest expense of $10,000 over the remaining life of the loan. This coincides with an expected 10-basis point decline in the 40 contracts held up until June 1987.

$$\text{Added interest expense} = (360/360) \times (\$10\text{MM}) \times 0.001$$

$$= \$10,000$$

If rates increase 20 basis points by September 1987, the added interest expense over the remaining 270 days of the loan equals $15,000. This coincides with an expected 20-basis point decline in the 30 contracts held up until September 1987.

$$\text{Added interest expense} = (270/360) \times (\$10\text{MM}) \times 0.002$$

$$= \$15,000$$

Stack Hedge

The strip hedge may be quite effective in that it matches a futures contract (the price of which should be reflected in implied forward rates) with a future interest rate exposure. As such, it may be quite precise in "matching up" an interest rate exposure with a hedging vehicle.

Notice, however, that the strip strategy will only work if futures are available with extended maturities which coincide with the maturity of the asset or liability to be hedged. To the extent that Eurodollar and T-bill futures are available with maturities every three months extended as far as three years into the future, it is relatively easy to develop this "match."

This strategy may be frustrated, however, to the extent that those deferred futures may be illiquid. This illiquidity may make it difficult if not impossible to execute orders at reasonable prices in deferred months. This may prompt the hedger to utilize a strategy known as a *stack hedge*.

In addition, if the short-term segment of the yield curve is relatively steep, the implied forward rate curve will be steeper. The effective interest rate(s) locked in at each reset date of the strip may be significantly higher than the current spot rate and therefore unacceptable to the hedger.

A stack requires a hedger to match the cash market risk exposure (measured in terms of BPV) with a position in the nearby month. Subsequently, that position is rolled over into the next month when the nearby contract matures.

Example: Return to the situation illustrated in the previous example. It is December 1986; you have taken out a $10 million 18-month LIBOR-based floating rate loan to June 1988; the rate is reset every three months. A stack hedge may be created by selling 50 futures in the nearby month.

Initial Transaction	BPV
Sell 50 Mar. '87 futures	$1,250

What will happen as the loan term draws near?

Date	Action	Net Short	BPV
Mar. '87	50 Mar. '87 cnts mature; sell 40 Jun. '87 cnts	40 cnts	$1,000
Jun. '87	40 Jun. '87 cnts mature; sell 30 Sep. '87 cnts	30 cnts	$750
Sep. '87	30 Sep. '87 cnts mature; sell 20 Dec. '87 cnts	20 cnts	$500
Dec. '87	20 Dec. '87 cnts mature; sell 10 Mar. '88 cnts	10 cnts	$250
Mar. '88	10 Mar. '88 cnts mature	Net flat	$0

By continually rolling forward, the hedger assures that he will always hold a futures position, the movements of which offset the risks associated with the floating rate loan. If rates increase 10 basis points by June 1987, for example, this implies added interest expense of $10,000 over the remaining life of the loan. This matches up with an expected 10-basis point decline in the 40 June 1987 contracts.

If rates increase 20 basis points by September 1987, the added interest expense over the remaining 270 days of the loan equals $15,000. This coincides with an expected 20-basis point decline in the 30 September 1987 contracts.

Strip/Stack

Obviously, there are advantages and disadvantages associated with both a strip and a stack. Notably, a strip allows one to match up one's risk exposure quite precisely over an extended period of time. To the extent that the hedge is self-liquidating, it requires very little management. Furthermore, the strip hedge generally requires fewer transactions and associated commissions, execution skids, the possibility of errors, and so on.

Unfortunately, if you go beyond the nearby into increasingly deferred contracts, liquidity becomes diminished, and it may become impossible to execute a strip. A stack addresses that problem at the risk of giving up some of the advantages of the strip.

As a result, the strip is generally the more favored of the two transactions—assuming sufficient liquidity. Thus many hedgers prefer to enjoy the benefits of a strip by extending their position as far as liquidity permits. As liquidity diminishes in deferred months, the hedger puts on a stack.

Example: Return to the situation illustrated in the previous example. Assume the market is considered too thin in the December 1987 futures contract to put on a position.

	Initial Transaction	BPV
Strip:	Sell 10 Mar. '87 futures	$250
	Sell 10 Jun. '87 futures	$250
	Sell 10 Sep. '87 futures	$250
Stack:	Sell 20 Sep. '87 futures	$500
	50	$1,250

What will happen as the loan term draws near?

Date	Action	Net Short	BPV
Mar. '87	10 Mar. '87 cnts mature; buy-back 20 Sep. '87 cnts; sell 20 Dec. '87 cnts	40 cnts	$1,000
Jun. '87	10 Jun. '87 cnts mature; buy-back 10 Dec. '87 cnts; sell 10 Mar. '88 cnts	30 cnts	$750
Sep. '87	10 Sep. '87 cnts mature	20 cnts	$500
Dec. '87	10 Dec. '87 cnts mature	10 cnts	$250
Mar. '88	10 Mar. '88 cnts mature	Net flat	$0

This technique also allows you to cover the diminishing risk exposure as measured by BPV.

It is difficult to compare the strip, stack, and strip/stack hedge insofar as there are numerous nonquantifiable advantages and disadvantages. One obvious way to quantify these features, however, is in terms of number of transactions (which is obviously highly correlated with the cost of commissions and the possibility of execution skids or errors).

The strip hedge involves the fewest number of "round-turn" transactions at 50. The stack entails the largest number of round-turns at 150. Finally, the strip/stack falls between at 80.

REGRESSION-WEIGHTED HEDGE TECHNIQUES

Our discussion of hedging techniques so far has been premised on the idea that the instrument to be hedged is very similar to the instrument which underlies the futures contract. As such, the problem of defining the relationship between the hedged instrument and the futures contract reduces to a matter of mathematics.

Sometimes, however, the relationship between the hedged security and a given futures contract cannot be anticipated very precisely. It can be difficult to anticipate the relationship when attempting to hedge the risks associated with a given stock or equity portfolio with a stock index futures contract, for example, hard to anticipate the relationship when hedging the risks associated with a mortgage against a Treasury futures contract. Let us see how regression analysis may be applied to these situations.

Measuring Equity Movements with Beta

Index based futures are often said to represent the stock market in the aggregate. This is true to the extent that the computation and composition of the index are representative of overall market movements.

Aggregate or general stock market risk is often referred to as "systematic" or "market" risk. "Unsystematic" risks are those uniquely associated with a specific firm. The total risk to which a particular stock is subject represents the summation of systematic and unsystematic risk:

$$\text{Total Risk} = \frac{\text{Systematic or}}{\text{Market Risk}} + \frac{\text{Unsystematic or}}{\text{Firm-Specific Risk}}$$

By diversifying a stock portfolio such that it includes stocks representative of many different sectors of the economy, one may reduce and virtually eliminate unsystematic risk from the portfolio. Unfortunately, diversification cannot reduce systematic risks.

To understand this, consider a portfolio composed of equal values of two stocks (A and B) where market returns average 10 percent. In one year, stock A generates a 5 percent return on investment, while stock B generates a 15 percent return on investment. Thus the portfolio yields a 10 percent return. In another year, stock A generates an 8 percent return, while stock B generates a 12 percent return and again the portfolio yields 10 percent.

Had the portfolio been devoted exclusively to either stock A or B, the investor's returns would have been quite variable. By diversifying, the investor minimizes the unique risks associated with one or the other stock. Thus the investor achieves a relatively stable return in each period.

Diversification works because these unsystematic market factors (by definition) influence stocks independently. So while some companies may experience a bad year due to unique factors, other companies may experience a good year. The poor performance of some stocks may be offset by the better than average performance of others.

An investor, therefore, is left with systematic market risk, or the general economic risk which affects all stocks. Because stock index based products reflect general market conditions, they may be used to hedge systematic risk. But how does one get a handle on these systematic risks?

Beta-Weighted Hedge

Beta analysis is a statistical technique which allows one to assess the degree to which a stock is affected by systematic and unsystematic market factors. This method calls for a statistical regression comparing the returns on a particular stock R(s) with market returns R(m):

$$R(s) = a + bR(m) + e$$

Where a is the regression constant, b or *beta* is the slope of the regression line, and e represents the error term. As mentioned above in our discussion of the risk-adjusted weighted hedge, two significant statistics arise from this analysis: beta or the slope of the regression line and R-squared.

Beta represents the expected sensitivity of a particular stock to fluctuating systematic factors. If the stock's beta is less than 1.0, the stock is considered a "conservative" investment because it can be expected to fluctuate less dramatically than the market. An "aggressive" investment with a beta greater than 1.0 moves more dramatically than the market.

For example, a conservative beta of 0.7 suggests that the stock will advance 7 percent if the market advances 10 percent. Not only will stocks follow market advances, but they will also parallel declines. An aggressive beta of 1.30, for example, suggests that the stock will decline 13 percent if the market declines 10 percent.

R-squared represents the degree to which stock movement may be attributed to systematic market factors. R-squared varies from 0 to 1.0.

A statistic of 0.90 suggests that about 90 percent of the movement associated with a stock may be attributed to systematic market factors; only about 10 percent of its movement is traced to unsystematic factors. A statistic of only 0.30 suggests that only about 30 percent of the stock's movement may be traced to systematic factors; 70 percent of that movement is traced to unsystematic factors.

Furthermore, R-squared provides an indication of the potential effectiveness of a hedge using index-based products. An R-squared of 0.90 suggests that about 90 percent of the stock's risk may be hedged using an index-based product. An R-squared of only 0.30 suggests that only about 30 percent of the risk may be hedged.

Beta is very useful in determining how many futures contracts with which one should hedge to offset the systematic risk associated with a stock or stock portfolio. (Be certain to calculate the beta of a stock using returns on the stock index, which is the subject of the futures contract in use, to represent market returns.) The hedge ratio may be identified as:

$$HR = [Value_{stock}/Value_{futures}] \times Beta$$

The value of the futures contract equals the index value multiplied by the contract size multiplier. (For example, the S&P 500 futures contract is based on a value of $500 times the index. If the index is at 250, the contract is valued at $125,000.)

Example: You hold 100,000 shares of stock ABC at $125.00 per share with a beta of 1.15. The S&P 500 is at 250.00. One may decide how many S&P 500 futures contracts with which to hedge by using the formula presented previously:

$$HR = [\$12,500,000/(\$500 \times 250.00)] \times 1.15$$

$$= 115 \text{ contracts}$$

The same analysis may be applied against any other stock or portfolio of equities. The prospective effectiveness of the hedge may be measured by R-squared. Presumably, as we diversify from a single stock to a multiple stock portfolio, R-squared will increase, suggesting that the effectiveness of the hedge is likely to be higher.

The beauty of this approach is that you need not attempt to predict the relationship between the equities and the stock index futures contract. Instead, this method simply examines the relationship between cash and futures over the recent past as an indication of the relationship which may exist in the near future.

Of course, a more effective hedge may be initiated between a portfolio of stocks and the stock index futures contract, as opposed to a hedge of a single stock. How can you identify the "portfolio beta" and, therefore, the number of futures with which to hedge? If you can identify the beta associated with each individual stock in the portfolio, then the hedge ratio becomes simple to calculate. The first step is to find the "beta-adjusted" value of all the stocks in the portfolio; that is, multiply the dollar value held in each issue by its beta. Take the sum of those beta-adjusted values and compare to the value of the futures contract.

$$HR = \sum_{i=1}^{n} (Beta_i \times Shares_i \times Price_i)/Value_{futures}$$

Example: Find the number of futures needed to hedge the portfolio of 20 blue-chip stocks described next. The S&P 500 futures contract (valued at $500 times the index) was at 292.75 at the time.

Ticker	Shares	Price ($)	Value ($)	Beta	Adj-Value ($)
AXP	18,200	50.875	925,925	1.70	1,574,073
CHV	12,300	59.500	731,850	1.09	797,717
DEC	14,700	166.500	2,447,550	1.52	3,720,276
DOW	21,000	82.625	1,735,125	1.31	2,273,014
EK	22,300	78.375	1,747,763	0.79	1,380,732
GE	8,900	108.000	961,200	1.10	1,057,320
GM	11,000	82.250	904,750	1.04	940,940
IBM	25,800	146.500	3,779,700	0.77	2,910,369
ITT	40,000	62.625	2,505,000	1.03	2,580,150
JNJ	13,400	88.750	1,189,250	1.05	1,248,713
MCD	4,400	80.625	354,750	1.01	358,298
MOB	33,500	49.625	1,662,438	0.83	1,379,823
MRK	27,700	160.750	4,452,775	0.87	3,873,914
PEP	14,900	34.000	506,600	0.86	435,676
S	34,700	53.750	1,865,125	1.31	2,443,314
XON	12,000	88.375	1,060,500	0.53	562,065
XRX	34,000	76.125	2,588,250	1.26	3,261,195
VO	3,300	76.500	252,450	1.18	297,891
			$29,671,000		$31,095,478

$$HR = \$31,095,478/(\$500 \times 292.75)$$
$$= 212.44 \text{ or } 212 \text{ futures contracts}$$

The effective beta associated with this portfolio equals 1.0480. This number may be derived by taking the beta-adjusted value of the portfolio ($31,095,478) divided by the nonadjusted value of the portfolio ($29,671,000).

Beta or Duration Tuning

It is clear that when you hedge a long equity portfolio by selling futures, you are reducing your exposure to the risk of price declines. This is analogous to the idea of hedging by selling high beta stocks, which are very sensitive to the risk of general market declines, and rolling into low beta stocks, which may be relatively less sensitive to the risk of price decline.

If you hold a low beta portfolio but believe that the market may rally, it is reasonable to roll the portfolio from low to high beta stocks in order to be poised to take maximal advantage of the anticipated advance. Buying futures provides a way of increasing the net beta of the portfolio.

In other words, stock index futures provide an alternate means of decreasing or increasing the effective beta of the portfolio, allowing the investor to position himself to take maximal advantage of anticipated price movements, without recourse to the cash market.

Assume that you would like to take on a portfolio with a higher or lower beta. If you can identify a "target beta" Beta(t) as well as the "current beta" Beta(c), you can identify the number of contracts that you must buy or sell in order to achieve that beta.

$$HR = [Beta(t) - Beta(c)] \times Value_{portfolio}/Value_{futures}$$

Example: Assume that you want to reduce the effective beta of the portfolio just described to 0.50 in anticipation of a price decline. Rather than rolling from higher to lower beta stocks, you may simply sell 111 futures.

$$HR = (0.50 - 1.048) \times \frac{\$29{,}671{,}000}{\$500 \times 292.75}$$

$$= -111.08 \text{ or } 111 \text{ short futures.}$$

Example: Assume that you want to increase the effective beta of the portfolio previously described to 1.20 in anticipation of a price advance. Rather than rolling from lower to higher beta stocks, you may simply buy 31 futures.

$$HR = (1.20 - 1.048) \times \frac{\$29{,}671{,}000}{\$500 \times 292.75}$$

$$= 30.81 \text{ or } 31 \text{ long futures.}$$

Similarly, a fixed income portfolio manager may measure the risk associated with his holdings in terms of the net duration of the portfolio. If rates are expected to advance, he will generally roll from long- to shorter-term securities in order to shorten the duration of the portfolio and, thereby, insulate it from the risk of falling prices. If rates are expected to decline, he may roll from short- to longer-term securities, increasing the duration of the portfolio in order to participate more fully in the anticipated price rally.

Buying or selling fixed income futures provides an alternate way of increasing or decreasing the effective duration of the portfolio, respectively, without recourse to the cash market. The duration of the futures contract itself may be represented by the duration of the cheapest-to-deliver cash security. The duration of a portfolio comprised of a cash bond hedged with short futures may be represented as follows:

$$\text{Duration}_{\text{portfolio}} = \text{Duration}_{\text{bond}} - (\text{Value}_{\text{futures}}/\text{Value}_{\text{bond}}) \times \text{Duration}_{\text{futures}}$$

Example: It is August 25, 1986. Assume you own $10 million face value of the 12 1/2 percent bond of 2009–14 with a modified duration of 9.74 years. The bond is priced at 148 17/32ds and is currently the cheapest to deliver against the December 1986 T-bond futures contract priced at 100–01. Assume you hedge in the ratio of the conversion factor (1.4662) by selling 147 bond futures. What is the duration of the portfolio?

$$\text{Duration}_{\text{portfolio}} = 9.74 - (\$14{,}704{,}594/\$14{,}853{,}125) \times 9.74$$
$$= 0.10 \text{ years}$$

This makes sense in that it suggests you can reduce your net duration practically to zero by hedging the cheapest-to-deliver security in the ratio of its conversion factor. But what if you hedge a noncheapest security?

Example: Assume you own $10 million face value of the 7 1/4 percent bond of 2016 with a modified duration of 11.97 years. The bond is priced at 101 00/32ds, but the cheapest to deliver remains the 12 1/2s with a duration of 9.74. December 1986 bond futures are at 100–01. Assume you apply a duration weighted hedge by selling 124 futures. What is the duration of the portfolio?

$$\text{Duration}_{\text{portfolio}} = 11.97 - (\$12{,}403{,}875/\$10{,}100{,}000) \times 9.74$$
$$= 0.01 \text{ years}$$

Again, you are able to reduce the net duration of the hedged bond practically to zero. What if your objective is simply to modify the effective net duration? What if you wish to decrease the net duration when rates are expected to advance and increase the duration when rates are expected to fall? Assuming you can identify a target duration or D(t), you may use the following formula to calculate the appropriate hedge ratio:

$$\text{HR} = [D(t) - D(h)] \times [Q(h)/CS] \times [P(h)/D(cd)P(f)]$$

Example: Earlier we calculated a duration-weighted hedge ratio of 124 contracts for the 7 1/4s of 2016. Assume the hedger's objective was to reduce the effective net duration from 11.97 years to five years. How many futures contracts must the hedger employ?

$$HR = [D(t) - D(h)] \times [Q(h)/CS] \times [P(h)/D(cd)P(f)]$$
$$= [5 - 11.97] \times [\$10,000,000/\$100,000] \times [101.00/9.74 \times 100.03125]$$
$$= -72.25 \text{ or sell } 72 \text{ futures}$$

Example: Assume the hedger's objective was to increase the effective net duration from 11.97 years to 14 years. How many futures contracts must the hedger employ?

$$HR = [D(t) - D(h)] \times [Q(h)/CS] \times [P(h)/D(cd)P(f)]$$
$$= [14 - 11.97] \times [\$10,000,000/\$100,000] \times [101.00/9.74 \times 100.03125]$$
$$= 21.04 \text{ or buy } 21 \text{ futures}$$

But why use futures to *tune* the beta or duration of an equity or fixed income portfolio, respectively, to be compatible with market forecasts? Why not simply use the cash market to accomplish these objectives? The reason futures enjoy a high level of acceptance on the part of cash market participants is that they can be used to achieve these investment objectives at reduced costs.

Consider the transaction costs associated with a roll from long-term to short-term Treasuries in anticipation of rising rates. Even for on-the-run Treasury securities, the bid/ask spread may be four to five 32ds at a minimum. But bond futures in near-term months generally trade at a $1/32d$ bid/ask spread. Thus it is generally cheaper to alter beta or duration using futures as opposed to more traditional means.

Hedging Current Production Fixed Rate Mortgages

Hedging fixed rate mortgages using existing interest rate futures contracts has proven to be a very difficult proposition over recent years. Fortunately, the techniques that were applied previously in the context of an equity hedge may be applied with equal force in the context of a mortgage hedge.

Superficially, hedging mortgages may appear to be very straightforward: Simply use GNMA futures! In fact, the very first interest rate futures was the GNMA futures contract introduced in 1975. This contract served the needs of the mortgage industry fairly effectively for many years, but by the fall of 1982, many difficulties associated with the contract became quite apparent.

The GNMA CDR contract was developed in the mid-1970s when fixed rate mortgages were being issued with rates near 8 percent. At the time, it was unthinkable that mortgage rates would jump into the high double digits as they did in the early 1980s, or that rates would subsequently drop sharply as they did in the fall of 1982, leaving large supplies of outstanding mortgages with above-market rates.

When rates fell, the GNMA CDR futures tracked or priced these high-coupon GNMAs, not current production or current market rate mortgages! (See Figure 8–1). To understand why, consider the nature of the mortgages which the GNMA CDR was intended to represent. GNMA securities represent a pool of federally insured Federal Housing Administration (FHA) or Veterans Administration (VA) fixed rate 29–30-year mortgages. Once the mortgage is taken out, the mortgagor has significant latitude which can affect the term of the security.

In particular, the mortgagor may elect to prepay the mortgage principal well before maturity. In fact, the standard industry assumption is that mortgages will be prepaid in their 12th year. Prepayment may come much sooner, however, if rates have fallen considerably relative to the original loan rate.

Prepayment forces the mortgage investor to accept the principal or par value of the mortgage. Thus mortgage investors may be reluctant to bid over par for fear of prepayment. Higher-coupon mortgages "cap out" or suffer price compression as their prices rise above par.

Because the GNMA CDR futures contract utilizes an invoicing system based upon an assumed 12-year average life, it ignores the potential for

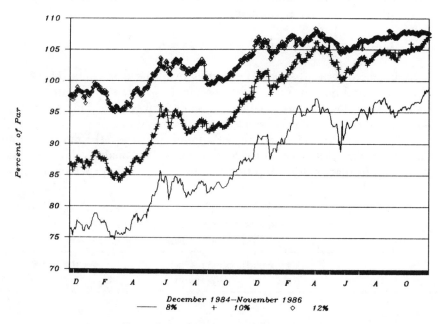

Figure 8–1   GNMA mortgage securities.

the effective maturity of mortgages to be shortened. As such, it encourages the delivery of high-coupon mortgages suffering from price compression.

The bulk of the risk faced by mortgage market participants is in "current production" mortgages. Mortgage "pipeline" risk is incurred during the period between the approval of the loan and the time it is packaged and sold off in the secondary markets.

Because GNMA CDR futures tend to track high-coupon mortgages, use of the contract to hedge current production generally entails considerable basis risks. As a result, growing interest has been witnessed in a cross-hedge between mortgage securities and Treasury bond or note futures contracts. The problem reduces to an assessment of the correct number of futures contracts to use and the prospects for a reliable hedge.

Unfortunately, FHA and VA mortgages which are pooled to create GNMA certificates are unlike Treasury securities on a number of counts: (1) many mortgages may be prepaid, decreasing the life of the obligation; (2) many mortgages may be assigned to other parties, generally lengthening the life of the obligation; and (3) mortgages call for monthly rather than semiannual interest payments.

These and other features suggest that it may be inappropriate to use the methods discussed earlier to construct a hedge ratio. An alternate method is to run a regression between the price of the mortgage or mortgage-backed security to be hedged P(h) and the price of the futures contract P(f) which will be used in the hedge.

$$P(h) = a + bP(f) + e$$

By inspecting the R-squared statistics resulting from such regressions using bond and note futures, one may decide whether the security to be hedged more closely tracks the note or bond futures market. The beta b or slope of the regression may be used as the hedge ratio.

This analysis asks: What has the relationship between the mortgage and the futures contract been in the recent past? This analysis does not ask: What *should* that relationship be? The following table provides information about these relationships over recent years.

GNMA Securities vs. Nearby Bond & Note Futures
(Raw Price Levels)

	Nearby Bonds		Nearby Notes	
	Beta	R-Squared	Beta	R-Squared
12/84–2/85				
GNMA 13%	0.57	0.73	0.68	0.83
GNMA 12-1/2%	0.67	0.87	0.74	0.84
GNMA 12%	0.78	0.88	0.84	0.80

GNMA Securities vs. Nearby Bond & Note Futures *(Continued)*

	Nearby Bonds		Nearby Notes	
	Beta	R-Squared	Beta	R-Squared
3/85–5/85				
GNMA 13%	0.62	0.94	0.64	0.96
GNMA 12-1/2%	0.70	0.98	0.69	0.97
GNMA 12%	0.78	0.98	0.80	0.99
GNMA 11-1/2%	0.85	0.99	0.87	0.99
GNMA 11%	0.90	0.99	0.91	0.99
6/85–8/85				
GNMA 12-1/2%	0.46	0.75	0.48	0.72
GNMA 12%	0.58	0.86	0.58	0.77
GNMA 11-1/2%	0.68	0.90	0.66	0.78
GNMA 11%	0.82	0.88	0.80	0.76
9/85–11/85				
GNMA 12%	0.58	0.96	0.76	0.97
GNMA 11-1/2%	0.63	0.98	0.82	0.98
GNMA 11%	0.67	0.98	0.87	0.98
GNMA 10-1/2%	0.81	0.98	1.04	0.98
GNMA 10%	0.80	0.98	1.03	0.97
12/85–2/86				
GNMA 10%	0.38	0.75	0.55	0.78
GNMA 9-1/2%	0.45	0.75	0.66	0.78
GNMA 9%	0.49	0.86	0.72	0.89
GNMA 8%	0.50	0.88	0.73	0.90
3/86–5/86				
GNMA 10%	0.28	0.64	0.49	0.66
GNMA 9-1/2%	0.30	0.63	0.55	0.74
GNMA 9%	0.33	0.56	0.62	0.70
GNMA 8%	0.29	0.49	0.56	0.65
6/86–8/86				
GNMA 10%	0.39	0.73	0.55	0.89
GNMA 9-1/2%	0.44	0.80	0.60	0.93
GNMA 9%	0.44	0.80	0.65	0.94
GNMA 8%	0.57	0.76	0.80	0.93
9/86–11/86				
GNMA 10%	0.35	0.61	0.49	0.63
GNMA 9-1/2%	0.45	0.63	0.62	0.60
GNMA 9%	0.52	0.78	0.69	0.72
GNMA 8%	0.53	0.82	0.70	0.74

This analysis utilizes near-par GNMA mortgage securities with coupons ranging from 8 percent to 13 percent. These mortgages were regressed against nearby bond and note futures over eight 3-month intervals from December 1984 through November 1986.

The term *nearby futures* refers to the futures contract closest to expiration rolled over as it enters the delivery month. In May, for example, the nearby contract is the one which calls for delivery of securities in June. But as you enter the month of June, the nearby contract rolls over into September.

The foregoing table provides betas and R-squared regressing mortgage price levels on future price levels. This is the most straightforward method of performing the analysis. Some analysts, however, point out that you want to hedge price *changes*, not the raw price *level*.

You may elect, therefore, to regress price changes against price changes. Results of such an analysis using the same securities over the same time periods is provided in the following table. This study does not utilize day-to-day price changes (daily lags). Instead, it utilizes week-to-week changes (weekly lags). The use of daily or similarly short-term lags in the context of a regression should be approached with caution in that they may incorporate a great deal of spurious "noise" or unexplained price fluctuations.

GNMA Securities vs. Nearby Bond & Note Futures
(Weekly Price Changes)

	Nearby Bonds		Nearby Notes	
	Beta	R-Squared	Beta	R-Squared
12/84–2/85				
GNMA 13%	0.53	0.71	0.61	0.75
GNMA 12-1/2%	0.60	0.80	0.69	0.82
GNMA 12%	0.72	0.87	0.83	0.90
3/85–5/85				
GNMA 13%	0.46	0.71	0.54	0.69
GNMA 12-1/2%	0.55	0.82	0.65	0.79
GNMA 12%	0.69	0.90	0.82	0.90
GNMA 11-1/2%	0.74	0.92	0.88	0.93
GNMA 11%	0.79	0.82	0.94	0.84
6/85–8/85				
GNMA 12-1/2%	0.58	0.84	0.62	0.82
GNMA 12%	0.70	0.90	0.75	0.88
GNMA 11-1/2%	0.74	0.92	0.89	0.79
GNMA 11%	0.83	0.93	0.89	0.90
9/85–11/85				
GNMA 12%	0.39	0.66	0.55	0.70
GNMA 11-/2%	0.47	0.72	0.66	0.75
GNMA 11%	0.60	0.79	0.84	0.80
GNMA 10-1/2%	0.67	0.80	0.92	0.80
GNMA 10%	0.70	0.79	0.97	0.81

GNMA Securities vs. Nearby Bond & Note Futures *(Continued)*

	Nearby Bonds		Nearby Notes	
	Beta	R-Squared	Beta	R-Squared
12/85–2/86				
GNMA 10%	0.60	0.67	0.90	0.75
GNMA 9-1/2%	0.65	0.54	0.96	0.59
GNMA 9%	0.70	0.80	1.04	0.88
GNMA 8%	0.72	0.84	1.05	0.91
3/86–5/86				
GNMA 10%	0.23	0.38	0.41	0.44
GNMA 9-1/2%	0.27	0.54	0.49	0.62
GNMA 9%	0.32	0.60	0.57	0.65
GNMA 8%	0.32	0.59	0.58	0.66
6/86–8/86				
GNMA 10%	0.29	0.59	0.50	0.62
GNMA 9-1/2%	0.36	0.74	0.63	0.80
GNMA 9%	0.40	0.69	0.72	0.80
GNMA 8%	0.43	0.65	0.80	0.77
9/86–11/86				
GNMA 10%	0.14	0.32	0.18	0.25
GNMA 9-1/2%	0.25	0.32	0.33	0.25
GNMA 9%	0.31	0.65	0.39	0.48
GNMA 8%	0.31	0.76	0.39	0.57

Mortgage Cross-Hedging Conclusions

These results suggest that a mortgage/Treasury cross-hedge may be implemented with some effectiveness from time to time. T-note futures tend to provide marginally greater hedge reliability than do bond futures. This is intuitive if you consider the maturities associated with these two futures markets. Note futures are based on a 6½ to 10 year security. Bonds are based on a 15-year plus maturity security.

Thus note futures more closely conform to the assumed 12-year average life of many mortgage securities which suggests the use of a cross-hedge with note rather than bond futures. This consideration must be balanced with the greater liquidity and depth in the bond market.

In many cases, however, T-bond futures provide a more effective cross-hedge versus lower-coupon mortgages. Low-coupon mortgages are less likely to be prepaid—they tend to lengthen in terms of effective maturity into longer-term ranges. High-coupon mortgages are more likely to be prepaid, shortening their effective maturities into the intermediate range.

As the mortgage coupon falls, volatility associated with the instrument (as measured by beta) advances. This is just the opposite of the situation in most fixed income markets where the prices of high-coupon instruments tend to be more responsive in an absolute sense to changing yield levels than low-coupon instruments.

This is traced to the price compression effect for mortgages over par. (As coupons get very high, volatility may start to fall as the price compression effect takes hold.) The implication is that you should reduce the hedge ratio as the mortgage value rises above par.

In general, the regression using price changes is more discriminating as evidenced by the generally lower correlation levels. Regressions using price levels tend to inflate the R-squareds particularly during heavily trending markets.

A good way of getting a feel for the basis risk associated with a cross-hedge of this nature is to examine a "scatter diagram" for the mortgage-backed security against the futures contract (see Figures 8–2 and 8–3).

In the March–May 1985 period, for example, our scatter plot suggests that there is a clear linear relationship between GNMA 12s and nearby T-note futures. But this relationship was much weaker in the subsequent June–August 1985 period.

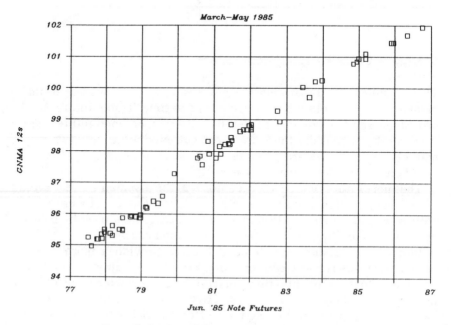

Figure 8–2   June '85 note futures vs. GNMA 12s.

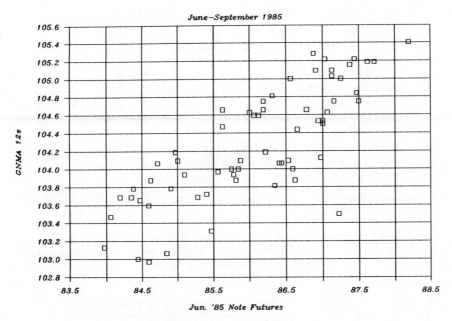

Figure 8–3   September '85 note futures vs. GNMA 12-½s.

One way of determining whether the basis relationship is remaining consistent is to examine the observations associated with the past few days. If those observations are beginning to fall below the line shown on the scatter plot, this suggests that one of three things is happening: (1) GNMAs are falling while futures are remaining stable; (2) futures are rising while GNMAs are remaining stable; or (3) there is some combination of the two. No matter which is true, if you are long GNMAs and short futures, this implies a basis loss.

If the observations start to rise above the linear plot, this suggests that (1) GNMAs are rising while futures remain stable; (2) futures are falling while GNMAs remain stable; or (3) there is some combination of the two. No matter which is true, if you are long GNMAs and short futures, this implies a basis profit.

QUESTIONS

1. The conversion factor hedge ratio . . .
   (a) Works well with any Treasury as long as it is deliverable against a Treasury-based futures contract.
   (b) Means that you should hedge in the ratio of the reciprocal of the conversion factor.

(c) Is best suited for a hedge of the cheapest-to-deliver futures contract.

(d) Works well when you are hedging a 90-day bill against the T-bill futures contract.

(e) None of the above.

2. Which is false? A conversion factor represents . . .

(a) The value of a particular bond or note to be delivered relative to the 8 percent $100,000 face value bond or note futures contract standard.

(b) An indication of the relative price movement of a bond or note relative to the futures contract given a parallel yield-curve shift.

(c) Relative price volatility given stable yield spreads.

(d) A net present value calculation which perfectly reconciles the value of a bond or note to the 8 percent, $100,000 face value futures contract standard.

(e) The price of a bond or note to yield 8 percent.

3. Find the basis point value for the following discount securities. How many T-bill futures are needed to hedge these instruments?

Face Value	Term	BPV	Number Contracts
$1 million	180 days		
$10 million	30 days		
$2.5 million	90 days		
$1 million	45 days		
$1 million	270 days		
$1 million	360 days		
$20 million	75 days		

4. A strip . . .

(a) Represents the sale (or purchase) of a number of T-bill or Eurodollar futures in successive months.

(b) May be valued by study of the spread between different delivery months in the long-term T-bond futures contract.

(c) Is preferable to a stack particularly when trading in deferred months.

(d) May be valued by study of the yield curve.

(e) All of the above.

5. What are the relative merits of a stack versus a strip?

Stack:

Strip:

6. (a) You represent a company borrowing $1 million for one year. The rate floats such that it is reevaluated every three months at the Libor rate. It is March, and you wish to hedge against the risk of

rising rates with three-month instruments. How would you hedge against the possibility of rising rates using a strip or a stack?
Strip:

Stack:

(b) How would the strip and stack outlined in (6a) be unwound?
Strip:

Stack:

7. A basis point value . . .
   (a) Represents the change in the dollar amount of an investment given a 1 percent change in yield.
   (b) Represents the change in yield given a one-tick ($1/32$d) change in the price of a bond.
   (c) Is a linear function of the term to maturity and face value of the investment.
   (d) Reflects the change in the value of a bond given a .01 percent change in yield.
   (e) Is the same as the duration of the bond.
8. The basis point value of the cheapest-to-deliver bond equals $94.75, the conversion factor equals 1.4074, and the BPV of a $100,000 face value lot of the bond you would like to hedge equals $85.40. Find the BPV weighted hedge ratio.

$$HR = [Q(h)/CS] \times CF(cd) \times [BPV(h)/BPV(cd)]$$

9. Which statement is false?
   (a) Regression analysis is most useful for finding relationships between two debt instruments which differ with respect to credit risk or debt structure.
   (b) Hedgers want to offset changes in the prices of a security, not price levels.
   (c) It is usually best to find hedge ratios with regression analysis using daily price lags.
   (d) R-squared varies from 0 to 1.0 and provides an indication of the tracking reliability between two debt securities.
   (e) The beta or slope from a regression equation may be used as a hedge ratio.
10. Match the method of identifying a hedge ratio with the circumstances under which it is most useful.

Method	*Circumstances*
1) Conversion factor	a) Varying credit risks
2) BPV weighting	b) Varying maturities and coupons of bonds
3) Regression analysis	c) Similar debt structures, varying credit risks
4) Risk-adjusted BPV	d) Most economic-to-deliver security
	e) Varying debt structure

11. Identify a portfolio of ten Treasury notes and bonds. For the duration of the course, assume that you own these securities and want to hedge against the possibility of rising interest rates. Devise an appropriate hedging strategy—identify appropriate hedge ratios, follow fundamental and technical events, etc. It is unnecessary to fully hedge your portfolio.) Keep a log on your paper hedge transactions. At the conclusion of the course, identify the difference between your results on a hedged basis versus possible results on an unhedged basis. Did you do better or worse on a hedged basis? Why?

9

Asset/Liability Management with Futures*

Many commercial banks and thrift institutions have adopted the financial futures concept with zeal over recent years, and for good reason: Profitability may be heavily dependent on fluctuations in the interest rate markets. Unfortunately, it is not always easy to develop an effective risk-management program. The problem lies first and foremost in the ability (or inability) of an institution to identify exactly what risks impact on the firm.

A bank or thrift typically holds a variety of investments and liabilities on its books. To a large extent, the risks and potential rewards associated with these assets and liabilities tend to offset, but often these risks and rewards do not match or offset. As such, an asset or liability "gap" is identified.

MACROASSET/LIABILITY MANAGEMENT

The primary concern of the stockholders, principals, and officers of a bank or thrift is profitability. The profitability of an entity, which operates by taking in deposits and lending them out, is a function of the difference between interest income and interest expense, often expressed as a percentage of earning assets. This figure is often referred to as the net interest margin (NIM).

* This material is excerpted with permission from *Interest Rate Futures for Institutional Investors* by John W. Labuszewski © 1986 Board of Trade of City of Chicago.

$$NIM = (\text{Interest Income} - \text{Interest Expense})/\text{Earning Assets}$$

Stockholders, principals, and officers in a financial institution prefer to see steady growth in an institution's profitability. Wild fluctuations in the NIM from month to month are not generally welcome. On occasion, however, an institution's NIM may fall to an extremely low or even a negative level. When might this occur?

The NIM associated with many institutions exhibits a clear correlation with short-term (S–T) rates. When S–T rates fall, NIMs generally advance, but when S–T rates increase, NIMs generally decline.

In order to understand why an institution's profitability may be affected in such a way, you must examine its balance sheet in detail. The first step may be to perform a "macrogap" analysis by taking an inventory of all short- and long-term assets and liabilities and lumping them into two categories: those which mature within six months and those which mature over six months.

> **Example:** In this example, short-term rate sensitive liabilities (RSL) are funding relatively longer-term rate sensitive assets (RSA). Effectively, this institution is exposed to a maturity mismatch or gap equal to $95 million or 21 percent of its $450 million in earning assets.

Macro Asset/Liability Gaps
(Thousands of $'s)

	< 6 Mos.	> 6 Mos.	Total
Rate Sensitive Assets (RSA)	$220,000	$280,000	$500,000
Rate Sensitive Liabilities (RSL)			
& Equity	$315,000	$185,000	$500,000
GAP	($ 95,000)	$ 95,000	0
Percent of Earning Assets (EA)	(21%)	21%	0

Like many banks and thrifts, the institution in our example borrows on a short-term basis and lends on a relatively longer-term basis. It is attempting to take advantage of the spread of long-term yields over short-term yields characteristic of a normal or upwardly sloping yield curve. This institution's balance sheet is said to be "liability sensitive" because it has more liabilities which will mature and be repriced than assets in the short-term. As such, it is exposed to the risk that rates will rise.

> **Example:** If all short-term RSAs and RSLs are repriced just 1 percent higher, while long-term rates remain stable, the institution's annualized net interest margin (interest income less interest expense) will decline on the order of

$950,000 or 21 basis points as a percentage of earning assets ($950,000/
$450,000,000):

Interest Rates Increase 1% . . .

RSA: $220,000 × 1% = $2,200 Interest Income

RSL: $315,000 × 1% = ($3,150) Interest Expense

GAP $95,000   = ($950) Net

Although this is a simplified measure of the institution's risks, it might
very well alarm the firm's officers. At a minimum, this analysis suggests
that further examination of the firm's risks is warranted. The risk is equally
troublesome on the long-term side. If long-term rates rise, the market
value of the institution's assets could plummet sharply.

MICROASSET/LIABILITY MANAGEMENT

By closely examining a maturity schedule of all rate sensitive assets and
liabilities, an asset/liability manager can pinpoint exactly where the institution's risks lie.

Table 9-1 provides a "microgap" analysis where the institution's assets
and liabilities are broken down by their maturities to the nearest month.
(Individual assets and liabilities are not noted in the table. Moreover, only
summary information of selected periods is provided to avoid complicating
the illustration.)

This technique is often known as a "bucket gap" approach to identifying where an institution's risks lie. Individual assets and liabilities are
classified or "bucketed" in accordance with their maturity.

By preparing this bucket gap analysis, the institution is able to pinpoint
"period gaps." These period gaps may be liability gaps (where liabilities to
be repriced exceed assets) or asset gaps (where assets to be repriced exceed liabilities). If you add up the institution's total asset gaps, it must
balance with its liability gaps plus equity; that is, assets must equal liabilities plus equity.

The Asset/Liability Management Committee (ALCO) of this institution
may decide that a macrogap of 21 percent of earning assets is unacceptably large. Many institutions may feel that they are able to sustain some
risk but would be more comfortable if they could reduce major macrogaps.
In this example, a target gap below 10 percent may be deemed reasonable.

In order to accomplish this objective, an institution must zero in on
significant period gaps. Period gaps which exceed 5 percent of earning
assets, for example, may be considered large. These excessively large period gaps may be identified as "primary risk centers."

TABLE 9–1 Micro Asset/Liability Gaps in Thousands (000)
(April 30, 19XX)

	0	May	Jun	Jul	Aug	Sep	Oct	6 Mos	5–6 Yrs	1		
Rate Sensitive Assets												
Fed funds												
Investments												
Commercial loans												
Real estate loans												
Installment loans												
Other assets												
Total RSA for period	25,000	25,000	42,000	38,000	34,000	32,000	24,000	220,000	38,000	105,000		500,000
Weighted ave yield percent	8.5%	7.3%	8.1%	7.7%	8.3%	8.6%	9.1%	8.2%	9.2%	8.1%		8.3%
Cumulative RSA												
Percent of Earning Assets												
Rate Sensitive Liabilities												
Money market												
6 month MMCs												
3 month CDs												
CDs $100M												
Other CDs												
Repurchase agreements												
Savings shift												
Other liabilities												
Total RSL for period	15,000	44,000	45,000	44,000	48,000	75,000	44,000	315,000	5,000	59,000		500,000
Weighted ave cost percent	6.0%	5.7%	6.9%	5.8%	5.5%	5.7%	6.7%	5.9%	6.0%	5.7%		7.5%
Cumulative RSL												
Percent of int. bearing liab.												
Summary Measures												
Period gap	10,000	(19,000)	(3,000)	(6,000)	(14,000)	(43,000)	(20,000)		33,000	46,000		0
Yield gap	2.5%	1.6%	1.2%	1.9%	2.8%	2.9%	2.4%	2.3%	3.2%	2.4%		0.8%
Cumulative gap								(95,000)				
Cum RSA/RSL												0
Gap as percent of EA	2.2%	4.2%	0.7%	1.3%	3.1%	9.6%	4.4%	21.1%	7.3%	8.9%		

228

	Primary Risk Centers			
	May–Aug	Sep	5–6 Yrs	10 Yrs +
RSA	$164,000	$32,000	$38,000	$105,000
RSL	$196,000	$75,000	$ 5,000	$ 59,000
GAP	($ 32,000)	($43,000)	$33,000	$ 46,000
Percent of EA	7.1%	9.5%	7.3%	10.2%
Major RSA or RSL	CDs	CDs	Treasuries munis	GNMAs mortgages
Rate Exposure	Increasing	Increasing	Increasing	Increasing

ASSET OR LIABILITY HEDGE?

Effectively, the liability gaps in the near-term are funding the asset gaps in the long-term. Thus we might say that the $32,000 liability gap in May-August is funding the $33,000 asset gap from five to six years out. Likewise, the $43,000 liability gap in September is funding the $46,000 asset gap in the 10 years plus maturity range. The institution's concern is to plug these gaps. But how can the institution approach this problem?

The institution has two basic ways to plug these gaps with futures: (1) effectively shorten the maturity of the long-term assets to match the short-term liabilities by selling futures based on long-term debt securities or (2) effectively lengthen the maturity of the short-term liabilities to match the long-term assets by selling futures based on short-term debt securities.

Either approach is valid. But which approach is most cost-efficient? There are a number of costs associated with a hedging program including commissions, margins, and basis risk. How would these costs differ in the event the institution decides to implement an asset or a liability hedge?

Commissions and margins are almost linearly related with the number of futures contracts the institution trades. As a general rule, it will require fewer futures contracts to shorten the maturity of a given face value of longer-term assets than to lengthen the effective maturity of shorter-term liabilities.

Upwards of 200 bill futures may be required in the context of a strip hedge* to extend the effective maturity of a $10 million face value

* A $10 million face value of six-month CDs could be lengthened to a five-year maturity by selling a strip of two hundred $1 million face value three-month T-bill futures. In other words, the institution could sell T-bill futures with staggered delivery dates every six months, assuming that the six-month CDs will continually roll over. Twenty three-month T-bill futures are needed for each of the staggered futures months because six-month instruments should be approximately twice as volatile as three-month instruments in a fluctuating interest rate environment. Unfortunately, it may be impossible to strip out five years. Other hedge techniques such as the stack or strip/stack requiring additional contracts may be necessary.

quantity of six-month CDs out five years. By contrast, it will typically require less than 100 note futures to shorten the effective maturity of a $10 million face value quantity of five-year notes.

Far and away the most significant cost associated with a hedging program is basis risk. Sometimes liability hedges have been likened to hitting a moving target. An institution's liabilities are often effectively dictated by changing customer preferences, so those CDs might change into money market funds within the next few months.

As a general rule, an intermediate-sized institution will have much more control over its assets than its liabilities. This suggests that an asset hedge may be more stable over time, possibly requiring less maintenance and worry. Sometimes, however, the basis risk is so severe that it becomes impossible to use futures to hedge specific types of investments. For example, that long-term asset gap in the 10 years plus range was attributable largely to fixed rate mortgages and GNMAs.

Unfortunately, the GNMA CDR futures contract had grown illiquid and finally dormant in the mid-1980s. A cross-hedge between cash mortgage instruments and Treasury futures is sometimes possible but often fraught with significant basis risk. It may be wiser to close that gap by lengthening the effective maturity of liabilities.

DURATION ANALYSIS

A topic which has attracted a great deal of interest in recent years is duration. Duration analysis goes beyond the simple bucket gap analysis previously illustrated. Rather than grouping assets and liabilities into buckets corresponding to their maturities, duration analysis attempts to define an institution's risks by comparing the average duration of its assets with the average duration of its liabilities. Macauley's duration may be thought of as the average life of a security. In most cases, the average life of a security is much less than its term to maturity.

Treasury bonds and notes entitle the holder to semiannual interest payments. These cash flows are received much in advance of the maturity date. Moreover, the present value of current coupon payments is greater than that of deferred coupon payments and, indeed, may be more than the present value of the final principal payment.

What is the duration of a six-month Treasury bill? Six months! The duration of any debt security which entails a single cash flow is the maturity of the instrument itself. Thus the duration of a T-bill which is sold on a discount basis must be the maturity of the bill.

More importantly, however, a modified duration may be used to provide a measure of the expected percentage change in the price of a security given a change in yield. Specifically, the percentage change in the price of a security is roughly equal to the product of its modified duration and the change in yield.

Example: If the modified duration of a security equals five years, a 100-basis point advance in yield should lead roughly to a 5 percent decline in the price of the security.

How can a financial institution use information regarding the duration of its assets and liabilities? By matching the duration of its assets and liabilities, an institution can effect a natural hedge without the use of interest rate futures.

Example: The modified duration of an institution's assets equals four years, while the modified duration of its liabilities equals three years. This suggests that the institution should shift a greater proportion of its liabilities into instruments with longer durations to bring up the average or shift a greater proportion of its assets into instruments with shorter durations to drive down the average.

But how does an institution use the concept of duration to shape its hedging program? By selling T-bond or T-note futures against longer-term assets, an institution may diminish the effective maturity and duration of those assets, presumably to match liabilities. By selling Euro or T-bill futures against shorter-term liabilities, an institution may increase the effective maturity and duration of those liabilities, presumably to match with longer-term assets.

QUESTIONS

1. An institution which has more assets that are to be repriced in the long-term (beyond six months) than liabilities is said to be _____ sensitive.
2. Which statement is true?
   (a) The institution's net interest margin equals the difference between its earning assets and its cost of liabilities.
   (b) The net interest margin for a liability sensitive institution will tend to rise when short-term rates rise and to fall as short-term rates fall.
   (c) A macrogap analysis gives the institution most of the information it needs to close its balance sheet gaps.
   (d) The institution's net interest margin equals its interest income less interest expense, expressed as a percentage of its assets or earning assets.
   (e) All savings and loan institutions are hurt when interest rates rise.
3. (a) A $1 billion institution (assume these are all earning assets) has $350 million in rate sensitive assets rolling over in less than six months and $450 in rate sensitive liabilities rolling over in the long-term (greater

than six months) period. Find the short-term RSLs, long-term RSAs and the macrogaps.

	< 6 Mos.	> 6 Mos.	Total
RSA			
RSL			
GAP			

(b) What would happen to the institution's bottom line if all its near-term assets and liabilities were repriced at a rate 1 percent higher during the next six months? One percent lower?

1% Higher . . .

    Interest Income:
    Interest Expense:

1% Lower . . .

    Interest Income:
    Interest Expense:

(c) How big is the institution's macrogap compared to earning assets?

4. A primary risk center . . .

  (a) Is a macrogap which may be hedged with either a long-term or a short-term interest rate futures contract.

  (b) Represents the risk associated with a 1 percent increase in interest rates.

  (c) Represents an unacceptably large asset or liability gap in a specific maturity period.

  (d) Is the same as a bucket gap.

  (e) Generally measures the magnitude of this risk by reference to duration.

5. Which statement is false?

  (a) In order to hedge a primary risk center, you must identify a specific asset or liability which gives rise to a significant portion of that gap.

  (b) Asset hedges are generally more desirable than liability hedges for accounting reasons.

  (c) The institution's interest rate forecast should play a role in the development of a reasonable hedge strategy.

  (d) It is usually unnecessary or undesirable to close *all* balance sheet gaps.

  (e) Futures generally provide a quicker and more efficient way to close balance sheet gaps relative to the possibility of restructuring the balance sheet.

6. What factors do *not* affect a decision to implement an asset versus a liability hedge?

  (a) Hedgeability of the asset or liability.

  (b) Margins and commissions, accounting practices.

  (c) Whether you are using a bucket gap or a duration analysis.

  (d) Management costs associated with monitoring and adjusting the hedge.

  (e) The correlation between available futures contracts and the instrument to be hedged.

Answers to Questions

INTRODUCTION TO FINANCIAL FUTURES

1. e
2. d
3. Japanese yen .... 12.5 million units
   British pounds .... 25,000 units
   S&P 500 futures .... $500 × index
   $6^1/_2$- to 10-year T-note ..... $100,000 face value
   90-day T-bill futures ...... $1 million face value
   West German mark .... 125,000 units
4. c
5. b
6. (a) Your account equity falls by $250, but no variation margins are required because you still have $2,250 in the account—$250 above the maintenance level.

   (b) Your account equity falls another $625 to $1,625. Because this is less than the maintenance margin level, you must post margin equal to $875 to bring your account equity up to the initial $2,500 level.

   (c) You have made $500; this amount is posted to your account in cash.
7. Fifteen years, no restriction.
8. S&P futures are marked-to-market each day including the last trading day subsequent to which the contract simply expires. Subsequent to the last trading day in yen futures, shorts are required to make delivery of 12.5 million yen.
9. a

FUNDAMENTAL MARKET FACTORS

1. c
2. a
3. (a) Fed does match sales: +
   (b) PPI is down: −
   (c) Housing starts up: +

(d) Personal income is down:	−
(e) Unemployment is down:	+
(f) GNP is up:	+
(g) CPI is down:	−
(h) Leading economic indicators are down:	−
(i) Corporate tax rates going up:	−
(j) Fed buying bills:	−
(k) Fed tightening:	+

TECHNICAL ANALYSIS WITH FUTURES

1. d
2. a
3. c
4. e
5. d
6. 1, 1, 2, 3, 5, 8, 13, 21, 34, 55, 89, 144, 233, 377, 610 . . .

COST OF CARRY

1. (a)

Cash bond	($100)
Financing	($ 4)
Coupon income	$ 5
Futures price	$ 99

(b)

Cash bond	($100.0)
Financing	($ 2.0)
Coupon income	$ 2.5
Futures price	$ 99.5

2. d
3. a
4. (a) $F = .0055 [1 + (.06 − .04)(30/360)] = .005509$
   (b) $F = .0055 [1 + (.06 − .04)(90/360)] = .005527$
   (c) $F = .0055e (.06 − .04)/(30/360) = .005509$
   $F = .0055e (.06 − .04)(90/360) = .005528$
   (d) 30 days: $1/.005509 = 181.52$
   90 days: $1/.005528 = 180.90$
5. d
6. d
7. e
8. d
9. $1 + 0.0655(270/360) = [1 + .064(180/360)] [1 + IFR(90/360)]$
   $IFR = 6.64\%$

10. #1: R = 6.18%
    #2: 1 + R(.5) = [1 + .0561(.25)] [1 + .0612(.25)]
        R = [[1 + .0561(.25)][1 + .0612(.25)] − 1]/.5 = 5.91%
    #3: 1 + R(.5) = [1 + .0620(.75)]/[1 + .0605(.25)]
        R = [[(1 + .0620(.75))/(1 + .0605(.25))] − 1]/.5 = 6.18%

Alternative #1 and #3 are roughly equal.

DISCOUNT AND INTEREST BEARING SECURITIES

1. e
2. e
3. 360, 365
4. d
5. (a) $114,000
   (b) $114,752
   (c) $115,027
6. d
7. Price = $9,687,500   MMY = 6.19%
   EBY = 6.28%   BPV = $500
8. 0.40%

PLAYING THE TREASURY FUTURES BASIS

1. b
2. c
3. d
4. (a) CF = 0.9155
   (b) Basis = 97.03125 − (0.9155 × 95.0625) = 10.00 or 320/32ds
5. c
6. d
7. d
8. c
9. c

FINANCIAL FUTURES SPREAD RELATIONSHIPS

1. b
2. 97–24 less 99–16 equals 1–24 or 56/32ds
3. d
4. d
5. b
6. c

HEDGING WITH FINANCIAL FUTURES

1. c
2. d
3.

Face Value	360 days	$100.00	Number Contracts
$1 million	180 days	$50.00	2
$10 million	30 days	$83.33	3
$2.5 million	90 days	$62.50	2 or 3
$1 million	45 days	$12.50	0 or 1
$1 million	270 days	$75.00	3
$1 million	360 days	$100.00	4
$20 million	75 days	$416.67	17

4. a
5. Stack: Uses near-term liquid futures.

   Strip: Fewer transactions, less commissions.
   More certainty with hedge as you use futures which correspond
   to the roll-over dates associated with your cash position.
6. (a) Strip: Sell 1 Jun. bill futures @ 6.12
                Sell 1 Sep. bill futures @ 6.05
                Sell 1 Dec. bill futures @ 6.12

                Average rate 6.10

           Stack: Sell 3 Jun. bill futures @ 6.12
    (b) Strip: In Jun. - Buy back 1 Jun. futures.
                In Sep. - Buy back 1 Sep. futures.
                In Dec. - Buy back 1 Dec. futures.

           Stack: In Jun. - Buy back 3 Jun. futures, sell 2 Sep. futures.
                In Sep. - Buy back 2 Sep. futures, sell 1 Dec. futures.
                In Dec. - Buy back 1 Dec. futures.
7. d
8. HR = BPV(h) × [CF(ctd)/BPV(ctd)]
      = $85.40 × [1.4074/$94.75]
      = 1.27 or 13 contracts per million face value.
9. c
10. 1) d; 2) b; 3) e; 4) c

ASSET/LIABILITY MANAGEMENT WITH FUTURES

1. liability
2. d
   (b) 1% Higher . . .

Interest Income: 1% × $350MM	=	$3.5MM
Interest Expense: 1% × ($550 MM)	=	($5.5MM)
		($2.5MM)

1% Lower . . .

Interest Income: $-1\% \times \$350$ MM $= (\$3.5\text{MM})$

Interest Expense: $-1\% \times (\$550$ MM$) =$ $\underline{\$5.5\text{MM}}$

$\$2.5\text{MM}$

(c) $\$200$ MM / $\$1,000$ MM $= \underline{20\%}$

3. (a)

	< 6 Mos.	> 6 Mos.	Total
RSA	$350 MM	$650 MM	$1 Billion
RSL	($550 MM)	($450 MM)	$1 Billion
GAP	($200 MM)	$200 MM	0

4. c

5. b

6. c

Index

Adjusted futures price, 137, 138, 139
American terms, 11
Annual percentage rate, 106
Annuity, 113
  ordinary, 113
  annuity due, 113
Anticipatory hedge, 191
Asset gap, 225
Asset-Liability management, 225
  asset hedge, 229
  duration hedge, 230
  liability hedge, 229
Auction tail, 102

Bar chart, 30
Basis, 132, 135, 136, 140, 149
  hedging, 189, 221
Basis point, 121
Basis point value (BPV), 121, 122, 123, 175, 195
  T-bond futures, 172
Bear spread, 157
Beta, 209
  aggressive, 209
  conservative, 209
  hedge ratio, 210
  tuning, 212

Bill/Bond spread, 170, 171
Bottom, 37
British pound futures, 10, 11
Bucket gap, 227
Bull spread, 157
Buying the basis, 150, 166

Canadian dollar futures, 10, 11
Capital asset pricing model (CAPM), 28
Capitalization weighted index, 7, 8
Carry, see cost of carry
Carry model, 88
Cash settlement, 8
CFTC, 2
Channel, 33
Cheapest to deliver bond, 6, 86, 134, 140, 165
Compound interest, 106
Consolidation pattern, 43, 44
Continuous compounding, 107
Conversion factor, 5, 135, 146
Convexity, 116
Correlation, 185
Cost of carry, 83, 84, 90, 93, 158, 159, 165
CPI, 19
Cross-hedge, 185, 219

Delivery bias, 146, 148
Deutsche mark futures, 10, 11
Discount yield, 117, 118
Discretion order, 14
Diversification, 208, 209
Double top, 41
Dow theory, 27, 28, 29
Duration, 126
  Macauley, 126, 127, 128
  modified, 128, 130
  tuning, 213, 214

Effective annual yield, 106
Elliott wave theory, 28, 29, 45, 47, 52, 53
Equally weighted geometric average, 7
Equivalent bond yield (EBY) 114, 116, 119, 120
Eurodollar futures, 9, 10, 96
Expectations hypothesis, 93

Fibonacci number, 36, 37, 54
Filter, 35
Flag pattern, 44
Foreign exchange futures, 10
Forward contract, 2
Fundamental analysis, 17, 25
Future interest factor (FIF), 105, 107
Futures contract, 1
  definition, 1
Futures margin, see margin

Gap, 30
  breakaway, 50
  common, 50
  exhaustion, 50, 51
  pattern, 50
  runaway, 50, 51
Gann; W.D., 30
GNMA futures, 214, 215
GNMA hedge ratio, 216, 217

Head and shoulder formation, 37, 38
Hedge ratio, 185
  beta adjusted, 210, 211
  BPV, 193, 194, 202
  conversion factor, 186, 188
  definition, 185
  duration based, 197, 198
  regression based, 200, 216
  yield adjusted, 199
  yield value of 1/32, 196

IMM index, 9
Implied forward rates (IFR), 94, 95, 96, 164, 167
Implied put option, 142, 152, 153
Implied repo rate, 150, 152, 165, 166, 167
  definition, 150
  calculation, 151
Intermarket spread, 156, 170
Intramarket spread, 144, 156
  pricing, 159

Japanese yen futures, 10, 11

Leading economic indicators (LEI), 20
Liability gap, 225
LIBOR rate, 9
Light bar/heavy bar delivery play, 144
Limit order, 13
Liquidity hypothesis, 93, 94
Local(s), 12
Long, 2

Macauley duration, see duration
Macrogap, 226
Margin, 6, 26, 27
  initial, 6, 27
  maintenance, 6
  variation, 6

Mark-to-market, 6
Market if touched (MIT) order, 14
Market order, 13
Matched sale agreement, 18,19
Microgap, 227
Momentum, 78
Monetary policy, 17
Money market yield, 118
Money supply, 17
Moving average, 70, 74
    arithmetic, 71
    double, 78
    exponential, 72, 73
    geometric, 71
    weighted, 71, 72

Nearby futures, 218
Negative carry, 85, 87, 157
Net interest margin (NIM),
    225, 226
NOB spread, 170, 172, 173
Note/bond ratio, 175
NYSE composite average, 7, 8, 9

One cancels the other (OCO)
    order, 14
Open outcry system, 12
Oscillator, 77
Out trade, 13

Pennant pattern, 44
Pivot point analysis, 68
Point and figure chart, 66
    box size, 66, 67
    reversal criterion, 67
Positive carry, 84, 87, 143, 157
PPI, 19
Present value, 110
Principle invoice price, 5, 135

R-squared, 209, 210
Random walk, 25
Rate sensitive assets (RSA), 226

Rate sensitive liabilities (RSL), 226
Rectangle pattern, 49
Regression, 209
Relative strength indicator (RSI),
    80, 81
Repo, see repurchase agreement
Repurchase agreement, 18
Resistance, 31, 68
Reversal, 37, 43
Reverse repurchase agreement,
    19
Rounded bottom, 40, 41
Running correction, 59, 61

Scalper, 12
Segmentation hypothesis, 93, 94
Selling the basis, 150, 166
Short, 2
Simple interest, 105
S&P 500 futures, 7, 8, 9
Spreads, 156
Stack, 201
    hedge, 205, 206
Stop loss order, 13
Strip, 98, 201
    hedge, 203, 204
Strip/stack, 206, 207
STRIPS, 103, 104, 146, 147
Stock index futures, 7
Support level, 31, 68
Swiss franc futures, 10, 11

Tail, conversion factor, 143
Technical analysis, 24, 26
TED spread, 170, 176, 177
Tick, 3, 178, 202
Time value, 104
T-bill futures, 9, 10
T-bills, 101
T-bond futures, 2, 3, 132
T-note futures, 2, 3
Trend, 30, 31
Trendline, 30, 35, 36

Triangle, 44, 45, 56
  ascending, 46, 65
  descending, 46, 65
  expanding, 48, 64
  symmetrical, 45, 46, 65
Triple top, 39, 40
Turtle spread, 168, 169
  ratio, 170

Unsystematic risk, 208

Value Line Composite Average
    (VLCA) futures, 7, 8, 9
Value Line/S&P 500 spread, 178

Wedge pattern, 48, 56
Wild card delivery play, 142, 153

Yen/mark spread, 181
Yield curve, 85, 93, 140, 141, 160
  flattening, 161, 165
  non-parallel shift, 160, 161
  parallel shift, 160, 161
  steepening, 161, 165
Yield value of 1/32, 125, 195

Zero coupon bond, 112, 147
Zigzag pattern, 58, 59, 65